*The Economics and Politics of Public Education* 3

# National Politics and

# Federal Aid to Education

FRANK J. MUNGER
RICHARD F. FENNO, JR.

SYRACUSE UNIVERSITY PRESS 1962

This study was made possible in part by funds granted by Carnegie Corporation of New York. The statements made and views expressed are solely the responsibility of the authors.

*Manufactured in the United States of America by
The Heffernan Press Inc., Worcester, Mass.*

*Library of Congress Catalog Card: 62-19364*

Additional copies of this monograph may be ordered from Syracuse University Press, Syracuse 10, New York, with prices as shown.

| | |
|---|---|
| 2–24 | $1.40 each |
| 25–99 | 1.15 each |
| 100–249 | 1.05 each |
| 250–499 | .90 each |
| 500–999 | .70 each |
| 1000 or more | Prices on request |

# Contents

# Contents

# Tables

# Figures

# Preface

EDUCATION and politics have ordinarily been studied as separate subjects; when political decisions affect educational programs, such separation is no longer possible. The study that follows is concerned with the political factors affecting general federal aid to elementary and secondary education. As such, it is aimed at a dual audience that includes both those interested in education and those interested in public affairs.

In the research for this monograph primary reliance was placed on the voluminous public record concerning federal aid; on the prior work of others, both educators and social scientists; and on interviews with individuals involved in the controversy, either as public officials or officers of the affected interest groups. It is a source of regret to the authors that the desire to protect the anonymity of the many persons who gave their time freely for these interviews prohibits individual acknowledgment of their courtesy.

The authors can and do acknowledge a number of other debts. The manuscript benefited substantially from readings by William W. Brickman, Professor of Education, University of Pennsylvania; Jesse Burkhead, Professor of Economics, Syracuse University; Hugh Douglas Price, Associate Professor of Political Science, Syracuse University; Robert Rosenzweig, Assistant to the Commissioner, U.S. Office of Education; Stanley Rothman, Assistant Professor of Political Science, Smith College; Joseph Cooper, Instructor in Government, Harvard University; George Goodwin, Professor of Political Science, University of Rhode Island; Nelson Polsby, Assistant Professor of Government, Wesleyan University; Donald Matthews, Associate Professor of Political Science, University of North Carolina; and Robert McCord, Staff Director of the General Subcommittee on Education of the House Committee on Education and Labor.

Research assistance was provided by Marian Lief Palley and Louise K. Margules. The final document profited from an editorial reading by Carol Julie Stein. Mrs. Edna Hockensmith served both as typist and shepherdess to the final manuscript. Additional secretarial assistance was provided by Marguerite Gross.

Final responsibility is, of course, the authors': Richard Fenno takes responsibility most particularly for chapters five and six, and Frank Munger, for the remainder.

*Syracuse, New York*
*Summer, 1962*

FRANK J. MUNGER
RICHARD F. FENNO, JR.

# I. Introduction:
# Ninety-four Years of Controversy

T HE FEDERAL GOVERNMENT today constitutes what is probably the last major untapped source of revenue for public school education in this country. Federal grants have been made for limited and specific purposes, as in the National Defense Education Act of 1958. Endowments of land have been given to the states for educational purposes, the most famous being the grants made under the Articles of Confederation through the Ordinances of 1785 and 1787. Emergency allocations of funds were made to local school systems by the federal government in the depression days of the 1930's. Under the Morrill Act of 1862 and later legislation, higher education has been encouraged through the establishment and support of land-grant colleges for agriculture and the mechanical arts. Areas especially affected by federal employment have been assisted under the Lanham Act and the subsequent impacted areas legislation. But no long-term, general federal aid program for elementary and secondary education has yet been approved.[1]

Inevitably, attempts have been made to secure such a program of federal aid to education. This study is concerned with the question why such efforts have failed. No attempt will be made to appraise the validity of the case for federal aid or to argue the form it should take. The focus will be upon the proposals made for general federal aid programs for operating expenses, for school construction, or both; the only answers offered will be suggestions as to why these proposals have failed of enactment by Congress.

Certainly it has not been for lack of trying. During the 1948 floor debate over federal aid, Senator Lister Hill (D., Ala.), one of the bill's sponsors, told his colleagues:

> Mr. President, bills similar to this one have been before the Senate for many years. Volumes of hearings have been taken. If we

---

[1] The many federal programs affecting education in the states are enumerated in many sources. One detailed description can be found in Charles A. Quattlebaum, *Federal Educational Activities and Educational Issues Before Congress*, H. Doc. 423, 82nd Congress, 2nd Session, 1952.

1

were to bring into the chamber from the Committee on Labor and Public Welfare the many volumes of hearings, they would be piled high on our desks. Year after year, the committee has held hearings. Year after year, the committee has spent weeks considering the bill, attempting to reconcile differences, attempting to wipe out inequities, attempting to bring forth the best possible bill to provide Federal aid, with the primary responsibility for education still continuing in the states.[2]

Senator Hill's statement did not exaggerate the amount of time that had already been given to the subject of federal aid. Yet since his statement the Senate has formally debated federal aid bills five additional times. During that period the relevant House and Senate committees have conducted hearings whose published record, by conservative estimate, runs to over 10,000 pages and includes more than six million words of testimony.

In the extent to which it has occupied the time of Congress and congressmen, federal aid to education is clearly one of the major issues of American politics today. As such it is intrinsically worthy of detailed study. But the length of time through which the federal aid debate has been carried on in American national politics suggests a broader framework for analysis, the process by which consensus is created for new departures in government policy. One of the most striking features of the issue has been the failure to secure such consensus; this study will attempt to suggest some of the reasons why.

### THE EARLY PHASES: 1870–1943

A full account of the proposals for federal aid to education would have to begin in the nineteenth century. The first major federal aid bill was the Hoar bill of 1870, providing for the establishment of national schools in all states where the state government failed to provide adequate public school instruction. Although no measure seriously considered since has been as far-reaching in its terms, the debate over the Hoar bill opened a period of two decades that has been described as the first phase of the federal aid struggle.[3]

[2] 80:2 *Congressional Record* (1948), 3290.

[3] Gordon Canfield Lee, *The Struggle for Federal Aid—First Phase: A History of the Attempts to Obtain Federal Aid for the Common Schools, 1870–1890* (New York: Columbia University Teachers College, 1949). The history of this early period of federal aid legislation is discussed also in William Alexander Mitchell, *Federal Aid for Primary and Secondary Education* (unpublished doctoral dissertation, Princeton University, 1948).

## The First Phase: The Battle Begins

Congressional action taken on the proposals of this period—as of the years since—is summarized in Figure 1. Although the bill introduced by Representative George Hoar (R., Mass.) was denounced by educational groups as unwarranted federal interference in public school education and withdrawn, it was followed by others, and federal aid bills were passed by both houses of Congress at one time or another—by the House once in 1872 and by the Senate four times. Unfortunately for the proponents of the legislation, the same bill was never passed by both houses in the same Congress. A federal aid bill came closest to success in 1880 when the Morrill bill was approved by the Senate, and the House Committee on Education offered a motion to suspend the rules and accept it. The House refused the motion, however, and though the Senate three times subsequently approved versions of the Blair bill for federal aid, none of the three passed the House. The only legislation to win approval from Congress was a measure concerning higher education, the second Morrill Act, passed in 1890 and augmenting the federal assistance provided to the land-grant colleges.

## The Second Phase: 1918 to 1925

With the defeat of the last Blair bill in the Senate in 1890, the struggle to secure general federal aid died. After a lapse of only a few years, however, Congress renewed its concern with educational legislation in a new guise. In the first two decades of the twentieth century Congress concentrated on problems of vocational education. From 1906 to 1917 bills for federal assistance to state programs for industrial, agricultural, or domestic education were continuously before Congress.[4] With the temporary disposition of the question by the passage of the Smith-Hughes Act in 1917, the way was cleared for the resumption of the general aid fight. Reconsideration of the issue was encouraged by World War I. The discovery by the draft boards that close to 25 per cent of the draftees were illiterate, that surprisingly large numbers did not speak English, and that the great majority of the one-third who were physically unfit suffered from defects that

---

[4] The development of a federal policy of aid to vocational education is described in Jack W. Morgan, *Factors Influencing the Passage of Federal Legislation for Vocational Education* (unpublished doctoral dissertation, University of Missouri, 1951); and Carl R. Bartel, *Origin, Development, and Work of the American Vocational Association* (unpublished doctoral dissertation, University of Missouri, 1959).

# FIGURE 1
## Congressional Action on General Federal Aid to Education Bills
### from the 40th (1867-69) to the 87th (1961-63) Congress

| HOUSE | | | CONGRESS | SENATE | | |
|---|---|---|---|---|---|---|
| Passed House | Passed House Committee | House Bill Introduced | | Senate Bill Introduced | Passed Senate Committee | Passed Senate |
| | | | 40 | | | |
| | | | 41 | | | |
| | | | 42 | | | |
| | | | 43 | | | |
| | | | 44 | | | |
| | | | 45 | | | |
| | | | 46 | | | |
| | | | 47 | | | |
| | | | 48 | | | |
| | | | 49 | | | |
| | | | 50 | | | |
| | | | 51 | | | |
| | | | 52 | | | |
| | | | 53 | | | |
| | | | 54 | | | |
| | | | 55 | | | |
| | | | 56 | | | |
| | | | 57 | | | |
| | | | 58 | | | |
| | | | 59 | | | |
| | | | 60 | | | |
| | | | 61 | | | |
| | | | 62 | | | |
| | | | 63 | | | |
| | | | 64 | | | |
| | | | 65 | | | |
| | | | 66 | | | |
| | | | 67 | | | |
| | | | 68 | | | |
| | | | 69 | | | |
| | | | 70 | | | |
| | | | 71 | | | |
| | | | 72 | | | |
| | | | 73 | | | |
| | | | 74 | | | |
| | | | 75 | | | |
| | | | 76 | | | |
| | | | 77 | | | |
| | | | 78 | | | |
| | | | 79 | | | |
| | | | 80 | | | |
| | | | 81 | | | |
| | | | 82 | | | |
| | | | 83 | | | |
| | | | 84 | | | |
| | | | 85 | | | |
| | | | 86 | | | |
| | | | 87 | | | |

could have been remedied if identified at school age, precipitated a demand for action.

Occasional federal aid bills had been offered before, but late in 1918 Senator Hoke Smith (D., Ga.), one of the sponsors of the vocational education law, introduced two bills into the 65th Congress, one to establish a Federal Department of Education, the second the so-called Americanization bill. The following year, in the first session of the 66th Congress, a new bill, the Smith-Towner bill, was introduced incorporating features of both; it provided for the establishment of a cabinet-level Department of Education and made appropriations for the removal of illiteracy, for the equalization of educational opportunities, for Americanization programs, for physical education, and for the preparation of teachers. Similar measures were introduced into the 67th and 68th congresses and the issue of federal educational policy was actively pending before the Congress continuously from October 10, 1918, to March 4, 1925.[5]

Despite endorsement by President Woodrow Wilson and support by the National Education Association and numerous women's organizations, none of these bills was even reported out of committee. Hearings were held by the Senate Committee on Education and Labor during the 65th Congress and a joint hearing by the Senate and House committees during the 66th, but no further action was taken. With the failure to secure a federal aid bill, the proponents of federal action for education turned to more limited goals. The Curtis-Reed bill in the 69th and 70th congresses and the Capper-Robinson bill in the 71st Congress all proposed the establishment of a Department of Education but were shorn of provisions for equalization funds, teacher education, and the like. Still no bill was reported from committee.

At President Herbert Hoover's direction, his Secretary of the Interior, Ray Lyman Wilbur, within whose department the Office of Education was then lodged, in 1929 appointed a 52-member committee to study the federal government's relations to education. The report of this National Advisory Committee on Education, published in 1931 as *Federal Relations to Education*,[6] although favorable to a

---

[5] A discussion of this second phase of the struggle to secure federal aid legislation and the subsequent effort to create a Department of Education without federal aid will be found in Anne Gibson Buis, *An Historical Study of the Role of the Federal Government in the Financial Support of Education, With Special Reference to Legislative Proposals and Action* (unpublished doctoral dissertation, Ohio State University, 1953).

[6] U. S. National Advisory Committee on Education, *Federal Relations to Education* (Washington, 1931).

program of general federal grants for educational purposes, spelled a kind of finish to the agitation of the twenties. The coming of the depression terminated concern for a permanent federal policy of aid to education by forcing immediate consideration of an emergency program of temporary aid.

## The Depression Decade: Emergency Assistance

The question of direct federal aid to education was forcibly reopened by the economic collapse that followed 1929. As local school financial problems multiplied, the 72nd Congress, meeting from 1931 to 1933, was urged to amend the Reconstruction Finance Corporation Act to authorize loans to states and municipalities for educational purposes. This effort was renewed by Senator Walter George ( D., Ga. ) in the first session of the 73rd Congress, but it was not until the second session in 1934, when the public school systems in many states were near collapse, that the rush of bills came. Twenty-five to thirty bills were introduced providing for aid in one form or another, usually on an emergency basis.

None of the earlier bills had emerged from committee, but in February and March of 1934 the House Committee on Education finally opened hearings on federal emergency relief for education. Although the Committee chairman, John J. Douglass ( D., Mass.), expressed great concern during the hearings over the possibility that emergency aid was likely to become permanent, he nevertheless introduced in May a bill earmarking $75 million in relief funds for education. The measure was reported out of committee, but no further action was taken on it during the session.

Much of the steam was taken from the drive for emergency aid at this time by the fact that the federal government was already assisting in the problem out of general relief funds. At the House hearings in February, 1934, Harry Hopkins, the Federal Emergency Relief Administrator, estimated that 40,000 teachers were being paid from relief funds. Many of these were employed to teach in adult education or in rural schools. Hopkins estimated that from $2 million to $3 million was being spent each month for federal educational relief work. The Congress eventually set aside $48 million of relief money to employ unemployed teachers and authorized the Reconstruction Finance Corporation to allocate $75 million for loans to meet overdue teachers' salaries. No direct aid to education on either a temporary or permanent basis was voted; money was to be provided either on a loan basis or in payment to individual teachers in the form of relief. School systems as such were not to be helped.

The 74th Congress, meeting from 1935 to 1937, again saw numerous bills introduced concerning education. Between thirty and forty were offered, a number of which provided for temporary or permanent grants-in-aid to the states. The House Committee on Education again held hearings, but the only bill passed was another RFC loan bill. In addition direct aid was provided to needy students through the National Youth Administration and a portion of federal relief funds earmarked for the employment of unemployed teachers. An unsuccessful effort was made by Senator Matthew Neely (D., W.Va.) to attach an allocation for school construction to the relief appropriation bill. In the face of repeated failures to secure an emergency program, its proponents turned back once more to proposals for a permanent and general federal aid program.

## The Third Phase: General Aid Revived

The return to a strategy of seeking long-term federal aid legislation was signalized by the introduction of companion bills by Senator Pat Harrison (D., Miss.), and Congressman Brooks Fletcher (D., Ohio), in the second session of the 74th Congress in 1936. The Harrison-Fletcher bill proved to be the first in a long series of bills providing for a permanent policy of federal grants-in-aid. No action was taken, but a similar bill was introduced into the 75th Congress, and hearings were held before the Senate Committee on Education and Labor in 1937. The bill was reported out of committee unanimously, but withdrawn by its sponsors after an advisory committee on education appointed by President Franklin D. Roosevelt brought in a recommendation for a combination of general and specific educational grants to the states. Through an amendment offered by Senator Elbert D. Thomas (D., Utah), the bill was rewritten to conform generally to the Committee's recommendations and again approved by the Senate Committee. But the Harrison-Thomas bill, as it was now called, remained upon the Senate calendar and in the House Committee on Education.

The federal aid fight was renewed in the 76th Congress with the principal proposal, largely unchanged, now called the Thomas-Harrison-Larrabee bill. Congressman John R. Murdock (D., Ariz.) informed his colleagues in the House: "Because I have been a schoolman and am now in the national legislature, some of my school friends regard me as a 'watchman on the tower.' They are saying to me: 'Watchman, how goes the battle?' "[7] The answer was: not so good. The

[7] 76:1 *Congressional Record* (1939), 516.

Senate Committee again approved the bill, but the House Committee pigeonholed it, refusing even to hold hearings. The only major educational legislation approved at this time was the Lanham Act providing funds for schools in areas sharply affected by federal activities, a measure made necessary by the rapidly expanding national defense effort.[8]

History was repeated in the 77th Congress as another federal aid bill was introduced, approved by the Senate Committee, and died. In the following Congress, however, for the first time in over fifty years, a federal aid to education bill was debated and acted upon in the United States Senate. This was the Educational Finance Act of 1943, introduced by Senators Thomas and Hill. After extensive hearings before the Senate Committee on Education and Labor, it was approved by the Committee and taken up for consideration by the Senate in October of 1943. The bill was debated for four days but, after the addition of an amendment requiring an equitable distribution of state funds between segregated schools, it was recommitted as its southern supporters deserted it. The House companion bill was never acted upon.[9]

## THE POSTWAR STRUGGLE: 1945–1961

The setback in the Senate in 1943 proved only temporary, and new federal aid legislation was soon before the Congress. Since 1945, in fact, federal educational legislation of some sort has been pending almost continuously. It is upon this latter period of controversy that subsequent chapters will primarily concentrate. Figure 2 provides a more detailed account of the treatment given these various bills by the two houses of Congress during these years. The separate stages of committee hearings, committee reports, floor debate, and floor approval are identified on a year-to-year basis. The fact that additional entries are required for action in the House of Representatives testifies to the greater complexity of the parliamentary procedure in that chamber, an important factor in explaining action—and non-action—during this seventeen-year period.

[8] The attempts to secure first emergency and then permanent general aid for education during the 1930's are described in Buis, *op. cit.*, 151–282.

[9] A detailed discussion of the 1943 attempt to pass a federal aid law will be found in Buis, *op. cit.*, 283–372.

FIGURE 2

CONGRESSIONAL ACTION ON GENERAL FEDERAL AID TO EDUCATION BILLS
FROM 1945 TO 1961

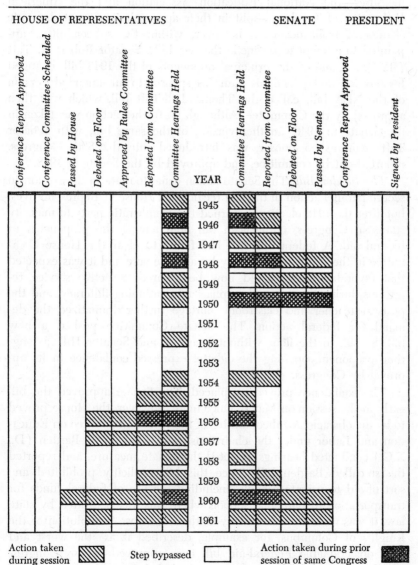

Action taken during session | Step bypassed | Action taken during prior session of same Congress

*The Truman Period: Religion and Other Problems*

During the first of these sessions, 1945, two major federal aid bills were offered to the 79th Congress as the principal sponsors of the measures—the National Education Association and the American Federation of Teachers—split in their approach. The most dramatic change of front occurred, however, within the subcommittee appointed to attempt to reconcile the two bills. Senator Robert A. Taft (R., Ohio), one of the principal opponents of the 1943 bill, changed his position and joined his name as sponsor to an amended version of the NEA bill, called the Thomas-Hill-Taft bill, which was then approved by the Committee. Although no further action was taken in the Senate in 1946, another version of the same bill, with Senator Taft again as co-sponsor, was introduced into the 80th Congress, reported out by committee, and approved by the Senate in 1948.

*The Barden Bill.* The Senate action came too late in the session to secure parallel action in the still recalcitrant House of Representatives, but after the 1948 elections returned the Democratic party to majority status in Congress, enthusiasm ran high among the proponents of federal aid. A federal aid bill had failed to clear the House Committee in the 79th Congress only by a single vote and it was expected that favorable action could now be secured. Selective service rejections during the war had emphasized continuing illiteracy, and the postwar teacher and classroom shortage further dramatized the demand for federal action. The Senate Committee pushed a new bill, S. 246, to the floor without hearings, and Senator Hill, a longtime proponent, opening the debate, expressed confidence in its approval by Congress.

The confidence proved misplaced. The Senate approved the bill early in the session on May 5. Once more, however, the House proved to be the obstacle. A subcommittee of the House Committee on Education and Labor under the chairmanship of Graham A. Barden (D., N.C.) conducted hearings, rejected the Senate measure, and reported the so-called Barden bill. Since this bill explicitly prohibited any sort of aid to private schools, including the use of federal funds for transportation to parochial schools where this was permitted by state law, it was violently attacked by Catholic groups. A resolution of the Knights of Columbus, for example, described it as "the worst and most objectionable Federal-aid bill ever approved by any Congressional committee." The controversy exploded into dramatic national headlines when Mrs. Eleanor Roosevelt criticized Francis Cardinal Spellman of New York City for precipitating the religious conflict and the Cardinal replied: "(Y)our record of anti-Catholicism stands for all to see. . . ." and described her newspaper columns as "documents of discrimination, unworthy of an American mother." The bill never emerged from the full House Committee.[10]

By 1951 the fervor of the push toward federal aid was declining. Although President Truman endorsed it in a message to Congress, fewer federal aid bills were introduced and none emerged from committee in either House or Senate. The heat of the religious controversy discouraged congressmen from acting further and for the next several years the movement for federal education support turned in other directions.

*Impacted Areas Legislation.* One such direction was the enactment of more permanent legislation for assistance to schools in the so-called impacted areas of heavy federal employment. During the 1950 session Congress passed two laws in this field, P.L. 815 for construction grants and P.L. 874 for operating costs "in areas affected by Federal activities."[11] The laws provided for the expansion and continuation of the same kinds of educational support begun under the Lanham Act, but as the number of communities assisted increased, the impacted areas program served as a substitute for general federal aid insofar as the affected communities were concerned.

A second change of direction involved an effort to secure funds for education through the use of income from the tidelands oil fields. After a Supreme Court decision vesting title in the federal government, efforts were made in Congress to secure legislation to transfer ownership to the adjacent states, but such attempts were frustrated by presidential veto. Following out a suggestion originally made by Secretary of the Interior Harold Ickes, a bill introduced in 1949 proposed to use the federal share of the oil revenues for grants to all the states for educational purposes. In the subsequent 82nd Congress the proposal was actively taken up by Senator Hill, but congressional

[10] A brief account of the 1949 religious controversy can be found in Jack Donald Vincent, *Specific Areas of Congressional Legislation Relating to Elementary and Secondary Education* (unpublished doctoral dissertation, George Peabody College for Teachers, 1958), 72–74. The text of Mrs. Roosevelt's original newspaper column, Cardinal Spellman's letter, and Mrs. Roosevelt's reply can be found in Buis, *op. cit.*, 665–72.

[11] The impacted areas program is the subject of another monograph in this series, I. M. Labovitz, *Aid for Federally Affected Public Schools.* The passage and contents of impacted areas legislation are discussed in Louie Reid Davis, *A Study of Federal Assistance to Federally Affected Schools with Special Attention to the State of Virginia* (unpublished doctoral dissertation, University of Virginia, 1953), 40–75.

support for a quitclaim bill proved too strong. In 1952 another bill was passed transferring title to the states, and again was vetoed by President Truman.[12]

*School Construction.* The most significant shift in 1950 in the direction of the movement for federal aid was the beginning of a concerted campaign to secure federal grants for school construction. Such an alternative had been proposed during the 1949 Senate debate by Senator John Bricker (R., Ohio), who had offered a substitute bill, authorizing appropriations of $250 million a year for five years for school construction. After a very sketchy debate, the amendment was defeated overwhelmingly, but subsequent hearings by a Senate Subcommittee on Construction of Educational Facilities, chaired by Senator Hubert Humphrey (D., Minn.), began the task of compiling a record to justify school construction legislation.

School construction bills were also pending in the House, and in 1950 a subcommittee of the House Committee on Education held hearings on one of these. The legislation was supported by the same general groups that had supported the federal aid bill, but all were insistent that construction funds should not be a substitute for general aid. The U.S. Commissioner of Education, Earl J. McGrath, testified: "I do not regard financial aid for school construction as in any sense a substitute for Federal financial aid for current expenses, particularly since such aid will be essential in attracting additional teachers to man the additional classrooms. Both types of Federal financial assistance to the States are desperately needed."[13] Spokesmen for the American Association of School Administrators, the CIO, and other groups echoed this sentiment.

From the objections made to the exclusive emphasis on construction, it seems clear that the decision to switch to an approach to federal support via school construction was made largely by the congressmen themselves. Various reasons could be and were given for the shift, but it seems obvious that the principal reason for the change was to avoid the religious issue. If such was the purpose of the strategy, it proved successful, for when a school construction bill finally reached the House floor in 1956, no amendments were presented

---

[12] The judicial and legislative ramifications of the dispute are described in William K. Metcalfe, *The Tidelands Controversy* (unpublished doctoral dissertation, Syracuse University, 1952). See also Ernest R. Bartley, *The Tidelands Oil Controversy: A Legal and Historical Analysis* (Austin: University of Texas Press, 1953).

[13] House Committee on Education and Labor, *Federal Aid to School Construction*, 81st Congress, 2nd Session (1950), 146.

relating to private schools. Although the bill failed, the primary causes lay elsewhere.

Despite their original opposition to the shift to school construction as the focus for attack, the executives of the NEA came to accept the change through most of the next decade. By late 1954 the NEA had moved so far toward emphasis on construction that an NEA witness was embarrassed by a question at a House hearing as to her personal opinion of federal aid for teachers' salaries. A friendly chairman ruled the question "not germane to the purpose of the hearing." A similar question to an NEA representative at a Senate hearing the same year produced the answer that the NEA had not given up hope of federal aid for teachers' salaries eventually, but also hoped that assistance for construction might release local funds for teachers.

## The Eisenhower Period: Race and Other Problems

The final factor confirming the new emphasis on aid to construction was partisan—the change in administration that followed the 1952 election. Insofar as the Eisenhower administration was willing to support federal aid for education at all, its preference was for construction assistance.

The initial position taken by President Eisenhower after his election was that no action of any kind should be taken until the newly appointed Commission on Intergovernmental Relations had prepared its report and until the White House conference on education, scheduled for 1954, had met. Neither the NEA, the American Federation of Teachers, nor the senatorial supporters of federal aid were willing to wait so patiently and a school construction bill was prepared and sent to the Senate floor in 1954. There it died.

*The Eisenhower Program.* Following the unexpected victory of the friends of federal aid at the White House conference on education, President Eisenhower proposed a school construction program in early 1955. The presidential proposals were relatively complicated in character, involving three alternative forms of assistance—purchase of local school bonds, federal backing for the bonds of state school building authorities, and, where nothing else would work, federal matching grants. The NEA and other educational groups objected to the form of the administration bill, protesting both that it provided too little federal assistance and that it imposed too many conditions on the aid authorized. Accordingly, the mid-fifties witnessed a series of annual struggles among the supporters of different kinds of school construction bills.

The central arena for this struggle, however, shifted to the

House of Representatives. In large part because of the impact of the school segregation decision on the southern senators, the Senate, previously the leader in seeking federal aid for education, now abandoned the stage to the other house. Although the Senate Committee conducted hearings in early 1955, no bill was reported to the floor. Instead, for the first time since the emergency Douglass bill of 1934, the House Committee gave its approval to a federal aid bill. This was the so-called Kelley bill which was reported from committee late in the 1955 session and brought up for debate in 1956 in the first formal House debate on a federal aid bill in the twentieth century.

*The Kelley Bill.* The Kelley bill was a compromise, combining some of the elements of the original Eisenhower administration bill with some of the counter-proposals of the NEA and similar groups. Unfortunately for its sponsors, the coalition of support that had brought it out of committee fell apart on the floor. Supporters of the administration approach broke away during the debate to push their own substitute, while the opponents of the bill combined with some of its proponents to attach the Powell Amendment restricting aid from segregated school systems. Shorn of all southern support and deserted by most administration Republicans, the bill was killed by a 30-vote margin.

The next year saw a repetition of the debacle. After another set of hearings a new House bill, HR 1, was reported out, debated, and defeated. Again the attempt was made to compromise with the administration proposals and the Democratic congressional sponsors insisted they were now going 70 to 85 per cent of the way with the President. Some administration Republicans accepted the argument and the bill; others, including Charles Halleck (R., Ind.), the party whip, did not. After the adoption of the Powell Amendment again imperiled the bill, the Democratic floor managers promised "to cross every 't' and dot every 'i'" and accepted a substitute that incorporated every particular of the Eisenhower plan. Before this substitute could be voted upon, a preferential motion by Rep. Howard Smith (D., Va.) to strike the enacting clause from the bill was adopted 208 to 203 as many Republicans refused the offer to join in support of the Eisenhower bill.

With the failure of a second successive school construction bill in the House, the proponents of federal aid began another reappraisal of their strategy. Such a reconsideration was further encouraged by the decision of the Eisenhower administration to withdraw its support from the school construction measures it had proposed in 1955, 1956, and 1957. Decreasing administration enthusiasm had already been evident in 1957 and had helped to explain the defeat of the bill.

*National Defense Education Act.* The revised position of President Eisenhower was now formalized. According to a letter from the acting Secretary of Health, Education, and Welfare, Elliott L. Richardson, to House Committee Chairman Barden, May 1, 1958, the administration still recognized the existence of "a serious shortage in school housing which adversely affects the quality of education," although it believed local and state construction programs were "keeping abreast of the rapid increase in enrollments" and making slow progress in remedying the backlog of need. The principal reason given for the withdrawal of support, however, was the need to concentrate attention on "other needs and deficiencies in our educational system" which were "brought into sharp focus" by "the events of the past year."[14]

These circumlocutions were references to the Soviet breakthroughs in space. By 1958 the Soviet scientific successes had begun to frighten and alarm Americans. One reaction was the passage of the National Defense Education Act, providing federal educational grants for a variety of specific programs, primarily connected with instruction in science. The concentration of interest on NDEA had the indirect effect of diminishing the interest shown in a general federal aid program. Hearings were held on general aid in both houses, but no new bills were reported.

*The Murray-Metcalf Bill.* The proposals made at these hearings were significant, however, for after a lapse of eight years the NEA now revived the question of federal aid for teachers' salaries as well as that of construction costs. In the form of the Murray-Metcalf bill this program was put before Congress again in 1959. An alternative to it was offered by the administration; after a year of silence the Eisenhower administration proposed another school construction bill, but on a sharply restricted basis due to budgetary stringencies. Although both education committees cleared bills, it was not until 1960 that either came up for floor action.

In 1960 the House passed a federal aid bill—for the first time in seventy-five years. Unhappily for its proponents, however, the bill approved by the Senate the same year differed materially. And, when

[14] House Committee on Education and Labor, *Federal Grants to States for Education*, 85th Congress, 2nd Session (1958), 252.

a conference between the houses became necessary to compromise the differences, the House Rules Committee refused to provide the necessary permission to appoint conferees.

## The Kennedy Period: The Religious Issue Returns

The nearness of victory in 1960 produced the same contagious optimism in 1961 that had been so deceptive twelve years before. Once more, as in 1949, the proponents of federal aid felt confident of success. With the strong support of a new president, it seemed inevitable that the near victory of 1960 would be turned into real victory in 1961. Federal aid to education bills were cleared promptly out of the Senate and House committees, and the Senate gave its approval soon after.

Once more, however, the House of Representatives disappointed the proponents of federal aid. And once more it was the House Rules Committee that exercised the veto. Despite a Kennedy administration victory early in the session that had expanded the membership of the Rules Committee, an 8-to-7 division tabled action on federal aid. The pivotal vote in opposition was provided by an advocate of federal aid to parochial as well as public schools as the religious issue was raised once again. When a truncated federal aid measure was brought to the House floor late in the 1961 session by a parliamentary maneuver that bypassed the Rules Committee, the bill was decisively beaten. With this defeat general federal aid appeared to be dead for the duration of the 87th Congress and—probably—for some time to come.

### SOME COMMENTS IN CONCLUSION

This chronological account of the history of federal aid legislation in Congress from 1870 to 1962 serves to suggest several characteristics of the controversy. It provides clear evidence for a frequently cited proposition, the importance of social crisis in encouraging government action. Repeatedly, it has been the emergence of some crisis that has forced consideration of action concerning federal aid to education.

More than any other single cause, the rate of selective service rejections produced the demands for federal aid in 1918. Strengthened by other forces, the repetition of the same events in the World War II draft produced the 1943 Senate debate on federal aid. The depression forced emergency aid to education in the 1930's. The severe postwar teacher shortage stimulated the federal aid proposals of the late 1940's. The baby boom of the 1950's—abetted by suburban sprawl—generated the school construction bills of the same decade. Impacted areas legislation followed one national defense crisis while the NDEA was called into existence by the cold war crisis that followed the launching of the Soviet Sputnik. Apparently, no crisis as yet has been big enough to justify general aid to education.

Reference to impacted areas legislation and to NDEA suggests, however, a second characteristic of the federal aid debate. For the purpose of this analysis primary attention will be given to general federal aid proposals rather than to such special purpose grants as these, but in practical political terms it is impossible to make a clear separation between the two types of educational assistance. In fact, both impacted areas legislation and the NDEA appear in large measure to be the products of the general federal aid fight.

The adoption of these two programs followed periods of maximum legislative pressure for general aid, the impacted areas laws of 1950 succeeding the struggles of the 1948-49 legislative sessions and NDEA in 1958 following the 1956-57 school construction controversy. Each bill served the purpose of satisfying a major part of the demands of some of the most active proponents of federal aid. This pattern, in which a specialized program serves as a lightning rod minimizing the pressure for general aid, seems in 1962 destined for repetition. The efforts made in 1960 and 1961 for general aid will apparently produce not a general aid bill but new measures of federal support at the college level.[15] It may well be that it takes the impact of an all-out struggle for general federal aid to generate sufficient support to secure approval even of such limited programs.

A third comment also seems justified. Mention has previously been made of the significance of the effort to win support for federal aid as an illustration of the problems faced in building consensus for any new program. The difficulties attending advocacy of federal aid for education are in this sense comparable to those faced by the proponents of any new governmental service although they are exaggerated by the magnitude of the service involved—education—and the magnitude of its total cost.

A glance at the history of the federal aid struggle, however, raises the real question whether the effort to build consensus for federal aid has made any headway whatsoever. Rather than a steady progression toward greater and greater evidences of strength, the

---

[15] The identical sequence of events occurred in 1890 when two decades of efforts to secure federal aid to common schooling terminated in the second Morrill Act for higher education.

federal aid movement betrays a cyclical character. For almost a full century efforts have been made to secure such legislation, but in each phase of the struggle support has been mobilized only to be lost again. Then, after a delay, the effort is renewed once more.

This is not the place, however, to attempt to determine whether such a pessimistic interpretation (pessimistic at least from the viewpoint of its proponents) is justified. Nor is it the place to attempt to draw conclusions as to the obstacles that have blocked a general federal aid program each time. Subsequent chapters will depart from the chronological record of events and dissect the handling of federal aid legislation, first by the multiple interest groups concerned, second by the executive department, third by the relevant congressional committees, and fourth by the Congress as a whole. Only then will it be appropriate to state some general conclusions regarding the forces influencing the treatment of federal aid to education in national politics.

# II. The Issue of Federal Aid

Even the briefest history of federal aid legislation makes clear one important fact, that the struggle over federal aid has not been a single conflict, but rather a multiplicity of controversies only loosely related to one another. The situation might be compared to a better-than-three-ring circus, although, in view of the tactics at times employed, a multiple barroom brawl might make a more apt analogy.

A number of these conflicts have already been suggested in the previous chapter. In addition to the primary struggle between the proponents and opponents of federal aid to education, subsidiary controversies over both race and religion have at times raged. Within the ranks of the supporters, conflicts have occurred as to the form under which assistance should be given: school construction *vs.* teachers' salaries, flat grants *vs.* equalization payments, and the like. Other conflicts have also become entangled with the federal aid issue. It is the purpose of this chapter to describe the principal among these conflicts and to identify the major interest groups involved in each.

Clearly, the starting point is the issue of federal aid itself. Although the controversies over religious schools and segregation may at times make more dramatic headlines, it is the pressure for federal aid to education as such that has created the issue. Similarly, the bulk of the opposition to any specific federal aid bill has ordinarily come from those who are opposed to all federal aid bills, even though they may take tactical advantage of additional opposition generated by the treatment accorded parochial schools, segregated systems, and the like, in the bill at hand.

## THE PROPONENTS

Of the organizations that have regularly provided the support for the federal aid drive, the leading position has always been occupied by the educational groups. And among these in turn the foremost has ordinarily been the National Education Association (NEA).

### The NEA

The importance of the role played by the National Education Association in the struggle for federal aid is perhaps best described in the words of one of its opponents. Testifying at a 1955 House hearing, John Burkhart of the U.S. Chamber of Commerce asserted:

> In good times and bad, in war and in peace, whether Treasury surplus or deficit, the NEA has pursued the notion of Federal aid to education with a singlemindedness of purpose that perhaps has never been equaled by any organization in any field over such a long period of time. It has sought to frighten the wits out of the citizenry with its dire predictions of educational catastrophe if our schools are left to the devices of State and local governments. It has sought to woo and win this same citizenry with persuasive pictures of an educational millenium to be achieved under the panacea of Federal aid.[1]

Although the tribute is a mixed one, corresponding closely to the kindly adage that "even the devil has perseverance," it would probably not be repudiated by the NEA. Since its foundation in 1857, the NEA has pursued as one of its major goals the recognition of a responsibility for education by the federal government. Although the NEA opposed the original Hoar bill, it supported the subsequent federal aid bills of the nineteenth century and has been in the thick of the fray each time that general aid has been proposed during the twentieth.[2]

The NEA is a large, but at times unwieldy organization. The size and distribution of its membership contribute to its political power. With about three-quarters of a million members, the NEA has affiliates of substantial size in each of the states, although it is most thoroughly organized in the Rocky Mountain West and the southeastern states. The maintenance of its southern membership has recently become a source of concern to the national leadership as the civil-rights-conscious memberships of the northern industrial states have pushed the NEA into a position of more and more uncompromising opposition to segregation.

The dues paid by its large membership have contributed to the NEA's strength. With them the NEA maintains a substantial staff in Washington housed in the NEA's own building. As one result NEA statistics and reports have usually been the starting point of most

---

[1] House Committee on Education and Labor, *Federal Aid to States for School Construction*, 84th Congress, 1st Session (1955), Vol. II, 436–37.

[2] See Albertina Adelheit Abrams, *The Policy of the National Education Association Toward Federal Aid to Education (1857–1953)* (unpublished doctoral dissertation, University of Michigan, 1955).

legislative debates on federal aid. The NEA's expenditures for lobbying activities have regularly placed it among the top spenders in Washington during recent years, at least as measured by reported expenditures.

Not satisfied with its present membership, the NEA has launched a recruiting drive with a goal of a million and more members. Since one of the major arguments for affiliation with the NEA is its asserted leadership in the fight for federal aid, this membership drive is closely related to the vigor of NEA pressure for legislation. While membership continues to be sold as support for federal aid, the NEA can neither abandon the issue nor—ordinarily—compromise with the demand for aid to teachers' salaries, although a minority among its leaders would like to de-emphasize political activity in favor of professional educational programs.

The large size of the NEA is, however, in some part deceptive. The NEA's strength is partly limited by its federal organization; the Association is actually a federation of state and professional units, many with a primary concern over separate interests of their own. More importantly, however, the NEA suffers from the casualness with which many of its members affiliate. Classroom teaching is still today primarily a woman's job, and many of its women members have only temporary employment in teaching. As transients in the NEA they pay minimal attention to its policies and add little to its political clout.[3]

---

[3] One source of tension within the NEA lies in the recurrent differences in outlook between the organizations of classroom teachers and the American Association of School Administrators, a component unit. At one time the Department of Superintendence, the precursor of the AASA, threatened to break away from the NEA; it eventually decided to remain in return for increased autonomy. A description of the current organization of the NEA, plus some account of past events, will be found in a centennial history sponsored by the organization itself, Edgar B. Wesley, *NEA: The First Hundred Years* (New York: Harper and Brothers, 1957). A more critical, but now badly dated, discussion of the internal politics of the Association is contained in Erwin Stevenson Selle, *The Organization and Activities of the National Education Association: A Case Study in Educational Sociology* (New York: Columbia University Teachers College, 1932). Selle's book deals only with the NEA in the period up to 1928. Additional information on the NEA and its member-organizations will be found in Walter D. Stille, *The Educational Policies Commission: A Leadership Organ in American Education* (unpublished doctoral dissertation, George Peabody College for Teachers, 1958); and John Martin Groebli, *National Organizations in the Education Profession at Mid-Twentieth Century: Present Status and Future Development* (unpublished doctoral dissertation, George Peabody College for Teachers, 1958).

*The AF of T*

The principal rival of the NEA as a mass organization of teachers is the American Federation of Teachers, affiliated with the AFL-CIO. Although only a fraction of the size of the NEA, the AF of T likes to describe itself as the largest voluntary teachers' organization in the country. A typical exchange of pleasantries between the organizations would be the testimony of Irvin Kuenzli of the Federation at the 1945 Senate hearing on federal aid:

> MR. KUENZLI. I think comparisons of organizations are a little odious and perhaps unfair. We claim to have the largest voluntary classroom teacher membership in the country. . . .
>
> SENATOR CHAVEZ. Is the NEA a voluntary institution, too?
>
> MR. KUENZLI. Again, I say comparisons are a little difficult, and I am a bit reluctant to answer that question for the record, but it is our contention, and I think a generally accepted fact that great pressure is brought upon classroom teachers by the administrators to compel them to join the National Education Association.
>
> SENATOR AIKEN. Do you include superintendents and other school officials in your organization?
>
> MR. KUENZLI. I often say to my audiences around the country that our constitution forbids membership to Nazis, Fascists, Communists, and superintendents, but I do not mean that they all belong to the same class.[4]

Numerous differences in tone divide the NEA and the AF of T. The NEA considers itself a professional organization and includes all members of the profession, whether teachers or administrators; the AF of T is proud of its affiliation with "the House of Labor," describes its rival as a "company union," talks the language of collective bargaining, and is willing at times to talk of teachers' strikes. The two groups actively compete with one another for the loyalties—and dues—of classroom teachers. As a result of its harder tone, the AF of T possesses a more militant and devoted membership, and finds its maximum strength within the big cities. In a recent election the American Federation of Teachers was chosen by the teachers of the city of New York as their collective bargaining agent, a major membership breakthrough with as yet unforseeable consequences.

Given their differences in emphasis and their competition for

---

[4] Senate Committee on Education and Labor, *Federal Aid for Education*, 79th Congress, 1st Session (1945), 675.

membership, it is hardly surprising that the AF of T and the NEA have at times had difficulty in working together on federal aid. Both organizations favor it, but often propose different conditions. In the late 1930's the two groups cooperated with fair success, but harmonious relationships broke down in the early 1940's. When the Senate Committee was considering federal aid legislation in 1945, two major bills were put before it, one sponsored by the NEA, the other by the AF of T. The differences between the two bills tell something about the differences between the organizations: the AF of T wanted (1) more money, (2) a guarantee that 75 per cent of the federal funds would go to teachers' salaries, and (3) provisions for assistance to parochial schools. As the testimony made clear, the inclusion of parochial schools within the AF of T bill resulted from pressure by the American Federation of Labor, many of whose leaders—and members —are Roman Catholics.

In 1947 and again in 1949 separate AF of T bills were prepared. Senator Taft commented at the time of the 1947 Senate hearing: "The principal danger to the present bill rests in the differences between the advocates of Federal aid to education."[5] Since the Barden bill and the collapse of the federal aid drive in 1950, the two organizations have cooperated somewhat more effectively in lobbying for federal aid. Each emphasizes different aspects of the problem and proposes its own amendments, but the mutual name-calling exhibitions of 1945 when the NEA bill was regularly described as "the bosses' bill" have not been repeated.

## Council of CSSO

The NEA and the AF of T are probably the two most widely known organizations seeking federal aid to education. A third group has also played a major part in the struggle. This is the Council of Chief State School Officers.

The Council is necessarily a small organization since its membership consists of only one person in each state, the constitutionally fixed chief state school officer. Its staff also is small. Although not affiliated with the NEA, it maintains an office in the NEA building with a staff of two, Dr. Edgar Fuller and an administrative secretary.

Despite its small size the Council wields very substantial political power as the collective spokesman for the state departments of education. Since many of its members are themselves elected office-

---

[5] Senate Committee on Labor and Public Welfare, *Federal Aid to Education,* 80th Congress, 1st Session (1947), 42.

holders, they are not inexperienced in the ways of politics. The major inherent limitation on the Council's influence lies in the frequency with which its members divide among themselves. In 1942, when the Educational Finance Act of that year was pending before the Senate, Senator Thomas presented a petition supporting the bill signed by the superintendents of education in 42 of the 48 states; abstaining, however, were the chief state school officers in Maryland, Massachusetts, New York, New Jersey, Ohio and Rhode Island. The identities of the dissenters may have changed, but the same kind of division continues today. Thus Dr. Fuller, testifying for the Council, told a 1958 House hearing that of 44 states expressing views, 22 preferred the Metcalf bill, 10 preferred the Hill-Elliott bill, 7 preferred the administration bill, and 5 were opposed to all further federal legislation for financial assistance to education. Under such circumstances individual congressmen are likely to look for guidance to the education commissioner in their own state, rather than to the CSSO Council.

Ordinarily, however, Dr. Fuller is able to report something nearer to unanimity among his members. The following year, for example, he placed the Council on record as endorsing the Murray-Metcalf bill. A bill of this kind, he testified, had the support of all nine of the officers and directors of the CSSO Council and had not been objected to by any state commissioner or superintendent. In view of the fact that almost all federal aid bills have proposed to disburse funds through the state departments of education, it is hardly surprising that the chief state school officers have been among their foremost supporters.

*Allies*

The principal steam behind the drive for federal aid has come from the educators themselves. Numerous other organizations, however, have come forward to give testimony in support of their position. Many of these have testified time and again through the years, but the most faithful have been the many womens' organizations. The offering of separate federal aid bills by the NEA and the AF of T in 1945 presented an unusual opportunity to distinguish between those who follow the lead of the NEA and those tied to the AF of L and the AF of T.

Supporting the NEA bill at that time were, of course, its own state educational associations plus the great majority of the national organizations endorsing the federal aid cause: the American Home Economics Association, the Vocational Education Association, the

National Council of Jewish Women, the Young Women's Christian Association, the National Federation of Business and Professional Women's Clubs, the General Federation of Women's Clubs, the American Association of University Women, the National Child Labor Committee, the Service Star Legion, the National Women's Christian Temperance Union, Alpha Kappa Alpha sorority, the National Congress of Parents and Teachers Associations, the American Farm Bureau Federation, and a number of Negro organizations—the NAACP, the American Teachers' Association, the National Council of Negro Women, Alpha Phi Alpha fraternity for college and professional Negro men, the Conference of Presidents of Negro Land-Grant Colleges, the National Association of Collegiate Deans and Registrars in Negro Schools, the National Medical Association, the Association of Colleges and Secondary Schools for Negroes, the National Bar Association, and the Improved, Benevolent, and Protective Order of Elks of the World. The Council of Chief State School Officers also supported the NEA bill.

To support its bill the AF of L produced from 25 to 30 national, state, and local union representatives. Of support from the other groups traditionally favoring federal aid the AF of L received backing only from the National Farmers Union. And this support was the more striking as a manifestation of symbolic organizational loyalty since it was coupled with several expressed reservations including a request for a larger appropriation and a preference for the mathematical formula for distribution contained in the NEA bill. In addition, however, the AF of L bill received endorsements from several organizations that had regularly opposed federal aid in the past, the National Council of Catholic Men, the National Council of Catholic Women, the Knights of Columbus and, at least in conditional form, the National Catholic Welfare Conference.

Testimony was also given by a representative of the CIO's New York City Teachers' Union (Local 555 of the State, County, and Municipal Workers), who, between the two bills, expressed a preference for that prepared by the NEA.

With but few exceptions, this list of names is identical with the list of organizations testifying for federal aid in most subsequent hearings. Indeed, for that matter, it was largely these same organizations that provided the support for the unsuccessful federal aid bills of the early 1920's and that unsuccessfully sought emergency federal aid for education in the 1930's. The most significant change since 1945 concerning the division between NEA and AF of T was the reunion of the AF of L and the CIO. Probably the strongest political card possessed by the Federation of Teachers is the fact that the AFL-CIO lobbyists take their cues on federal aid from the AF of T.[6]

THE OPPOSITION

At the 1950 House hearing on federal aid Representative Roy Wier (D., Minn.) suggested: "We have a situation here where education is caught between two groups in the Congress. One is termed the economy-minded group, and the other is termed the spendthrift group." With unusual frankness, he added: "I belong to the latter group."[7] Consistently through the years the foremost exponent of "the former group" has been the U.S. Chamber of Commerce, the bellwether of the economy bloc.

### The Chamber of Commerce

The U.S. Chamber of Commerce is modest in evaluating its own role. At a 1955 congressional hearing one spokesman for the Chamber described the NEA as "a powerfully financed, powerfully organized organization" and added: "As far as I know, there is no other organization that has devoted much time or thought to this, and I think it is unfortunate that we have not some other organization that has taken time, set up the staff and the money and the resources to furnish the people with a different point of view." When Congresswoman Green inquired whether he seriously intended to suggest that the NEA was better organized and financed than the Chamber of Commerce, Mr. Burkhart acknowledged:

> No, I do not think so, but I think that the Chamber has not done much in this field. I think it has been an incidental field as far as the Chamber of Commerce has been concerned, whereas it has been a main field as far as the NEA is concerned.[8]

---

[6] The early history of the relationship between the AF of T and the AF of L is discussed in detail in Philip R. V. Curoe, *Educational Attitudes and Policies of Organized Labor in the United States* (New York: Columbia University Teachers College, 1926). In understanding the importance that AFL-CIO support possesses for the AF of T in pressing its case on federal aid it is not irrelevant to note that such legislation comes for action to the House Committee on Education and *Labor* and the Senate Committee on *Labor* and Public Welfare. Some further effects of committee jurisdictions upon the struggle over federal aid are discussed in Chapter V.

[7] House Committee on Education and Labor, *Federal Aid to School Construction*, 81st Congress, 2nd Session (1950), 79.

[8] House Committee on Education and Labor, *Federal Aid to States for School Construction*, 84th Congress, 1st Session (1955), Vol. II. 463.

Few other observers would be inclined so to minimize the part played by the Chamber in fortifying the opposition to federal aid legislation. Year in and year out the Education Department of the U.S. Chamber of Commerce has provided the principal staff support for the effort to block federal aid. The Chamber's active interest in the question dates all the way back to the effort to secure federal aid for education after World War I. After a special committee on education appointed by the U.S. Chamber of Commerce had recommended that education be left a state and local responsibility, questions concerning education were submitted to a referendum of the membership in 1922. By the requisite two-thirds vote the referendum committed the Chamber to oppose both a cabinet-level federal Department of Education and the principle of federal aid to education in the states.

Only once since that time did the Chamber of Commerce appear to be weakening in its firm opposition to federal aid. Under the impact of the teacher shortage of the late war and immediate postwar period, the Chamber reconsidered its position. Testifying before the Senate hearing on federal aid in February of 1945 the Chamber's representative, Thomas C. Boushall, refused to take a stand either for or against the pending federal aid bill, holding firm only to the proposition that education should be upgraded by the expenditure of more money from some source. A Chamber report prepared by the staff at this time argued that an expansion of educational opportunities would be good for business, while the Chamber gave sympathetic support to one bill providing emergency federal assistance for education on a self-terminating basis.

By late 1945, however, the Chamber of Commerce was already returning to its earlier position and a policy declaration adopted late in the year asserted: "The public education system of each state should be financed from funds raised within the state."[9] At the 1947 Senate hearings Mr. Boushall again appeared for the Chamber and, while he was unwilling to make a flat statement in opposition to the pending bill, he acknowledged that the general opposition of his organization to federal grants-in-aid led it to oppose federal aid for education. By the 1949 House hearings Boushall was serving as floor manager for a parade of witnesses opposing federal aid, a role the Chamber of Commerce has maintained ever since.

[9] Quoted in Anne Gibson Buis, *An Historical Study of the Role of the Federal Government in the Financial Support of Education, with Special Reference to Legislative Proposals and Action* (unpublished doctoral dissertation, Ohio State University, 1953), 464–65.

## Allies of the Chamber

Support for the stand of the Chamber of Commerce in opposition to federal aid has come from other business and industrial groups, some of them offshoots of the Chamber itself, state chambers of commerce, the Southern States Industrial Council, the Investment Bankers Association, state public expenditures councils, taxpayers organizations, and so forth. The National Association of Manufacturers, likewise, has consistently opposed federal aid for education, but in a less conspicuous role than the Chamber.

The most impressive allies of the U.S. Chamber of Commerce, however, in terms of numbers of members, have been the farm and veterans' groups which have joined it in opposing federal aid. Behind their opposition lies a story of shifting stands.

The American Legion had been one of the organizations endorsing the federal aid proposals of the 1930's. In 1938 the Legion's national convention had, in fact, authorized establishment of a cooperative committee to work with the NEA. This support continued through the postwar period and a Legion representative quoted the pledge of his national executive committee to the 1947 Senate hearing: "The American Legion now resolves that, in view of the present serious situation, its support will be vigorous and continuous."[10]

With the return of the U.S. Chamber of Commerce to active opposition to federal aid, this position of the Legion was exposed to considerable re-examination. The Chamber and the Legion are regular legislative allies and, although a 1950 national convention reiterated its support of federal aid, the National Executive Committee in 1952 moved Legion policy into conformity with that of the Chamber. Since 1952 the Legion has regularly opposed proposals for federal aid to education, describing them as "unnecessary, unreasonable, unsound, and dangerous to the preservation of local initiative and vitality."[11]

The evolution of the policy of the American Farm Bureau Federation in the postwar years was similar. Like the Legion the Farm Bureau had supported federal aid to education in the 1930's. W. R. Ogg, director of the Bureau's Washington office, assured the Senate Committee in 1945: "For many years the American Farm Bureau Federation has advocated the establishment of a system of Federal grants-in-aid to the States for the purpose of equalizing

[10] Senate Committee on Labor and Public Welfare, *Federal Aid to Education*, 80th Congress, 1st Session (1947), 346.

[11] House Committee on Education and Labor, *School Support Act of 1959*, 86th Congress, 1st Session (1959), 220.

educational opportunity. . . ."[12] Throughout the House Committee hearings of 1949 the AFBF maintained the same stand.

In the 1950's, however, the Farm Bureau shifted its position to one of opposition to federal aid. The charge that this reversal was the result of pressure from the Chamber of Commerce was made directly in the 1957 House hearings. Rep. Cleveland Bailey (D., W.Va.), one of the bill's sponsors, told an AFBF witness: "There is a growing feeling among members of the Congress that your group is not functioning fully for the benefit of the farm folks. There is a feeling that you are functioning somewhat as an auxiliary of the United States Chamber of Commerce. I am forced to the conclusion that nothing in your testimony has changed my opinion the least bit."[13]

The other major farm organizations have displayed greater consistency in their positions: the National Farmers Union, as noted above, regularly in support of federal aid; the National Grange generally in opposition.

### The Patriots

The most zealous and faithful opponents of federal aid to education have probably not been any of the organizations so far mentioned. That distinction rightly should go to the so-called women's patriotic organizations, particularly to the Daughters of the American Revolution. Just as the issue of "progressive education" has aroused the members of such groups to vigorous action on the community level, so too have they taken an active part in the national debate over federal aid.

In some ways this position as taken by the DAR is a curious one. As earlier indicated such women's groups as the General Federation of Women's Clubs, the American Association of University Women, the League of Women Voters, and the like, have been very active in support of federal aid. Yet many women belong to the DAR and to one or more of these groups. The separation in the stands the respective organizations have taken on national issues dates back to the 1920's.

---

[12] Senate Committee on Education and Labor, *Federal Aid for Education*, 79th Congress, 1st Session (1945), 148.

[13] House Committee on Education and Labor, *Federal Aid to States for School Construction*, 85th Congress, 1st Session (1957), Vol. II, 648. Many of the statements made on education by the U. S. Chamber of Commerce, the National Association of Manufacturers, and the American Farm Bureau Federation are brought together in Everest John Michael Farnand, *A Study of the Social Philosophies of Three Major Interest Groups Opposed to Federal Aid to Education* (unpublished doctoral dissertation, St. Louis University, 1959).

For the first quarter of the twentieth century the DAR usually acted in concert with other women's organizations in matters concerning federal legislation. During this period the DAR supported such measures as the creation of the U.S. Children's Bureau, federal child labor and compulsory education laws, the regulation of working hours for women, expansion of the national park system, a federal highway program, uniform marriage and divorce laws, and the like. In 1921 on the recommendation of its committee on legislation the DAR voted endorsement both of a U.S. Department of Education and of federal aid to the states for educational purposes. This vote of approval was repeated in 1922.

The shift in the DAR's educational policy occurred later in the 1920's but was only a minor part of a drastic reorientation of the DAR's position on national and international politics. Its then President General, Mrs. Anthony Wayne Cook, was much impressed by a book called *Reds in America* arguing the existence of a massive communist conspiracy in the United States. Under her leadership the DAR set out to fight the communist menace. Since many of the organizations alleged to be under communist control were women's groups, the DAR was soon embroiled in controversy with its sister groups.

By the late 1920's the women's patriotic societies, led by the DAR, were holding grandly aloof from the Women's Joint Congressional Committee which united virtually all the other women's groups. Each step divided the organizations further. Denunciations of leaders of other women's groups by DAR executives and such episodes as the expulsion from the DAR of the president of the New Jersey branch of the American Association of University Women, an officer also of the National League of Women Voters, further widened the gap between the two types of women's organizations.

Through the 1930's the local activities of the DAR brought them into increasingly frequent conflict with the NEA and the American Federation of Teachers as DAR groups sought state legislation to require loyalty oaths from teachers. Louis M. Hacker described them as "busy-bodies and witch hunters" at a convention of the Federation of Teachers while Dr. George S. Counts told a meeting of school administrators at an NEA conference: "Their patriotism is a combination of thinly veiled snobbery and the protection of privilege." The DAR replied in kind. A publication of its National Defense Committee described progressive education as a "plan of collectivists at Columbia Teachers College, New York City, to propagate alien ideologies through the public schools from coast to coast," while another DAR statement called the periodical *Building America,* issued by the NEA's Association for Supervision and Curriculum Development, "a series of subversive textbooks."[14]

With such a background of conflict it is hardly surprising that the DAR failed to support the NEA in its effort to revive federal aid as an issue after World War II. Even when the Chamber of Commerce was wavering, the DAR was unswerving. A 1946 resolution opposed federal aid on the ground that it "would tend toward the further regimentation and centralization of government." Groups sharing similar suspicions of the federal government and of "educators" in general provided most of the testimony against federal aid at the 1945 Senate hearing: the National Economic Council, the Church League of America, the Friends of the Public Schools, and—all represented by a single spokesman—the Ladies of the Grand Army of the Republic, the Wheel of Progress, the Society for Constitutional Security, the Spengler Unit of the American Legion Auxiliary, and the Nineteenth Women's Patriotic Conference on Defense.

## THE BATTLEGROUND

The organizations so far described have fallen into one or the other of two groups, those firmly supporting federal aid legislation and those opposing it. A third group must also be identified, consisting of organizations deeply interested in American public school education, yet not so deeply committed to either position. Two organizations in particular fall in this category, the National Congress of Parent-Teacher Associations and the National School Boards Association.

### The PTA Congress

In point of size the National Congress of Parent-Teacher Associations is the most impressive of all organizations concerned with education. In testimony in 1961 a Congress spokesman estimated its then total membership at 12 million persons. Clearly this is an impressive audience of persons interested in education and an obvious target for those seeking federal aid.

In general the proponents of federal aid have been successful in securing the support of the PTA Congress at the national level. In the

---

[14] The political history of the Daughters of the American Revolution is discussed at scattered points in Martha Strayer, *The D.A.R.: An Informal History* (Washington, D. C.: Public Affairs Press, 1958).

1918-1925 effort to secure a Federal Department of Education plus federal aid the PTA Congress gave its support. In the struggle for emergency federal aid in the 1930's the PTA Congress provided support again. And consistently through the lengthy campaign for federal aid since the war, the PTA has testified favorably.

The problem of the proponents has not been so much one of securing an endorsement as of communicating the enthusiasm for federal aid far enough down the hierarchy of PTA committees to provide the kind of mass support that will determine the result. In this they have been less successful.

One obstacle has been the direct opposition of some state PTA units. In 1952, for example, the Indiana State Parent-Teachers Association criticized the national organization for having endorsed federal aid without polling its millions of members and declared: "The Federal aid to education bill, no matter what safe-guards are set up, would be the first step toward moving control to Washington."[15]

More frequently the difficulty has been a lack of interest on the part of many state and local units. The strength of the PTA movement lies in its focus on local school problems; this very characteristic, however, makes it difficult to mobilize the membership in support of national educational goals. The PTA leaders are aware of the problem, but profess to be unable to do much about it. When at the 1959 House hearing Representative Bailey thanked the National PTA Congress for their support in the 1957 fight, but criticized them for not acting more vigorously, the PTA representative, Mrs. Fred Bull, acknowledged the truth of the statement but explained that there was little to be done when many state organizations were less than enthusiastic.[16]

## National School Boards Association

A more enigmatic role has been played by the National School Boards Association. Although school boards or school trustees have existed since the beginnings of public schooling in the United States, their organization into state or national associations came relatively

---

[15] Quoted in Buis, *op. cit.*, 636.

[16] House Committee on Education and Labor, *School Support Act of 1959*, 86th Congress, 1st Session (1959), 529. The close cooperation between the PTA and professional educators at the national level is, of course, a parallel to similar harmonious relationships in the local community. In "The PTA as a Pressure Group," William W. Brickman has suggested that more conflict has occurred at the local level between school administrators and PTA's in recent years. This too, presumably, finds its reflection in national disharmony produced by dissident state and local PTA units. 85 *School and Society* (December 22, 1956), 218-19.

late. The first effective state teachers' association was organized in Rhode Island in 1845, but it was not until 1895-96 that the first state-wide federation of school board members was formed, in Pennsylvania. Other states gradually followed, but by 1920 there were still less than a dozen federations in existence and it was not until 1940 that a majority of the states were organized.

The National School Boards Association was established in 1938. Its creation was the work of a group of members of boards of education who were attending the annual convention of the NEA. From the first it was contemplated that the Association would take positions on legislation at the national level, and the provisional committee charged with organizing the group listed as its second objective: "To advocate needed national legislation and to carefully scrutinize all national proposed educational bills."[17] Paul Mort, addressing the first annual meeting, told the board members: "The school boards, not the teachers, are the true leaders of public opinion and support of education."[18]

Despite this initial commitment and despite the fact that many of the state school board associations play an active role in seeking legislation at the state level,[19] the National School Boards Association was a long time in making up its mind to express opinions on national issues. This hesitancy appears to have reflected the wishes of the state associations which saw the national organization primarily as a service, rather than a representative agency.[20] Not until 1961 did the National School Boards Association vote to become an "action" organization that would vote resolutions on national policy matters.

Both supporters and opponents of federal aid have sought to line up support among the school boards. Although the national membership is far less than that of the PTA—the Association claimed in 1961 to speak for 150,000 board members—it is nevertheless substantial, given the large number of school districts and their numerous

[17] Quoted in Leslie Guy Carter, *State School Board Associations in Twelve Selected States* (unpublished doctoral dissertation, University of Missouri, 1954), 31.

[18] *Ibid.*, quoted, 34.

[19] See, for examples, Roald F. Campbell, "State School Board Associations," 62 *School and Society* (October 1945), 276-77.

[20] This conclusion emerges, at least, from Carter's study of 12 states. Although the national association did disseminate information concerning proposed federal legislation among its affiliates, Carter provides no evidence to show that during the 1950's the state groups wanted a more active role in federal law-making and little evidence to show they were much interested in the information they were receiving. *Op. cit.*

trustees. More importantly, school board members are likely to be persons of weight in their own communities whose opinions will be respected by their representatives in Congress.[21] On the issue of federal aid, therefore, the National Association finds itself caught in a cross-fire. The ties between school board members and professional educators are close, yet many board members belong to the U.S. Chamber of Commerce, its state affiliates, or similar organizations.

The 1961 annual convention approved a resolution opposing federal aid to education, but the tone was tentative and conditional in character. Neither side in the struggle accepted the resolution as final. Before the 1962 convention the Association polled board members across the country. The results showed majority approval for the federal school lunch program, for aid to impacted areas, for the National Defense Education Act, and for vocational education, but a majority opposed a new general federal aid program. Of the 13,500 board members replying, 55 per cent opposed federal aid, 31 per cent approved it, 8 per cent were undecided, and 6 per cent did not answer.[22] At least for the immediate future, the Association appears to be committed to opposition to federal aid.

## FISCAL ISSUES

It would be a dangerous oversimplification to categorize these various interest groups solely as opponents, proponents, or in doubt. Other issues cut across that of support for federal aid as a principle. Some of these, such as federal control, aid to parochial schools, and toleration of racial segregation involve in their turn almost the full range of contemporary domestic political issues. These will be treated in the next section. First, however, attention should be given to the disputes over the terms under which federal aid should be made available if federal aid is to be approved.[23]

### The Extent of Equalization

Every federal aid bill seriously considered in Congress has contained some equalization features. Equalization, *i.e.*, a redistribution of funds under which some areas pay more in taxes than they

[21] The character of the local school board finds further discussion in an accompanying monograph in this series, Roscoe C. Martin, *Government and the Suburban School.*

[22] *New York Times,* April 12, 1962, 22.

[23] These same questions are discussed within a different context in another monograph in this series, *Issues in Federal Aid to Education,* by Sidney C. Sufrin.

receive in federal payments, is in fact the principal argument used to justify federal aid for education. Individual proposals, however, have varied widely in the extent to which the equalization principle is applied.

At one extreme are those distribution formulas based strictly upon some criteria of need. Ordinarily such measures provide assistance only to those states which fall below a minimum capacity to support a minimum foundation education program. In contrast to such proposals, often called "equalization" measures, are the so-called "flat grant" bills. These have usually taken one of two forms: either a flat sum in aid is authorized to be distributed among the states in proportion to school-age children, or a per capita payment is fixed, e.g., $30 per child, to be paid to the state for every school-age child within its borders. The two alternatives differ in their budgetary impacts since the latter produces an open-ended budget item, but both involve the same proportionate distribution of funds among the states.

Even the distribution formulas described as "flat grants" involve some equalization, since wealth and school-age children are not distributed in equal measure among the states. If wealthy states pay federal taxes according to the schedule of the graduated income tax and receive federal payments according to their numbers of school-age children, money will flow from the states with higher tax payments per school-age child to the poorer states as measured by this standard. Actually, the only formula for federal aid that would entirely eliminate equalization would be an arrangement under which each state would receive for educational purposes a percentage share of its federal tax payments. While amendments to this effect are regularly offered to federal aid bills, they have been as regularly rejected.

Such a catalogue of types of federal aid formulas drastically over-simplifies the situation since it ignores the many modifications and combinations of these basic types.[24] However, it is at once apparent from even a brief description that the adoption of one formula rather than another is a matter of great concern to the individual states since the formula will determine the degree of relative benefit to the state.

---

[24] A catalogue of the various distribution formulas proposed between 1947 and 1958, together with some analysis of their probable impacts, will be found in Ray O. Werner, *Federal Aid to Education: Some Economic Aspects of Major Legislative Proposals for Support of Primary and Secondary Schools in the United States, 1946–1958* (unpublished doctoral dissertation, University of Nebraska, 1959).

Probably the most significant "interest groups" in the consideration of this question are the alliances of congressmen representing similar constituencies and seeking to maximize the fiscal advantage to their own congressional districts or states. Although individual congressmen may occasionally support a particular formula on principle against constituency interest, the greater number have treated the issue as one on which their responsibility is to serve as delegates protecting their constituents' welfare. In most instances, therefore, a preference for flat grants or equalization reflects the relative wealth or poverty of the state represented. Representatives of wealthy northeastern states want flat grants; representatives of poorer southern states seek a formula. And because of the character of their respective constituencies, the Senate has usually favored equalization, while the House has been more receptive to the flat-grant approach.

In general, the major educational interest groups outside Congress have hesitated to take clear-cut positions in either direction. As national organizations they possess internally the same conflicts of interest that bedevil Congress. An NEA affiliate in a wealthy state will find flat grants advantageous, while an affiliate in a poor state will seek equalization. Nevertheless, significant differences in emphasis appear among the major groups supporting federal aid in their reaction to the formula problem.

Ordinarily both the NEA and the Council of Chief State School Officers have tended to favor the flat-grant approach in their official national positions. The reasons are not far to seek. Flat grants promise some aid for everybody; as such they are likely to be the lowest common denominator on which a national organization with national membership can agree. The Council of Chief State School Officers may serve as an illustration. In 1958 its executive director, Dr. Fuller, testified that of 44 members of the Council expressing opinions, 22 preferred the Murray-Metcalf bill, a flat-grant measure; 10 preferred the Hill-Elliott bill, with an equalization formula; 7 supported the administration bill, combining an equalization formula with provisions for loans; and 5 opposed all federal aid. Dr. Fuller's own proposal, an entirely new bill, was based on the flat-grant principle. Before and after 1958 the CSSO Council usually supported flat-grant measures.

The NEA, too, has supported flat-grant measures, although NEA-sponsored bills have often incorporated complex formulas combining flat-grant and equalization provisions and intended to maximize their political acceptability. Such formulas have their weaknesses too, for congressmen are quick to resent mathematical formulas which they cannot follow and which seem to lack common sense criteria of judgment. When Representative Bailey at a House committee hearing in 1955 expressed his displeasure at complicated formulas "where you reached up in the air here and picked up the figure 17 and square it and multiply it by the weighted pupils," Dr. Francis Cornell, the witness, acknowledged that the current NEA formula "did not have much political savoir-faire."[25]

Unfortunately for their proponents, however, flat-grant formulas suffer one serious defect, namely, that they are almost impossible to justify except in power terms. The usual argument presented to support a federal aid bill is the need to help poor states with good intentions but without the tax resources to provide adequate educational facilities. Why, then, provide per capita assistance at the same time to wealthy states well able to pay their own way? Attempts have been made to answer this question: all states have some poor areas within them; it is "unhealthy" for some states to fail to share in a program of federal aid, etc. But the final, convincing argument used time and time again is that it is politically impossible to secure a majority for a bill that leaves some states out of its benefits altogether.

A question by Senator Hubert Humphrey at the 1949 Senate hearings is typical. Asked Senator Humphrey: "What do you provide as a sort of come-on to assure some acceptance of this on the part of people who are just a little sick and tired of paying all the bills for everybody else? (That) is a practical question. It runs against my social instincts, I want you to know, but it does not run against my understanding of the area of politics."[26]

Partly because the logic of the case for flat grants lies in the power structure of Congress, the executive department ordinarily has been more disposed to favor an equalization measure. This was particularly true under President Eisenhower, for equalization promised a way to reduce the cost of the total program. As a result the question of the formula to be used became one of the major sources of friction between legislative and administrative supporters of federal aid. President Kennedy proved more favorable to flat grants, and the combined formula proposed in his administration's education recommendations did not go far enough toward equalization to satisfy the Senate.

The equalization approach has received some support also from

[25] House Committee on Education and Labor, *Federal Aid to States for School Construction*, 84th Congress, 1st Session (1955), Vol. III, 1006.

[26] Senate Committee on Labor and Public Welfare, *Federal Assistance for Construction of Public Schools*, 81st Congress, 1st Session (1949), Vol. II, 100.

extra-governmental interest groups. The American Farm Bureau Federation during the period of its support for federal aid strongly endorsed equalization. An early federal aid bill, the Brand-Nye bill of 1929, had proposed to distribute federal aid for education among the states in proportion to their rural school populations, and the Farm Bureau continued to support this or similar formulas throughout the 1930's. Largely as a result of AFBF pressure the 1939 version of the federal aid bill provided for counting rural inhabitants as 1.4 persons in calculating the educational load of the state. The Farm Bureau continued this policy as long as it continued to support federal aid, asserting in 1945, for example, that it would support a federal aid bill with an equalization formula, but would oppose one based on flat grants.

The American Federation of Teachers has also tended to show more sympathy for the equalization approach than has the NEA. With a national membership more unequally distributed among the states, the AF of T is not under the same pressure as the NEA to adopt a policy of flat grants. There is no reason to believe, however, that AF of T membership is concentrated in the states that will receive maximum benefit from equalization; quite the reverse is probably the case. Nevertheless, separate AF of T federal aid bills have usually given greater emphasis to equalization provisions.

## The Goal of the Grants

A second controversy over the conditions under which federal aid is to be granted has already been referred to, the conflict between those favoring federal assistance in meeting the costs of school construction and those seeking federal support to raise teachers' salaries. Actually more than these two alternatives exist as purposes for which federal grants might be made, and conflicts of this kind have arisen in different forms at separate times in the federal aid story.

Before 1940 this issue arose in most virulent form in the assumed conflict between general aid to education and the various specialized programs, especially those for vocational education. As a result of a report in 1931 of President Hoover's National Advisory Committee on Education, sympathetic to general aid but recommending curtailment of specific grants, the two programs were considered as conflicting alternatives throughout the early thirties. Although the Federal Board for Vocational Education was transferred to the Office of Education in 1933 and the Office made responsible for the administration of the National Vocational Education Acts, the tension between supporters of general aid and of vocational education continued.

By the 1940's, however, the Vocational Education Association was supporting NEA bills for federal aid which were now drawn to leave the vocational programs untouched.

By this time a new dispute over purposes had taken the place of the old. The new disputants were the NEA and the AF of T and the subject of the controversy was the earmarking of federal funds for salary support. The NEA-supported bill of 1945 provided for federal aid grants to be used at the discretion of the state and the school district; the AF of T insisted that this did not provide sufficient protection for the classroom teacher, and the Federation-sponsored bill required that at least 75 per cent of the federal funds be used to raise teachers' salaries. The controversy was renewed in 1947 when alternate bills were again offered and once more in 1949 during the Senate debate on federal aid when Senator Johnson of Colorado proposed an amendment to earmark 75 per cent of the funds for salaries.

During the same 1949 debate a third variation of the issue was raised when Senator Bricker offered as a substitute a school construction bill. Despite initial misgivings the NEA, Council of CSSO, and even the AF of T came by the mid-fifties to accept this as the only feasible program. There is every reason to believe, however, that passage of a construction bill would have been followed by immediate efforts to add operating costs to the federal support funds. In any event, passage never came and the educational organizations shifted back to the support of aid bills combining construction and salary costs.

Neither the Eisenhower administration nor the Republican friends of federal aid in Congress made the same change; both continued to support bills for construction only. As Republican Congressman Frelinghuysen indicated in 1959: "(To) include subsidies for teachers in a construction program seems to me to invite disaster. Strongly as I feel that there is a role involved for the federal government, it seems to me to include teachers as something that the federal government should presently subsidize on a large scale is just an invitation to trouble."[27] Involved also was the question of the permanence of the program since only aid for construction could even conceivably be imagined as temporary.

The two positions of construction or of construction plus teachers were by no means the only possible alternatives. Still a third position

---

[27] House Committee on Education and Labor, *School Support Act of 1959*, 86th Congress, 1st Session (1959), 9–10.

was in fact taken by the Council of Chief State School Officers whose director, Dr. Fuller, sought the inclusion of other operating costs in the 1961 federal aid bill. And the preference for special programs over general aid continues in some quarters; each of the NDEA programs has its own supporters who regard general aid as a potential competitor for a limited number of education dollars.

## The Size of the Sum

A third example of a question still left open after agreement in principle on federal aid is the obvious one of "how much?" Even among the supporters of federal aid there will be room left for disagreement as to the appropriate amount to spend.

Through the years considerable variations have occurred in the sums fixed for federal aid to education bills. Table 1 records the amounts allocated for annual general aid in bills sponsored by the NEA and the AF of T from the 74th to the 81st Congress. Most of the year-to-year variations have been tactical in character and designed to increase political palatability. After President Roosevelt's

TABLE 1

NEA AND AF OF T PROPOSALS FOR GENERAL, PERMANENT AID TO EDUCATION BY
THE FEDERAL GOVERNMENT 74TH TO 81ST CONGRESSES

| Congress | NEA (in millions) | AF of T (in millions) |
|---|---|---|
| 74th | $300 | |
| 75th | $300 | |
| 75th | $140 | |
| 76th | $140 | |
| 77th | $300 | |
| 78th | $100 | |
| 79th | $100 | $400 |
| 79th | $250 | |
| 80th | $300 | $1,000 |
| 81st | $300 | |

Advisory Committee on Education recommended in 1938 a general aid program pegged at $140 million a year, the NEA bill was revised to follow suit. Not until 1941 did the NEA revert to the $300 million figure. Then, under the impact of the war a new revision was made and the NEA now asked for $100 million a year in a permanent equalization fund plus $200 million in emergency grants. When Senator Taft joined the ranks of federal aid supporters in 1946 another rewriting took place with an upward revision to $250 million. With the addition of a flat-grant provision in the 80th Congress the total reached $300 million once more.

Two consistencies are suggested by the table. One is the tendency for federal aid bills to hover around a figure of $300 million despite the substantial downward shift in the purchasing power of the dollar during the period. This sum seems to represent a kind of consensus as to the size program that Congress is likely to accept rather than any consistent estimate of the share of the educational burden the federal government might be expected to carry. From this viewpoint it is an interesting coincidence that a decade later, when the Kennedy administration was attempting to devise a federal aid bill to salvage something from its 1961 defeat in the House of Representatives, the unsuccessful compromise proved to be a school construction bill set at $325 million for one year.

The second uniformity is the consistent tendency of the AF of T bills to seek larger federal grants. Through the 1930's the AF of T had criticized the small sums asked in NEA bills even while supporting them and in 1945, when the Federation offered its own bill, it sought $300 million in permanent general aid plus another $100 million in special services. Two years later "labor's bill" called for the then startling sum of $1 billion per year in federal aid to education.

Other organizations, such as the National Farmers Union and the Congress of Parent-Teacher Associations, at times joined the AF of T in tugging toward higher amounts. Simultaneously, however, pressures were exerted on the NEA to reduce its requests. Thus in 1947 Senator Taft told the Senate: "There are some bills providing a general contribution by the federal government and proposing very large appropriations for federal assistance to education. I do not believe that Congress under the present budget conditions could possibly adopt any such bills. In fact even with S. 472 we may have to postpone its first effective year until the Appropriation Committee certifies that the program can be begun with the over-all limitation set up by the provisions of the LaFollette-Monroney bill."[28]

With the shift to school construction legislation in the 1950's a new set of problems appeared. Since none of the construction bills was visualized as permanent legislation, two questions had to be answered, the sum to be spent each year by the federal government and the number of years the program should run. The answers were many and various. In general, however, the legislation seriously considered fell within the same cost range as the bills previously

---

[28] 80:1 *Congressional Record* (1947), 1028.

proposed. The Kelley bill, for example, reported from the House Committee in 1955, called for $400 million a year for four years, while HR 1, the subject of House debate in 1957, provided $300 million a year for five years. The school construction bill finally approved by the House in 1960 authorized an appropriation for $325 million a year for four years.

By this time, however, the NEA had begun to express dissatisfaction with the smallness of the sum proposed. The Murray-Metcalf bill, endorsed by the NEA in 1958, was bigger even than the old AF of T proposals, and called for $1,100 million a year in a permanent aid program. The sums sought grew still higher in the succeeding years. President Kennedy's Education Task Force in 1961 asked for $1,460 million a year in federal aid, although the Kennedy administration's own formal proposal to Congress was $866 million a year. And in February of 1962 the annual convention of the American Association of School Administrators adopted a resolution favoring a staggering $8 billion each year in federal aid.

This escalation in the sums sought in aid proposals accords with the prophecies expressed by such conservative critics of federal aid to education as Roger Freeman. Freeman has estimated that the total public school budget comes to $16 billion a year at the present time and predicts that within the decade it will increase to a figure between $24 billion and $31 billion a year. With such magnitudes, he argues, the small federal grants so far proposed must be regarded either as token payments or as the first installment on what will become steadily rising federal appropriations for education.[29]

Precisely because its $8 billion proposal encouraged such prophecies, the AASA was sharply criticized by other advocates of federal aid. It is clear, however, that differences of opinion still exist as to the appropriate point at which to peg a bill for federal aid to education.

### Conciliation and Compromise

Similar fiscal issues that have produced fissures among the proponents of federal aid could also be identified. The Eisenhower administration, while supporting federal aid, sought to require matching

---

[29] Such was one of the principal points made in his testimony in 1961. House Committee on Education and Labor, *Federal Aid to Schools*, 87th Congress, 1st Session (1961), 208–227. See also: Roger A. Freeman, *School Needs in the Decade Ahead* (Washington, D. C.: Institute for Social Science Research, 1958); and Roger A. Freeman, *Taxes for the Schools* (Washington, D. C.: Institute for Social Science Research, 1960).

of federal grants by state and local governments. One reply was that given by Dr. Fuller for the Council of CSSO: "Many people argue ad infinitum over matching, shall it be this much and shall it be that much—and how shall we arrange it. It complicates the bill, and it holds up action, and it has been before the Congress for years."[30] The use of matching requirements is, of course, complicated by the very point cited by Freeman, that federal aid will carry only a small share of the total cost of education. The Eisenhower administration's preference for federal loans rather than grants also met with suspicion from educational groups.

Other problems could also be noted, e.g., whether grants for construction should go to state departments of education, state school building authorities, or both; but these are probably sufficient to demonstrate the possibilities for conflict in working out the details of federal aid legislation.[31] Some of these conflicts are easy to resolve, but others are not.

The size of the sum to be appropriated is, for example, relatively easy to bargain over since support is ordinarily cumulative. The congressman who favors $800 million a year will accept $600 million if his own proposal fails; and if $600 million also is unacceptable, he will join with the supporters of a $600 million program to vote for a $400 million bill. The principal complications arise in deciding which sum to take to the floor. Parliamentary procedure and congressional patience limit the number of votes that can be taken, and the proponents of federal aid may differ among themselves in their estimates of the maximum sum that can be secured without endangering the bill by losing the votes of those who will accept only a small program.[32] And there is in addition the further problem that too small a figure may also lose some votes or at least some enthusiasm.

The question of the formula to be applied is often treated by the same kind of hard-headed bargaining. Thus, Dr. Fuller of the

---

[30] House Committee on Education and Labor, *Federal Grants to States for Education*, 85th Congress, 2nd Session (1958), 183.

[31] A related problem of administration has not produced controversy; almost universally general federal aid bills have called for payments to the school districts to be made through the state departments of education, as the state departments insist should be the case. There are exceptions—S. 81 in the 80th Congress, introduced by Senators Green and McGrath, provided for per capita grants to be made direct to the local district—but these have been few.

[32] For an example of a difference of opinion of this kind see: House Committee on Education and Labor, *Federal Aid to States for School Construction*, 85th Congress, 1st Session (1957), Vol. II, 785.

Council of CSSO described the political situation in a blunt statement in 1957:

> Personally, I think with the large delegations from the populous states in the House, the House would in the nature of things probably favor the flat grant. I think with two Senators from each state, the Senate would tend in the nature of things to favor an equalization type formula, probably the administration's bill.
>
> Then, if there were a compromise in a joint conference committee on the formula to use a combination of the flat grant and the equalization formula, I do not think any of our people would complain very much.[33]

The development of such a compromise is, however, easier to describe than to accomplish. At times it has not been accomplished at all. After the defeat of the 1956 construction bill in the House, two major alternative explanations were offered for the bill's defeat. One placed the blame on the Powell Amendment which, by driving off southern support, prevented a majority. The other, favored by such varied authorities as James Reston of the *New York Times*, David Lawrence of *U.S. News and World Report*, and Congressman Adam Clayton Powell (D., N.Y.), attributed the bill's defeat to the failure of its sponsors to include the equalization formula sought by President Eisenhower, thus turning administration Republicans against it.

Irreconcilable differences have also appeared over the purposes for which grants may be made. After accepting school construction as a satisfactory beginning to federal aid through much of the fifties, the NEA late in the decade began to insist that teachers' salaries be included as well. One of the reasons, among others, for the failure of federal aid in 1960, despite its passage in separate bills by both houses of Congress, was the lack of enthusiasm shown by the NEA for a bill for construction only. And when late in 1961 the Kennedy administration tried to push a school construction bill through the House of Representatives, the NEA flatly opposed it.

After the election of 1958 with increased Democratic strength in Congress and with administration support for a federal aid bill, it might have seemed the chances for passage were excellent. But divisions sharpened among the proponents as to the type of federal aid to be provided. Some wanted to include teachers' salaries; others regarded the addition of salaries to a construction bill as disastrous. Some felt that the states had already demonstrated their willingness to

[33] *Ibid.*, Vol. I, 153.

do their maximum to meet educational needs; others insisted that matching provisions be included in a federal aid bill to stimulate still greater efforts by states and localities. Some proponents were interested in a bill, permanent in character, based upon the flat-grant principle, while others insisted that the only acceptable legislation would be a measure focused on the existing emergency situation in the shortage of classrooms and designed through an equalization formula to pinpoint the areas of greatest need.

These disputes were perhaps less striking and more technical than the widely publicized controversies over race or religion, but were equally or even more effective in blocking action. Faced with such conflicts, some congressmen were willing to compromise. Others, however, convinced that they knew the one best way, were insistent on the particular measure which they favored. In one variant or another they took the position expressed by Representative Carroll Kearns (R., Penna.), when he told his colleagues on the Committee on Education and Labor:

> And I want to say this, that I have told the President and I have told everyone, if they want to go back—and I even told Drew Pearson—if they want to build schools they will build them under the proposals that Mr. Bailey and I had in HR 14 and HR 15.[34]

[34] House Committee on Education and Labor, *School Support Act of 1959,* 86th Congress, 1st Session (1959), 340–43.

# III. Other Controversies

In the debates over federal aid to education between 1870 and 1890 no opposition was expressed to the general goal of increasing educational opportunities. Rather the debate concentrated on three major subsidiary issues: the likelihood that federal aid would lead to federal control of education, the impact that federal aid would make on the parochial school system, and the effect that federal aid might have on the racial situation in the South.

In the course of ninety-four years not one of these issues has been resolved. The debate still stands where it did a century ago and the same three issues dominate the stage.

## FEDERAL AID AND FEDERAL CONTROL

Some would deny, however, that federal control exists as an issue apart from federal aid. The danger of federal control, they would say, is simply the argument used to justify a position of opposition to any proposal for federal aid to education. Anne Gibson Buis concluded, for example, in her study of federal educational policy:

> From the proceedings . . . there is evidence that the often expressed fear of federal control regarding education is a "red herring." It has been effectively used again and again to frighten the uninformed and gain support for positions which might be considered as selfish or socially unacceptable without the shelter of a great fear. . . . In the letters included in the *Record* from the various groups, and in the speeches made by the Senators opposing the bill, they often listed their objections. Usually the first six or eight objections listed would pertain to fear of federal control. These included statements pointing out the dangers of bureaucracy, nationalization, regulations, regimentation, centralization, destruction of state and local initiative, and federal dictation as to what to teach and how to teach. Near the end of these objections the Taxpayers Associations have reminded of the state of the federal treasury, the burden of taxation, and the imminence of bankruptcy; the National Catholic Welfare Conference has referred to the need for Catholic schools to participate in the benefits with-

out interference with the purposes and processes of that education; and the representatives of the rich states have pointed out that it would be more economical for that state to raise its own teachers' salaries if it became absolutely necessary.[1]

The plausibility of such an interpretation is reinforced by the fact that the controversy over federal control appears to be a controversy without controversialists. Uniformly, the supporters of federal aid have professed their strong desire to avoid federal control. The U.S. Office of Education, for example, has disavowed any desire to exercise educational controls. A typical exchange would be that at the 1950 House subcommittee hearing on school construction between Representative Wingate Lucas ( D. Tex.) and the Commissioner of Education, Earl McGrath:

> Mr. Lucas. There is no intention on the part of the Office of Education or yourself, Dr. McGrath, to direct the local school districts or the state educational authorities as to what is best within the state is there?
>
> Dr. McGrath. No sir, I have repeatedly testified before this and other committees to that effect but I am glad you give me an opportunity to repeat this statement that the Commissioner of Education, nor any of his staff, has any desire or intention to interfere with the internal operation of education in the 48 states, nor to impose any standards or programs or teaching methods or techniques or books on those states.[2]

Similar statements have been made by many others. Dr. Worth McClure, the executive secretary of the American Association of School Administrators, a component of the NEA, asserted the same year: "There is no administrator in the nation who wishes to see violated the principle of local control of education granted by our federal constitution and claimed in the constitutions of our 48 states."[3] Or as Dr. Fuller of the Council of CSSO put it: "There are almost as many people opposed to federal control of education as are opposed to communism. I do not know of a single educator or school board official

---

[1] Anne Gibson Buis, *An Historical Study of the Role of the Federal Government in the Financial Support of Education, With Special Reference to Legislative Proposals and Action* (unpublished doctoral dissertation, Ohio State University, 1953), 371–72.

[2] House Committee on Education and Labor, *Federal Aid to School Construction*, 81st Congress, 2nd Session (1950), 169.

[3] *Ibid.*, 77.

who favors federal control of education. All of us are against it. We will not tolerate it. Any federal assistance law we support must indisputably prevent federal control of educational programs in local districts."[4] Congressman Barden's summary seems only a little overstated: "I have never yet heard anybody make a speech or even dare to advocate any federal control and interference. . . ."[5]

## Congressional Attitudes

Despite this apparent unanimity many congressmen insist that federal control is an issue. For those who regard federal control as synonymous with any grant program it becomes a matter of indifference whether they are really concerned about federal control or whether their concern over federal control is a convenient argument to justify not spending any money. Regardless of the motive, they are opposed to any aid. But for other congressmen it would appear that the two things are divisible and that their attitudes on (1) control and (2) expenditures can be separated. Some who are willing to spend at least a little money are only willing to support a federal aid bill if it provides sufficient guarantees against federal control.

It would be difficult to believe that all congressional statements concerned with federal control are misleading or incorrect. Typical might be the position taken by Graham Barden, chairman of the House Committee on Education and Labor through most of the 1950's. Only reluctantly convinced of the necessity for federal aid, Congressman Barden demanded the minimum possible federal control. One of his proposals was a federal aid bill containing only the stipulation that the money be spent by the state on construction costs with no enforcement procedure except an authorization to bring action in the appropriate federal district court. Yet Barden insisted that the possibility of federal control should not bar all federal aid. As he told his colleagues on the House Committee in 1949:

> If I were to say, "Well, if I go on a plane, I am liable to break my neck; if I go on the train, it is liable to be wrecked; if I go in an automobile, some fool is liable to run over me; if I try to walk, it will probably kill me," and I keep on, the first thing I know, I would say, "Well, if I start down the elevator, it is liable to fall," and I could build a fence up here around me until I would sit

[4] Senate Committee on Labor and Public Welfare, *Construction of School Facilities*, 83rd Congress, 2nd Session (1954), 206.

[5] House Committee on Education and Labor, *Public School Assistance Act of 1949*, 81st Congress, 1st Session (1949), 653-54.

right there in my office and starve to death, I reckon, and figure that would be the longest way to live.

I am not going to build any such wall of fear around me on an undertaking of this kind, when if there is any one thing on earth established it is that a dollar spent in education is a good investment locally, nationally, and otherwise.[6]

A part of the confusion over the significance of the federal control issue probably arises from the failure to attach any precise meaning to the term "federal control." Thus, for example, in 1945 AF of L Vice-President Matthew Woll told a Senate committee: "We are unalterably opposed to any federal control of education or direction over the education process," while presenting a set of resolutions by his organization urging that federal aid to any state be made contingent on: (1) a school year of at least nine months; (2) distribution of federal funds within the state without discrimination by race; (3) a requirement that funds given any state be available to all political subdivisions of the state; (4) a requirement that a fixed proportion of federal funds be used for teachers' salaries; (5) a requirement that federal funds be treated as an addition to existing state appropriations; (6) a state minimum salary of $1,500 for any professionally qualified teacher, to be achieved within five years; (7) an equitable state aid program within the state, to be achieved within five years; and (8) maintenance of a state tenure system based upon recognition of professional fitness and applying to all teachers in the state.[7]

Realistically, federal control might be considered to describe any kind of federally induced limitation on the free choice among policy alternatives by the local school district. In practice, however, this is not the case. "Undesirable" limitations on local choice are "federal controls"; "desirable" limitations on local choice are usually described as "federal standards." A more sensible distinction might be drawn between "reasonable" and "unreasonable" federal controls, but such language cannot be used by proponents of federal aid because it would give the advantage of the battleground—and a loaded word—to the opponents.

## Proposals for Controls

This arbitrary use of words is by no means confined to the proponents of federal aid legislation. One of the curiosities of the dispute

[6] *Ibid.*, 238.
[7] Senate Committee on Education and Labor, *Federal Aid for Education*, 79th Congress, 1st Session (1945), 440.

over federal control lies in the fact that its strongest critics have been responsible for the most far-reaching proposals for controls. Thus in the 1948 Senate debate on federal aid Senator Hawkes of New Jersey proposed an amendment requiring the teaching of the Constitution of the United States "not less than two hours of classroom instruction during each four-week period within the school year above the fifth, excluding kindergarten." When Senator Taft described the amendment as violating every principle of the bill, Senator Hawkes acknowledged the general undesirability of prescribing curriculum, but argued that the teaching of the Constitution was so important that an exception should be made in its case. Most of the votes cast for the amendment came from senators who opposed federal aid because it would bring federal controls.[8]

A similar paradox appears in the position of the American Legion, which has regularly coupled resolutions deploring federal aid to education as a step toward inevitable federal control with other resolutions proposing that federal aid, if it is to exist, be accompanied by a requirement that all local school districts secure non-Communist oaths from their teachers and administrative personnel.

Even Congressman Barden, vigorous foe of federal control though he was, abandoned his position long enough to propose that the states be prohibited from using federal funds to pay the transportation costs of children attending parochial schools. And Barden likewise was a vigorous and effective supporter of federal vocational education, a program that goes further toward imposing curriculum upon the states than any proposals so far made concerning general school aid.

This dilemma was faced by the Eisenhower administration when it prepared its school construction program in the 1950's. Although strongly opposed to federal control, the administration was determined that federal funds go only to areas of proven need. In the effort to limit the responsibility of the federal government, federal assistance was made contingent upon a number of conditions. As a result, the argument of federal control was turned around upon the administration and one of the principal objections made by the NEA was that the administration plan of 1955 involved "much too little aid and much too much control."

[8] The fourteen Senators supporting the proposed amendment were: Baldwin (R., Conn.); Bricker (R., Ohio); Bridges (R., N.H.); Brooks (R., Ill.); Buck (R., Del.); Byrd (D., Va.); Capehart (R., Ind.); Hawkes (R., N.J.); Hickenlooper (R., Iowa); Langer (R., N.D.); McCarran (D., Nev.); O'Daniel (D., Tex.); Wherry (R., Neb.); and Williams (R., Del.). 80:2 *Congressional Record* (1948), 3912.

President Eisenhower's supporters in Congress acknowledged the fact that there was an element of federal control in his education program. As Congressman Samuel K. McConnell (R. Penna.), explained the testimony of the then Commissioner of Education Samuel M. Brownell: "I think that what we are trying to get at here, and I think what Dr. Brownell is saying is this, and I think he is right, that we as representatives of the people in the federal government have a right to set up certain standards before money is passed out. In other words, we just cannot leave it float according to the word of someone in a different state. . . There is a certain amount of control or direction in the beginning and there has to be in any federal program."[9]

A second source of confusion in the discussion of federal control is also suggested by the Eisenhower proposals. "Federal control" is a bad idea. "Stimulation of local effort" is a good idea. But the stimulation of local effort by the grant of federal funds for education contingent on local or state matching, as proposed by President Eisenhower, is a federal control over local budgeting practice. Although contingent grants may not be coercive in form, they frequently amount to controls in practice when funds secured by taxation in the states are returned only after agreement to federally established conditions.

Conditions of this sort have regularly accompanied federal aid bills. During the struggle for federal aid between 1918 and 1925, for example, the Smith-Towner bill assigned three-fortieths of the federal funds within any state to the eradication of illiteracy, three-fortieths to the education of immigrants, five-tenths to the equalization of educational opportunities, two-tenths to physical education, and three-twentieths to teacher preparation. One of the conclusions reached by President Hoover's National Advisory Committee on Education was that any attempt to specify the particular use to which federal funds should be put constituted federal control. The Committee concluded, however, that federal aid could be given without federal control by means of general grants.

Despite the Committee's recommendations, contingent educational grants continued to be proposed and to be made. Federal funds for vocational education are given on such a basis, as are the grants made under the National Defense Education Act. Indeed it is precisely for this reason that the Council of Chief State School Officers has criticized NDEA. In what is clearly an echo of the conclusions of the National

Advisory Committee in 1931, Dr. Fuller of the CSSO Council has insisted that federal control can only be avoided by intermingling general federal grants with state aid funds and distributing them through the state departments of education. His own proposals for federal aid have been as extreme as those of Representative Barden; in 1958 Dr. Fuller suggested that $100 million be appropriated and divided among the states in proportion to school-age population. The money could be used for construction, for salaries, or for equipment. No state plan for its use would be required, but at the end of the year each state would report what it had done with the money to the Commissioner of Education. In this way the "big nose of the Bureau of the Budget" and of the General Accounting Office could be kept out of "the local school districts."

## The Educators

As a representative of the heads of the state education departments, the Council of Chief State School Officers has shown a good deal of concern over the issue of federal control. The American Association of School Administrators has taken a similar position, criticizing the "control features" of NDEA-type progams. Although the AASA is part of NEA, the National Education Association itself has displayed less excitement and has tended to dismiss the danger of federal control as a "bogey" invented to justify the rejection of all federal aid. The NEA represents, of course, a national educational leadership that has enjoyed very close relationships with the U.S. Office of Education, the federal agency which would presumably be charged with enforcing any federal standards. The NEA has, for its part, been more disturbed at proposals to vest any authority over federal educational programs elsewhere than in the Office of Education.

A third and final source of confusion over the issue of federal control may be identified. Ordinarily, the issue has been discussed in terms of federal versus non-federal control; realistically, at least three sources of authority must be identified: federal, state, and local school district. And local school boards may be as reluctant to accept dictation from their state department of education as from the federal government. The Council of Chief State School Officers may see no sign of federal control in a particular federal aid bill, the local districts may predict much, and both may be right. For the result of the federal grant may be to increase the power of the state school officer, acting as disbursing officer for the federal government, and to permit the state department of education to control more effectively the local district.

All this suggests that federal control means different things to different people. To the local school board member it may mean any limitation on his freedom to choose among the program alternatives available within the fiscal resources of the school district. From such a viewpoint, it is probably true that any federal aid bill will result in some increase in external control. To the state school official the threat of federal control may appear to lie in the detailed prescription of conditions and standards by the Office of Education and the Bureau of the Budget; such a threat may be offset by minimizing the requirements for reporting within a program of general grants. To the National Education Association, the greatest worry may be that control over federal educational policy will be exercised not by the professional educators of the Office of Education, but by legislators or by other administrators.

Whatever the nature of the concern, however, it seems clear that federal control constitutes a real issue in the sense that it has served to separate out the support of some who have been willing to spend federal money on education, but are genuinely fearful of the possibilities of "federal control" implicit within some specific program. Yet the simple solution of eliminating all federal standards is not altogether satisfactory either. As the Eisenhower administration discovered, the standards may be necessary to insure that the money is used for the purpose intended. Whatever they may be called, "reasonable" federal controls are necessary. Without standards of any kind a federal aid to education bill might be converted into a bill for the relief of the tax burdens of local communities and produce no increase in educational expenditures at all.

Senator Taft pointed out the problem in opposing the Educational Finance Act of 1943. An effective equalization bill, he argued, would have to contain controls. To meet its own stated goal, the bill should require the states to spend a fixed minimum proportion of their income on education, pursue an internal equalization policy between sections and between races, and the like.

> In my opinion, if the federal government is going to subsidize common-school education, the federal government is going to have to control expenditures. I would be glad to guard, as far as possible, against any extension of the federal power to the subjects which are taught, but certainly if the purpose of the federal subsidy is equalization, then we must necessarily impose federal

regulation which will bring about equalization. That seems to me to be a necessary concomitant of any federal subsidy.[10]

Almost twenty years later the problem remains the same, to balance "federal standards" against "federal control" in a politically acceptable formula.

## FEDERAL AID AND PAROCHIAL SCHOOLS

Explaining the newspaper criticism of his federal aid to education bill in 1888, Senator Blair asserted: "Upon the staff of every great paper of this country today is a Jesuit, and the business of that man is to see that a blow is struck whenever there is an opportunity to strike at the common school system of America. . . ."[11] One proponent of federal aid during the 1918-25 struggle, Senator Hoke Smith of Georgia, declared a generation later: "There has been but one active opposition to the measure. It has come from organizations of Roman Catholics."[12] Although both statements substantially exaggerate the influence of the Catholic church, they testify to the length of time through which the issue of federal aid has been intertwined with that of parochial school education.

In this context, within the United States "parochial schools" refers in popular usage almost exclusively to the Catholic parochial system. It is sometimes overlooked that the absence of a widespread Protestant parochial system is a unique characteristic of the American scene. In the countries of western Europe, in Great Britain, the Netherlands, Germany, and Scandinavia, substantial numbers of Protestant religious schools exist and the Protestant churches have never relinquished to the state their claims to control of the educational system. In the early nineteenth century several of the Protestant churches made similar claims in the United States and at one time or another extensive parochial school systems were maintained by Quakers, Episcopalians, Presbyterians, and Lutherans. None of these systems kept pace with increases in population and most were abandoned.[13]

---

[10] 78:1 *Congressional Record* (1943), 8425.

[11] Quoted in Gordon Canfield Lee, *The Struggle for Federal Aid—First Phase: A History of the Attempts to Obtain Federal Aid for the Common Schools, 1870–1890* (New York: Columbia University Teachers College, 1949), 121.

[12] 66:3 *Congressional Record* (1921), 3039.

[13] The causes of this development are discussed in Francis X. Curran, *The Churches and the Schools: American Protestantism and Popular Elementary Edu-*

Meanwhile the Catholic parochial system has flourished and continued to expand. Table 2 summarizes data on the Catholic school system compiled by Peter and Alice Rossi. As it indicates, the Roman Catholic church has made no appreciable progress toward its self-imposed goal of a school in every parish, but Catholic parochial schools have enrolled a steadily increasing share of the elementary school children in the country. Although not all the children in non-public schools are in Catholic schools, the Rossis' estimate that about 85 per cent are. Father Neil G. McCluskey, education editor of *America*, a Jesuit periodical, has reported that in the 1958-59 school year 4.9 million students were enrolled in Catholic primary and secondary schools and predicted that by 1965, 6.5 million students will be so enrolled.

TABLE 2

GROWTH OF THE ROMAN CATHOLIC PAROCHIAL SCHOOL SYSTEM 1900 TO 1959

| Year | Number of Catholic Parishes | Number With Schools | % of Parishes With Schools | % of Elementary School Children in Non-Public Schools |
|------|------|------|------|------|
| 1900 | 6,127 | 3,812 | 63 | 7.6 |
| 1930 | 12,475 | 7,387 | 59 | 9.8 |
| 1938 | 13,132 | 7,597 | 58 | 10.2 |
| 1952 | 15,164 | 8,493 | 56 | 13.2 |
| 1959 | 16,753 | 9,814 | 58 | 14.8 |

SOURCE: Peter H. and Alice S. Rossi, "Some Effects of Parochial School Education in America," 90 *Daedalus: Journal of the American Academy of Arts and Sciences* (Spring 1961) 300-328, at 306.

The decline of non-Catholic parochial school systems has not meant the elimination of all non-Catholic religious day-schools. Although accurate statistics on attendance at Lutheran, Jewish, and other religious schools are difficult to secure, Father McCluskey noted that in 1958 eight religious groups, apart from the Catholic church, were operating school systems of some size: the Lutheran Church-Missouri Synod, the Protestant Episcopal church, the Jewish congregations, the Evangelical Lutheran Joint Synod of Wisconsin and other states, the Seventh-Day Adventists, the Mennonite churches (including the Amish), the Society of Friends, and the Christian Reformed Church. In addition about 150 schools were sponsored by local churches, some belonging to denominations without general school programs. The

*cation* (Chicago: Loyola University Press, 1954); see also Jerome Edward Diffley, *Catholic Reaction to American Public Education 1792-1852* (unpublished doctoral dissertation, University of Notre Dame, 1959).

aggregate enrollment of these school systems was about 500,000.[14]

The largest of the non-Catholic parochial systems by far is that of the Lutheran Missouri Synod, drawing upon the support of a rural German population in the Midwest. The most rapid growth, however, appears to be occurring within Jewish and Episcopalian schools. By the fall of 1960 there were 268 Jewish day schools reported with an estimated total enrollment of 50,000.[15] Episcopalians also have been establishing an increasing number of separate, religious schools. A further potential for an increase in the number of Protestant schools exists in the desire to escape court-ordered integration in the southern states. But all the non-Catholic private school programs are dwarfed by the Catholic parochial system, the one major non-public school system in the country. Accordingly, it is the position of the Catholic church that is of most critical importance in the debate over federal aid and parochial schools.

## The Catholics

It is impossible to identify a single viewpoint as the Catholic position on federal aid to education, both because the viewpoint has changed over time and because it may vary from one individual Catholic to another and from one Catholic organization to another. Ordinarily, however, the position of the National Catholic Welfare Conference is taken as the position of the Roman Catholic hierarchy.

Officially and publicly, the NCWC opposed federal aid to education altogether from 1919 to 1944, just as Catholic publications and spokesmen had opposed the federal aid bills of the nineteenth century. A part of this opposition was based upon fear of competition from a better-financed public school system, but the major component was a quite genuine fear that federal money would bring federal control. Based upon unhappy experience in Europe, a secular, national school system was seen as a source of grave danger by many of the bishops.

Throughout this period, however, some equivocation was evident in the Catholic hierarchy's position. The arguments presented by Catholic spokesmen were not totally consistent; on the one hand they condemned federal aid to education as unnecessary and threatening federal control, and on the other hand they objected to the exclusion of Catholic schools from the benefits of the bill.[16] Thus in

---

14 Neil G. McCluskey, *Catholic Viewpoint on Education* (Garden City, New York: Hanover House, 1959), 35, 176.

15 89 *School and Society* (May 1961), 219.

16 The various expressions of Catholic views are chronicled in William A.

the Senate Committee hearings on the Educational Finance Act of 1943, the director of the NCWC submitted a letter declaring: "The Catholic position is one of opposition to any measure for federal aid to education that would: (a) interfere with local control of the purposes and processes of education, and (b) fail to make mandatory the inclusion of Catholic schools in its benefits."[17] The question left unanswered, however, was this: what would be the position of the NCWC on a bill that satisfied requirement (b) and not (a)?

Following the 1943 debate the NCWC sought to clarify its stand, and shifted to the view that the adoption of federal aid to education in itself was a matter of indifference, but that no federal aid program would be acceptable that excluded assistance for private schools. The contrast in position was made clearly apparent in the hearings on the two separate federal aid bills submitted in 1945. Monsignor Frederick G. Hochwalt, testifying on the NEA bill, declared that the department of education of the NCWC was opposed to any federal aid bill that excluded parochial schools, while Father William E. McManus, the NCWC spokesman in the hearings on the AF of L bill, declared: "(T)his bill recognizes that public and non-public schools are equally important in the educational system of the United States . . . eliminates objectionable features of other proposals and frankly looks to the welfare and need of all children regardless of the school to which their parents choose to send them."[18] The National Council of Catholic Men and the National Council of Catholic Women directly endorsed the AF of L bill.

As was recognized by the NCWC in advance, this shift of front exposed the Catholic organizations to attack. One critic, for example, told the 1945 Senate hearing: "What a glaring contradiction there is in the arguments of the proponents of this measure who have heretofore appeared at congressional hearings to oppose federal aid for schools because federal aid would inevitably, they said, lead to federal control of the state's schools. They are now saying, in effect, 'We do not mind federal control, if we can have a goodly share of federal funds.' "[19]

Despite such criticisms the NCWC has stood consistently by this

---

Mitchell, "Religion and Federal Aid to Education," 14 *Law and Contemporary Problems* (Winter 1949), 113-143.

[17] Reprinted in: 78:1 *Congressional Record* (1943), 8562.

[18] Senate Committee on Education and Labor, *Federal Aid for Education*, 79th Congress, 1st Session (1945), 592.

[19] *Ibid.*, 954–56, statement of Charles J. Handley, president of a local of the CIO's State, County and Municipal Workers Union.

revised position since 1945. The precise form of the assistance to be sought for private schools within a federal aid bill has varied, but has not included salaries or construction grants. That position was stated in 1949 by Francis Cardinal Spellman of New York at the height of the controversy over the Barden bill: "We are not asking for general public support of religious schools. Under the Constitution we do not ask nor can we expect public funds for the construction or repair of parochial school buildings, or for the support of teachers or for other maintenance costs."[20] The language used by Cardinal Spellman in subsequent statements and by other Catholic spokesmen has frequently been less explicit in its self-denial, but the hierarchy has never yet mounted a concerted campaign for such direct forms of aid.

What Cardinal Spellman did enumerate as appropriate incidental expenses for which federal aid was sought included non-religious textbooks, health services, and transportation costs. Monsignor Hochwalt's later list includes transportation, certain reading materials, health services, and long-term, low-interest loans for school construction. Father McCluskey cites transportation; health services; counseling, testing, and guidance programs; programs for the physically incapacitated or mentally handicapped; and some form of income tax adjustment for tuition paid at private schools.[21] Catholic schools have already been included within the benefits of the school lunch program, some vocational education programs, and a few of the NDEA programs,

As previously noted, one of the principal reasons for the shift of congressional attention from general aid to aid for school construction was the controversy touched off by these demands. With the change in approach, the demands for aid to private schools were temporarily shelved. During the House debate on the 1956 school construction bill, assistance to parochial schools was not raised as an issue.

However, the return to a strategy of seeking federal support for teachers' salaries reopened the conflict and in a new, more acute form. From 1946 to 1959 the number of lay teachers in Catholic schools had increased from an insignificant 2,786 to 22,051, and one estimate indicated that by 1971 lay teachers would outnumber religious in the entire parochial school system.[22] Since salaries are competitive between public and parochial schools, an increase in public school teachers' salaries means increased operating costs for the parochial systems.

[20] McCluskey, *op. cit.,* quoted.
[21] *Ibid.,* 10, 168–174.
[22] *Ibid.,* 104–105.

At the time of the 1959 Senate hearings on federal aid a letter to Senator Murray from the NCWC expressed "serious misgivings about the intrusion of the federal government into the area of teachers' salaries. . . . A federal subsidy for teachers' salaries appears incompatible with the idea of temporary aid; for such a proposal, as a practical matter, is inherently nonterminable." The letter expressed a preference for temporary federal grants "to meet existing emergencies for school house construction," recommending, as a matter of equity, "long-term, low-interest loans for school construction" to private nonprofit schools.[23]

Such criticisms were renewed in 1961 when the Kennedy administration submitted its school program to Congress. To the President's program of grants for public schools, an official statement of the NCWC reiterated its counter-proposal of loans to private schools. And, the NCWC added, federal aid to education would be unacceptable without such a loan program. An attempt at compromise was made by a proposed broadening of the NDEA programs providing aid to private schools, but the effort was unsuccessful and it was actually over the religious issue that the Kennedy school bills foundered.

Despite the consistency of the official position of the Catholic hierarchy since 1945, it would be inaccurate to assume that the views formally presented by the NCWC represent the unanimous opinion either of American Catholics or of the hierarchy. Even among the Catholic bishops, differences of opinion occur. There are a number of bishops who remain unhappy over the concession to liberalism made in 1944, and still believe the Church should oppose all federal aid to education. A majority support the present NCWC stand to accept federal aid if accompanied by aid to private schools, but other clerics take a third, more advanced position—that the NCWC should work actively for federal aid for public and private schools on the assumption that the psychological impact of an appeal for federal aid to parochial schools will be greater if the Catholics are themselves a part of the group supporting federal aid.

Since the hierarchy's position is not binding as a matter of faith, an even wider range of views is found among lay Catholics. The most extreme in their support of government aid for parochial schools are those affiliated with the Citizens for Educational Freedom, a national organization, officially non-sectarian, but with a substantial following of Catholics, especially in the Midwest. CEF argues for

[23] Senate Committee on Labor and Public Welfare, *Federal Grants to States for Elementary and Secondary Schools*, 86th Congress, 1st Session (1959), 528.

a position based on parental right, namely, that every parent should have the freedom to choose his or her own kind of school and receive tax support for it. From this standpoint, CEF seeks both federal and state aid for parochial schools as a matter of right. After nearly successful intervention in a special congressional election in New York City in early 1962, Citizens for Educational Freedom promised to expand its political efforts to force recognition of its position.

That position is by no means, however, the viewpoint of all lay Catholics nor probably even a majority. One source suggests that the great majority of the Catholic laity is divided between two opinions, neither of which has yet been mentioned and both of which result from the personal popularity of their coreligionist, John F. Kennedy. One opinion might be summarized: give the President what he wants for public schools. The other: give the President what he wants for public schools but ask for assistance for parochial schools.

Beyond the personal factor, two persuasive arguments lead Catholics in such a direction. The first argument might be described as acceptance of the full dimensions of the principle of separation of church and state. It was expressed by a Catholic congressman, Andrew Jacobs of Indiana, when he declared:

> As long as we have the same right to send our children to public schools as everyone else, we are not discriminated against. . . . Our parochial schools are an adjunct of our religion. The issue is clear— either you keep parochial schools and maintain them or accept public funds and convert the schools into public schools. . . . As Catholics, we do not have the right to a separate publicly supported school system nor does any other group of people have such a right.[24]

For obvious reasons, such a viewpoint is most likely to be expressed by Catholics dependent upon non-Catholics for support, whether politically, financially, or socially. But it is by no means confined to such Catholics alone.

The second argument leads in the same direction, the fear that government aid will mean eventual control. To proposals for possible government aid for parochial schools one Cardinal, Archbishop of Boston Richard Cushing, has replied:

> I would absolutely refuse the offer for I cannot see how any government or state would build schools, without expecting to

[24] 81:1 *Congressional Record* (1949), 4606.

control them in whole or in part. We are not looking to any government for any assistance in building our system of education.[25]

Although Cardinal Cushing has been the most forceful in expressing such a view, it may be suspected that many within the Catholic hierarchy, having grown up in the American educational system, share his opinion and prefer parochial schools which are private rather than state, which can administer their own programs, determine their own curricula, and grant their own degrees. If incidental assistance can be obtained from the government without imperiling that private position, it will be sought. If not, so be it.

## Labor

The most reliable allies of the Catholic church in seeking benefits for parochial schools have been the labor organizations, and the most dramatic offer of assistance to the parochial school system was the AF of L version of a federal aid bill offered in 1945 as S. 717. This bill provided for the appointment of trustees in states barred by their own constitutions from disbursing money to religious schools; the trustee would distribute federal funds to non-public, non-profit schools in such states. Elsewhere the funds made available by the federal government would be distributed to both public and private schools by the state education authorities. The division of funds between public and non-public schools was to be determined by a National Board of Apportionment which was directed to "take into consideration the extent to which the burden of the educational needs of the state are borne by non-public schools." The National Farmers Union also expressed its approval of the trustee device, describing it as an "ingenious requirement" that "goes far to solve the problem that has baffled serious searchers for a solution in the past."[26]

In the Senate Committee hearing on federal aid, Senator Forrest Donnell (R., Mo.) suggested that the practical reason for the inclusion of aid to parochial schools was to get the votes to pass the bill; this AF of L Vice-President Woll denied. Another explanation for the Federation's position was suggested by the spokesman for the National Council of Catholic Men who attributed it to the large number of Catholics in the union movement.

Whatever the reason for its inclusion, the trustee proposal produced a divisive split in the ranks of the AF of L. At a time when the AF of L

---

[25] McCluskey, *op. cit.*, quoted, 180.

[26] Senate Committee on Education and Labor, *Federal Aid for Education*, 79th Congress, 1st Session (1945), 617.

was presenting a counter-proposal to the NEA federal aid bill, and when the AF of L bill was not supported by even the CIO, the Federation was further hampered by this internal dispute. The Commission on Educational Reconstruction of the American Federation of Teachers by a majority vote had favored legislation that would exclude funds for non-public schools. The bill actually introduced by the AF of L, however, included such aid. One AF of T witness admitted that he had not known the provision was in the bill until he saw it in print. As a result, conflicting evidence on this critical point was given by the AF of L witnesses. Floyd Reeves, speaking for the AF of T's Commission on Educational Reconstruction, opposed aid to parochial schools. Woll, for the AF of L, favored it. Another AF of T witness described the matter as "quite debatable" and when pressed to express his own views, replied: "My own attitude is that my feeling is not strong on that point."[27] Other AF of T spokesmen made clear that in a choice between no bill and a bill with aid to parochial schools, they would prefer aid to parochial schools.

Despite these differences of opinion, it is clear from the record that organized labor has been more receptive to the claims of parochial schools than other supporters of federal aid. Yet the support shown by the AF of L for aid to religious schools cannot be equated with the position taken by the Catholic church groups themselves. To labor, aid to parochial schools is a position that can be compromised. To the NCWC, the position is unalterable. The distinction was clear in 1949 when both the CIO and the AF of L showed their readiness to accept the so-called Taft compromise on the issue, leaving a decision on aid to religious schools to the school authorities in each state pursuant to the state's own constitution and laws. To the NCWC such a compromise was unacceptable and Father McManus assured the 1949 House hearing that he would prefer no federal aid to a bill embodying Taft's proposal.

*The Opposition*

The Catholic church was not alone, however, in objecting to such a compromise. The arrangement proposed by Senator Taft was equally unacceptable to those groups which have struggled to prevent any federal assistance to parochial schools.

The groups which have concentrated their energies primarily on this goal are in most cases religious organizations. Among those who

[27] Senate Committee on Education and Labor, *Federal Aid for Education*, 79th Congress, 1st Session (1945), 681.

have at one time or another testified in favor of absolute pro-
hibitions on the use of federal funds in religious schools are such
organizations as the Supreme Council of the Scottish Rite Order,
Southern Jurisdiction; the American Christian Foundation; the American Protestant Defense League; and the National Association of
Evangelicals. Catholic statements have usually identified their principal antagonist, however, as Protestants and Other Americans United
for the Separation of Church and State; the Barden bill, for example,
was attributed by many Catholic sources to the work of Protestants
and Other Americans.[28]

Of special interest has been the testimony of those non-Catholic
religious groups, which, like the Catholic church, operate parochial
schools. Of these the largest, the Missouri Synod of the Lutheran
church, generally supported the Catholic opposition to federal aid in
the period from 1918 to 1925. Since the war, however, the Missouri
Synod position has changed as Lutherans have worked more closely
with other Protestant communions. After the bid by Catholic groups in
1961 for a share in President Kennedy's federal aid program, Oswald
Hoffman of the Missouri Synod declared that "federal assistance should
be restricted to public schools."[29] The Seventh-Day Adventists have
been equally vehement in denying that they wish or would accept
public support for their schools.

A somewhat more complicated situation exists within the Jewish
community. Traditionally, Jewish groups have testified in opposition
to any public assistance to religious schools. As the number of Jewish
day schools has grown, however, some reconsideration of this position
has taken place, especially within the Orthodox Jewish congregations
that support the day-school movement. Although Reformed, Conservative, and Reconstructionist groups continue to oppose aid to
religious schools, the future action of the Orthodox community is
uncertain.[30]

The largest of all church groups taking positions on legislation
is the National Council of the Churches of Christ in the United States.
When the religious issue was raised in respect to federal aid in the
late 1940's, the Federal Council of Churches, predecessor of today's
National Council, took an intermediate position. At the 1947 Senate

[28] See, for example, Lawrence P. Creedon and William D. Falcon, *United for
Separation: An Analysis of POAU Assaults on Catholicism* (Milwaukee, Wis.:
Bruce Publishing Co., 1959).

[29] 42 *Phi Delta Kappan* (March 1961), 249.

[30] William W. Brickman, "Public Aid to Jewish Day Schools," 3 *Tradition:
A Journal of Orthodox Jewish Thought* (Spring 1961), 151-90.

hearings, for example, the Federal Council expressed support for federal aid but urged that it be restricted to "such schools as the constitution or statutes of the several States make eligible for State support." This was equivalent to endorsement of the Taft compromise and brought criticism from those who insisted that no loopholes be left by which parochial education might enter a federal program.[31]

Under pressure the Federal Council reconsidered its position. The 1949 hearings on the Barden bill came and went without the Council's participation. Late in the year the Executive Committee of the Council approved a new formulation of policy, hardly less equivocal than the old. The Federal Council's new position called for a separation of programs involving aid to schools from programs supplying welfare services to children. Each, the Council suggested, should be considered on its merits, but no aid should be given to parochial schools.

With this statement by the Federal Council ground was left for discussion as to what types of programs actually constituted aid to the child. Until late in the 1950's the Committee on Religion and Public Education of the National Council of Churches continued to support bus transportation for children attending parochial schools although it opposed all other types of support. The Committee subsequently changed its position to one of opposition to all kinds of aid, including transportation, largely on the "camel's nose argument" that aid for transportation could not safely be granted without opening the door to other assistance.[32]

Mention only of the religious groups that have directly concerned themselves with the parochial school issue would provide a distorted picture of the situation. Probably the strongest barrier against a program of federal aid that would include parochial schools is the vigorous opposition of many public school educators. Suspicions of a divisive and competitive parochial school system are widespread within both the NEA and the CSSO Council. They are reflected also in the PTA National Congress which in 1956 adopted a resolution asserting: "All funds appropriated by the federal government for

[31] The situation is discussed in Kenneth Nelson Vines, *The Role of the Federal Council of the Churches of Christ in America in the Formation of American National Policy* (unpublished doctoral dissertation, University of Minnesota, 1953), 149–51. See also Luke Eugene Ebersole, *Church Lobbying in the Nation's Capital* (New York: MacMillan, 1951); and Gordon Lichty Shull, *The Presbyterian Church in American Politics: A Study in Contemporary Church-State Relations* (unpublished doctoral dissertation, University of Illinois, 1955).

[32] R. L. Hunt, "Why Bus Transportation?" 42 *Phi Delta Kappan* (May 1961) 356–60.

support of education within the states and territories should go to publicly controlled, tax-supported schools only."[33] Similar resolutions have been adopted by the National School Boards Association. It is indeed not uncommon to hear the position expressed by public school educators at the national level that federal aid is desirable, but is less important than preventing any assistance to religious schools.[34]

### FEDERAL AID AND RACIAL SEGREGATION

One of the few instances in which the federal government has been directly involved in the operation of schools followed the War Between the States. At that time the Freedmen's Bureau sponsored and conducted schools for Negroes in the South. It was largely out of that experience and the desire to continue the expansion of public schooling for Negroes that the Hoar bill was prepared in 1870. Throughout the federal aid debate of the two decades that followed, the education of southern Negroes was one of the foremost concerns.

Ever since that time the effect of federal aid to education upon relations between whites and Negroes has been a major ingredient in the congressional debate. One major change has occurred in the terms of the debate, however. In the 1870's and 1880's the Republican party posed as the champion of the Negro. Today the Negro speaks for himself and through his own organizations. The principal Negro organization that has provided leadership on the federal aid question

[33] Theodore Powell, *The School Bus Law* (Middletown, Conn.: Wesleyan University Press, 1960), quoted, 193. Powell's account of the conflict over bus transportation for children attending parochial schools is confined to Connecticut, but serves as an effective reminder that the national positions of organizations do not always reflect their positions at the state and local level. Although the position of the National Council of Churches was favorable to transportation of parochial pupils at the time of which Powell wrote, the opposition to transportation in Connecticut was led by the Connecticut Council of Churches. And although the position of the National Congress of Parent-Teacher Associations was opposed to transportation, the Parent-Teacher Associations of Connecticut, due to internal differences, sat out the controversy.

[34] An interesting contrast exists between the religious problems faced in federal educational programs sponsored by educators, e.g., general aid bills, and those sponsored by non-educators, e.g., the emergency programs of the 1930's. Difficulties over non-public schools have plagued the former, but were largely ignored in the latter and parochial schools were included as a matter of course in the benefits of such programs as school lunches and the NYA. The contrast strongly suggests that the basic obstacle has been the—not surprising— strong public-school orientation of public-school educators.

has been the National Association For the Advancement of the Colored People (NAACP).

## The NAACP

Throughout its history the NAACP has consistently supported the principle of federal aid to education. The conditions under which it has desired federal aid, however, have frequently offered obstacles to its approval.

The interest of the NAACP in federal aid might almost be said to predate the creation of the organization. In 1905, at a time when the national movement for federal aid was quiescent, the first meeting of the Niagara Movement, a precursor of the NAACP, adopted a Declaration of Principles, stating among other things: "We believe that, in defense of our own institutions, the United States should aid common school education, particularly in the South, and we especially recommend concerted agitation to this end."[35] Similarly the opening address by William E. Walling at the First National Conference on the Negro Question, held in 1909, a conference which led directly to the foundation of the NAACP, listed as the second of the steps immediately needed: "That there be equal educational opportunities for all and in all the states, and that public school expenditure be the same for the Negro and the white child."[36]

Implicit in these two statements is a conflict which has plagued the NAACP throughout its history. When the goal of federal aid to common school education comes into conflict with the goal of equal expenditures for white and Negro education, which should be given priority? To which has been added subsequently another dilemma: should the goal of equal educational expenditures precede the goal of the elimination of segregation? The NAACP has never tolerated segregated education; the first annual report in 1911 rejected segregation as a way of life and this rejection has been reiterated frequently since. But the organization has frequently been forced to struggle with the question whether a temporary toleration of segregation is justified by the amelioration of conditions that can be attained within it.

This dilemma has applied in the making of NAACP policy concerning many matters, including housing, recreation, and local education. It

---

[35] Quoted in Herman H. Bozeman, *Attitudes of Selected Racial Leadership Organizations Towards Educational Policies and Practices for Negroes During the Twentieth Century* (unpublished doctoral dissertation, University of Michigan, 1955), 157.

[36] *Ibid.*, quoted, 154.

has had particular force in respect to federal aid. The original endorsement of aid to education had been coupled with demands for guarantees
of an equal distribution of funds for Negro schools. Thus the 1920 annual conference resolved: "We urge upon Congress such legislation as
will give federal aid to common school training, with such provision as
will insure each colored child its full proportionate share."[37] Because of
the absence of such guarantees the NAACP opposed the Smith-
Towner and the Sterling federal aid bills in the 1920's. This was at
the time, however, a minor part of the organization's overall program.

By 1929 the editorials of *The Crisis*, official publication of the
NAACP, indicated an increasing concern with educational problems.
Although the Association was still pursuing partially incompatible
goals—a 1930 statement listed both "better education" and "the
absolute ending of segregation of all sorts based on race and color"
among the first five aims of the NAACP—a strategy was devised
to resolve them temporarily. Segregation in schools would be attacked directly where possible, but elsewhere the attempt would
be made to bring Negro schools to "an absolute equality with white
schools." Charles H. Houston, vice-dean of Howard University Law
School, was added to the Association's national staff to direct the legal
effort to this end. In effect the NAACP took the position he stated:
"Equality of educational opportunities in separate school systems
is the greatest immediate educational problem of the Negro masses."[38]

NAACP policy concerning federal aid was shaped accordingly.
After the revival of the federal aid issue in the late 1930's the NAACP
expressed approval of the goal of aiding common schools, but remained
skeptical of any distribution formula that left the apportionment of
funds in the hands of state school authorities. The 1937 annual conference endorsed a "federal subsidy to education with the provision
that Negroes be guaranteed a just and proportionate share of the
funds based upon the population, and that the state make report of
the disbursement of such funds to the secretary of the Department
of the Interior." When the Hill-Thomas bill incorporated such provisions the NAACP professed itself satisfied and supported the bill.
Nonetheless it failed.

The most severe test for the NAACP's policy came in the Senate
debate on the Educational Finance Act of 1943. During the debate
Senator Langer offered an amendment to the bill: "*Provided,* that
there shall be no discrimination in the administration of the benefits

[37] *Ibid.,* 201–2.
[38] *Ibid.,* quoted, 187.

and appropriations made under the respective provisions of this act, or in the state funds supplemented thereby on account of race, creed, or color." The critical phrase was "in the state funds supplemented thereby," which would have had the effect of requiring an equalization of state educational expenditures throughout the South. Despite its attractiveness in principle, the NAACP opposed the Langer amendment on the ground it would endanger passage of the bill. The prophecy proved correct; after the adoption of the amendment, the bill was recommitted as its southern supporters deserted it. The NAACP reaffirmed its position at the 1945 Senate hearing when its representative described the requirement of a "just and equitable apportionment" as an adequate safeguard, and opposed any amendment that would seek to legislate a similar apportionment of the state funds themselves. As late as 1948 the NAACP annual report continued to note the organization's support of a federal aid bill of this type.

The change came in 1949, although it had been preceded by a gradual shift in the NAACP's general educational policy. Federal aid had never been the principal strategic goal of the NAACP in its effort to equalize educational opportunities for Negroes. The Association relied principally on the use of the federal courts in suits brought by its national legal staff. Through the 1930's and 1940's these suits continued in the states in the South; teacher salaries were equalized, equal transportation facilities were provided, and expenditures on Negro education brought closer to the per capita figures for white schools. It is difficult to identify the date at which the NAACP transformed its legal effort from an attempt to secure equality to an attack on segregation as such. In 1933 and 1935 the Association's lawyers joined in litigation seeking to force the admission of Negroes to professional schools in southern and border-state universities. Other cases followed, but all involved situations in which no truly equal, but separate, facilities were available to Negroes. It was not until mid-century that the NAACP at last turned to a direct legal attack upon segregated schools. In 1950 the recommendations and resolutions of a meeting of presidents of the state conferences, of the NAACP's lawyers, and of the Association's Board of Directors were all in accord; under the new policy no relief other than education on a non-segregated basis would be acceptable. In that same year cases were brought by the Association's attorneys which provided the basis for the famous school segregation decision in 1954.

Policy on federal aid was altered to parallel the change in legal strategy. During the Senate consideration of federal aid to education in 1949 Senator Henry Cabot Lodge (R., Mass.) offered an amendment to prohibit segregation in districts where federal aid was received, and produced a telegram from Leslie S. Perry of the NAACP seeking the amendment. The Barden bill, which failed even to require a "just and equitable apportionment" between the races, was denounced in *The Crisis* as "anti-Negro and wholly unacceptable." And resolutions at the 1950 and 1951 annual conventions reaffirmed the new position, supporting federal aid to education "provided no such federal aid is given to states where racially segregated education is practiced."[39]

The redefinition of the issue from the equal division of funds to segregation versus integration vastly reduced the chances of a satisfactory compromise over the wording of a specific bill. Previously the alternatives could be put in terms of sums of money: a Langer amendment promised the most money, but might be regarded as unattainable; if so, the best available alternative was a federal aid bill that would at least diminish the disproportionality of expenditures on Negro schools. The raising of the issue of segregation as such, however, transformed a money issue into a moral one. It might well be considered that no sum of federal money was worth a bill that tacitly accepted segregated schools as the status quo.

Whatever its inconvenience to the managers of federal aid bills, the NAACP has maintained this position consistently since. The only inconsistencies have been in the policies of other racially liberal organizations which have sometimes joined the NAACP in its stand and sometimes criticized it. Nor was the NAACP satisfied with its legal victory in the Supreme Court decision of 1954; the following year Clarence Mitchell, speaking for the Association, urged the Senate Committee to write into the school bill a requirement that every state receiving grants certify its conformance with the Supreme Court's orders. In response to questions, Mitchell acknowledged that his organization would prefer no federal aid bill at all to a bill with no prohibition against segregation.

## Other Negro Organizations

Ordinarily at hearings today the NAACP speaks as the representative of the Negro community. This has not always been the case, however. In earlier years the NAACP testified, but only as one voice among other Negro organizations. Thus in the 1937 hearings on federal aid appearances were made by the Colored Benevolent Protective Order of the Elks, the Negro Society of Virginia, and the National Council of Negro Women of America, as well as the NAACP. In 1943 the

[39] *Ibid.*, quoted, 209–10.

federal aid bill—without the Langer amendment—was endorsed by the National Urban League, the Association of Colleges and Secondary Schools for Negroes, and the American Teachers' Association, a professional organization of teachers interested in Negro education. And in 1945, when a concerted effort was being made to disavow the Langer amendment, appearances were made or statements filed by ten different Negro organizations.

Despite their multiple appearances these Negro organizations showed striking unanimity in their positions. More recently, however, the NAACP has usually served as sole spokesman for Negro organizations. This reflects in part the increased prestige of the Association; it results in part from the shift in strategy, for Negro educational organizations find it more difficult to attack segregation directly than to endorse federal aid.

Negro teachers' associations have rarely been in an effective position to lead the fight for equal educational opportunities. The dependence of the Negro teachers on school boards of southern whites makes vigorous leadership too dangerous. Thus in its efforts to equalize Negro teachers' salaries in North Carolina in the early 1930's the NAACP felt it necessary to denounce the North Carolina State Teachers Association, an organization of Negro teachers, for its "stupid backslapping sessions" and dominance by "weasel-worded petty school politicians."[40]

Similar denunciations of Negro teachers' groups accompanied the NAACP's legal attack on school segregation at mid-century. An editorial in *The Crisis* warned: "Inertia, fear, white pressure, and vested interest in the segregated system are going to make some Negroes, among whom will be many teachers, throw their weight against any suits attacking the discrimination system."[41] Such charges are common on the part of the NAACP; it is difficult to determine how much credence to give them. Certainly a basis exists for concern. At the time the segregation cases were brought to court the state of Virginia alone employed as many Negro teachers as the 31 non-segregated states together. Although a somewhat different situation surrounds Negro educators in the North, they too have been limited in their ability to exercise racial leadership by their environment. Particularly at the college level they have often represented institutions whose existence would be threatened by the effective ending of segregation.

[40] *Ibid.*, 189–93.
[41] *Ibid.*, quoted, 251.

*The Opposition*

The NAACP has been the principal exponent of Negro demands with respect to federal aid legislation. The NAACP has faced, however, two oppositions, arguing on different premises and pursuing different strategies.

The first and most obvious of the opponents to NAACP claims are the southern congressmen, the representatives of a white community seeking to preserve racially segregated education. Southern congressmen can usually be depended upon to speak and vote against the NAACP proposed amendments and to speak and vote against federal aid bills to which they are attached. The exceptions are few. It is notable, however, that many southern congressmen now appear to assume that any federal aid bill, no matter what its immediate wording, will eventually be used as an instrument to enforce integration.

This argument has been advanced long and often. Even during the earlier period of agitation for federal aid, 1918-25, it was expressed. Congressman Henry St. George Tucker of Virginia, for example, told his colleagues in the 68th Congress that although the administration might be fair for the first few years, the Secretary of Education, "in order to minimize the number of schools," might then require that "these millions of dollars that are to go to the schools could only go on condition that no separate schools recognizing racial differences in the states should exist in the states."[42]

This might be described as the fixed opposition to the NAACP position. The second kind of opposition consists of the enthusiastic advocates of federal aid who, in their zeal, seek to secure southern votes by "compromising" the racial issue. This group includes not only such educational associations as the NEA and CSSO Council, but also many liberal congressmen and organizations.

In 1955, for instance, both the American Jewish Congress and the CIO supported the NAACP in its stand that any school construction bill should prohibit the use of federal funds for segregated facilities. Two years later at the House hearings on federal aid, Andrew Biemiller, representing the AFL-CIO, reported that his executive council had adopted a statement deploring segregation in the schools, but opposing an anti-segregation amendment to the school construction bill. Liberals assumed this position particularly after the 1956 House debate on federal aid had shown the extent to which support

[42] 68:1 *Congressional Record* (1923), 544-45.

for the bill could be divided and destroyed by an anti-segregation rider. Even the Negro congressmen split on the issue, Representative Powell of New York introducing the amendment, Charles Diggs of Detroit supporting it, but William Dawson of Chicago opposing it.

The controversy created considerable bitterness between the educators and the NAACP. Spokesmen for both the NEA and the CSSO Council deplored the intransigent attitude of the NAACP and urged Congress to bypass the issue, treating school construction in the same fashion as previous educational programs, e.g., school lunches or vocational education, and simply making no reference to segregation. The NAACP replied sharply, and Clarence Mitchell told the 1955 Senate hearing: "One of the most cruel, reprehensible, and dishonest things I have ever heard before a committee of Congress was the statement made by that gentleman who left here a short time ago, I believe his name was Mr. Fuller. His statement is part of the vicious campaign of slander that the people he represents have tried to spread around the country."[43]

In the mid-fifties opinions differed as to whether it was the race issue, the equalization formula, or some other problem that was blocking a school construction bill. Whether or not it can be counted as the principal tangle, it is clear that racial segregation is one of the serious obstacles to agreement on some specific federal aid bill.

## THE ISSUE(S) OF FEDERAL AID

As this account has made clear, federal aid to education is not a simple, single controversy. Rather the issue of federal aid is a conglomeration of issues, all existing within a single framework, but each with its own controversialists. This complexity, one of the most significant features of the federal aid issue, has been the most serious impediment to passage of legislation.

Actually, the enumeration of issues above does not exhaust the list of controversies. In addition to the major conflicts—those concerning religion, race, and federal control—numerous other issues, some extraneous and some relevant, have found their way into the debate over federal aid.

One such issue has been that of teacher loyalty. During the consideration of federal aid bills in the 1930's, for example, the Children of the American Revolution, a youth organization sponsored by the DAR,

---

[43] Senate Committee on Labor and Public Welfare, *Emergency Federal Aid for School Construction*, 84th Congress, 1st Session (1955), 246.

adopted a resolution demanding congressional legislation "making it necessary for all teachers to subscribe to the oath of allegiance to our country or resign the certificate to teach."[44] In the postwar period the loyalty issue was taken up in turn by the American Legion. In 1953 the same Legion national convention that reversed the traditional stand in favor of federal aid also adopted a resolution urging Congress "to withhold aids and grants of federal funds to educational institutions at all levels failing to furnish satisfactory evidence guaranteeing that all administrative personnel, teachers, and instructors in said institutions have executed an oath of allegiance or a non-Communist oath or have otherwise proved their loyalty to this country and its constitution, and that the textbooks and courses of study within such institutions are of a non-subversive character. . . ."[45]

Or on a somewhat different level, a 1955 session of the House Committee on Education and Labor, conducting hearings on school construction, produced a sharp exchange among the Committee members over possible inclusion of a Davis-Bacon-type provision, guaranteeing prevailing wage rates. The Committee members flatly contradicted each other over the politics of the situation. Representative Kearns' comment: "You are going to have it in any bill that goes through" was at once challenged by Chairman Barden: "I have no record of predictions, but the gentleman might think a little bit further about what is going to pass. I would offer just a little weak prediction that if it is put in you will have no school construction bill." Regardless of the accuracy of the predictions or of Kearns' final shot, "I will give you 40 votes on the floor," the altercation clearly demonstrates the divisive effect upon the proponents of some federal aid legislation of the multiple issues raised by any specific bill."[46]

Disputes of this kind involve different possible uses of money; on the broadest level the same problem is raised when some critics suggest that the improvement of education—the accepted end for all—does not require more money, but the better use of it. Thus the whole controversy over curriculum, educational fundamentals, phonics, and all the rest, probably weakens the support for federal aid by dividing and distracting those who share the common goal of seeking improvement of the educational process.

[44] Martha Strayer, *The D. A. R.: An Informal History* (Washington, D. C.: Public Affairs Press, 1958), 73.

[45] Senate Committee on Labor and Public Welfare, *Construction of School Facilities*, 83rd Congress, 2nd Session (1954), 276.

[46] House Committee on Education and Labor, *Federal Aid to States for School Construction*, 84th Congress, 1st Session (1951), Vol. I, 49-50.

Raising such multiple conflicts was once described by Congress-man Barden as "digging up more snakes than we can kill."[47] Never-theless, it seems to be an inevitable ingredient of a federal educational program in a society in which education encompasses the full range of man's problems and aspirations. However, the multiplicity of con-flicts has important consequences on the character of the debate. One of these, the continual emphasis upon the need to bargain if legislation is to be approved has already been mentioned. Because of the multi-plicity of issues constant reference is made in the congressional debate to the need to take some particular position not because it is preferred but because it will accomplish the broader goal of getting some federal aid bill.

A second effect upon the debate is less clear from a discussion that has separated the issues into compartments. In reality it is impossible thus to separate the issues because they affect one another, and this interaction is an important element in the controversy. The fear of federal control encourages some congressmen to prefer a construction program in preference to salary aid because it supplies less leverage to federal administrators. The opposition of congressmen from the needy southern states to all federal aid, based upon the fear that it will endanger racial segregation, encourages the adoption of a flat-grant formula to secure compensating northern votes. The pressure of Catholic representatives for aid to parochial schools stimulates support for a construction program that will minimize the competitive impact upon the parochial system of salary raises for public school teachers. Other examples could be offered.

The most significant of these interactions, however, begins with the effective elimination of substantial southern support for federal aid by virtue of the racial issue. It is difficult to say to what extent the fear is genuine and to what extent the racial issue provides a cover behind which an economically conservative policy can be concealed from low-income constituents. But the result is to force the creation of a majority for federal aid based primarily upon the northern and western states. Yet in these states the Catholic populations are larger, the parochial schools more numerous, and the pressure for assistance to them great. Within these states are found politically effective Negro populations, anxious to strike a blow at segregation. These are also the states of strictest two-party competition, where the identification of a construction program as Republican and a salary program as Democratic is most divisive. And to provide in-

47 *Ibid.*, 159.

centive to reconcile these differences, less need for federal aid exists since these are the wealthier states that are likely to pay more in federal taxes than they will receive in federal payments. In one very realistic sense, the goal of the educational lobbyist is to write a bill to aid the public school systems of the South, and to do it without southern votes. And when, as in the case of the Eisenhower program, all this is to be done through an equalization formula that further minimizes the beneficial effect in the wealthy states, the objective becomes still less attainable.

In view of the multiplicity of conflicts it is hardly surprising that it has proven impossible to mobilize a majority in Congress for federal aid to education. Nor are the managers of federal aid bills to be envied their tasks. But before analyzing further the problems raised in the congressional treatment of federal aid bills, it may be appropriate to look first at the position taken by the executive on the federal aid question, the positions both of the President and of the affected executive departments within which responsibilities for educational programs are lodged.

# IV.  Action by the Executive

For a believer in progress the record of governmental action concerning federal aid to education is a discouraging thing to follow. Even without a personal commitment to the approval of federal aid, it is disheartening to read of a dispute that has continued for almost a full century with so little change. Whether the time be the 1880's, the 1920's, or the 1960's, the arguments are much the same, the controversial issues identical, and the positions expressed by the affected interest groups relatively inflexible.

A comparison, for example, between the alignment of interest groups for and against federal aid to education in the 1920's with the line of battle in the 1950's shows an almost total identity. On one side are ranged educators, women's groups, and labor. On the other side are arrayed businessmen and Catholics. Indeed the only substantial change that appears in such a comparison—and it is hardly to be described as of major consequence—is that the DAR has switched from support to opposition.

Such a contrast suggests the general stability of group alignments regarding federal aid. At the same time it may be grossly misleading if it ignores the massive shift in power positions that has resulted from the transformation of the Presidency from a hostile influence to the strongest support of the federal aid cause. That change in the position of the President is the single, major dynamic factor in the struggle for federal aid.

Formal responsibility for making a decision with respect to education is, of course, vested in the Congress. In the terms of the Constitution the executive department need only be involved through the decision of the President to approve or disapprove legislation approved by Congress. Inevitably, however, the President and his subordinates are deeply concerned in the totality of the policy-making process, and executive recommendations and actions play a major part in determining what Congress does.

The most important single individual in deciding the direction in which executive influence will be employed is, naturally, the President. Only he can make the final authoritative commitment of the political resources of his administration. However, the President's decision to support, oppose, or ignore federal aid legislation will result from the interaction of many factors including his own personal convictions, his estimate of public opinion on the subject, and his conception of his role as a party leader, setting policy for his party and choosing attractive issues on which to campaign.

One of the most important factors affecting the President's decision will be the recommendations made by his subordinates, both the administrative specialists on education and the other executive agencies concerned. Even if the President prefers a posture of relative neutrality, individual administrators may seek to affect congressional policy-making. Indeed at times, as the record demonstrates, nominal subordinates of the President have employed their influence to oppose a position taken by their chieftain, and have pushed contrary views upon the Congress.

Accordingly, this chapter will examine the positions taken on federal aid both by the President and by his executive departments, and will also take account of the relationship of public opinion and party policy to the stands finally taken by the many presidents who have been compelled to deal with the problem.

## THE OFFICE OF EDUCATION

Consideration of administrative attitudes with respect to federal aid might logically begin with the Office of Education. Although numerous other federal agencies carry on educational functions of one type or another, the formal link between the federal government and the world of education is the Office of Education, lodged within the Department of Health, Education, and Welfare.

Today's Office of Education is a little less than a century old, but the demands for the creation of a federal educational agency originated at least as early as the 1830's. As a result of pressure by many educators, statistics on education and illiteracy were obtained in the census of 1840, but the creation of a permanent federal agency to carry on the work was delayed first by other events and then by the War Between the States. The campaign for action was renewed in 1866 with the presentation of a memorial to Congress by the National Association of School Superintendents. By this time the federal government had become more deeply involved in educational matters, first through the Morrill Act of 1862 at the college level, and then through the work of the Freedman's Bureau in the field of Negro education. A bill, based upon the recommendations of the school superintendents, was prepared and introduced by Congressman James A. Garfield (R., Ohio).

The bill proposed by Garfield called for the establishment of "a department of education for the purpose of collecting such statistics and facts as shall show the condition and progress of education in the several states and territories, and of diffusing such information. . . ." Although Garfield saw the agency as only a limited one, with data-gathering purposes and the power only to publish, others of its advocates hoped to give the Department authority to enforce minimum standards for education on the states. It was partly the opposition generated by such far-reaching suggestions that made the bill's passage controversial. In spite of criticism the bill was approved and the Department of Education established in 1867. Within a year's time, renewed attacks by its opponents succeeded in reducing the status of the agency from a department to a bureau, sharply cutting its salaries and staff, and subordinating its commissioner to the Secretary of the Interior.

Despite its inauspicious beginnings the Office of Education was soon actively engaged in the first phase of the struggle for federal aid to education. One of the most forceful spokesmen for federal aid in the 1870's—Lee calls him the most forceful—was the second Commissioner of Education, General John Eaton.[1] If federal aid had been approved, the history of the Office of Education would presumably have been very different. It was not, however, and the Office languished. Even with the creation of new federal educational programs, most were lodged in other agencies. Thus, for example, the vocational educational program established in 1917 by the Smith-Hughes Act was lodged in a separate board, the Federal Board for Vocational Education. The Office of Education remained largely without administrative responsibilities, engaged in research and publication.

In the 1930's the scope of the Office was somewhat broadened. The Federal Board for Vocational Education was transferred to the Department of the Interior by executive order in 1933 and its functions assigned to the Office of Education. As originally established, the National Youth Administration carried on its own independent educational programs, but an amendment approved in the 76th Congress required that all NYA educational programs be subject to control by the state boards for vocational education and paid for from funds appropriated to the Office of Education. Comparable review pro-

---

[1] Gordon Canfield Lee, *The Struggle for Federal Aid, First Phase: A History of the Attempts to Obtain Federal Aid for the Common Schools, 1870–1890* (New York: Columbia University Teachers College, 1949).

cedures were incorporated in the Lanham Act of 1939, providing for assistance to federally affected school districts. The program was administered by the Federal Works Agency, but the Office of Education was authorized to review all applications for funds. In the same year the Office of Education was transferred from the Department of the Interior to the Federal Security Agency. The FSA served in turn as the basis of the Department of Health, Education, and Welfare, created in 1953 by a reorganization plan of President Eisenhower.

These changes and subsequent events have had a substantial impact upon the internal organization of the Office of Education. A very small agency before 1933, the Office was considerably enlarged by the assignment of responsibility for the programs of vocational education. In the late 1940's, for example, about 40 per cent of the professional staff were employed by the vocational education division.[2] In 1950, however, when a permanent program of federal aid to impacted areas replaced the Lanham Act and its subsequent extensions, the administration of the new program was vested entirely in the Office of Education and a large new division was created. In 1958 the passage of the National Defense Education Act, assigning new responsibilities to the Office, altered once again the internal staff balance.

Through these shifts and changes one constant factor has remained, a close collaboration between the Office of Education and the organized educational groups in the country. The associations of professional educators supplied most of the pressure for the creation of a federal agency for education and have retained a keen and sympathetic interest in its operations ever since. A representative indication of the attitude of the National Education Association toward the Office may be found in a set of resolutions concerning federal aid, adopted by the NEA and inserted into the *Congressional Record* in 1943. The first three points were:

1. The United States Office of Education should be made an independent federal agency. The Office would be directed by a national lay board of education, appointed by the President with the approval of the Senate. This board would select the Commissioner of Education.

2. The Office of Education should be strengthened in funds and personnel, should be the one federal agency in contact with state and

---

[2] The organization of the Office of Education at this time is described in detail in William Alexander Mitchell, *Federal Aid for Primary and Secondary Education* (unpublished doctoral dissertation, Princeton University, 1948), 337–403.

local school systems, and should administer all federal funds for state and local school purposes.

3. The Commissioner of Education should act as chairman of a coordinating council including all federal agencies with educational programs.[3]

Similar views have been expressed at other times and by other educational groups. Almost uniformly, the NEA, its affiliates, and its allies have sought to expand the role of the Office of Education as the educational spokesman for the federal government, to resist any efforts to lodge educational programs elsewhere within the executive establishment, and to insulate the Office from political control, preserving it for professional educators. In this last goal they have been particularly successful, and intimate personal relationships have existed through the years between the Office and the NEA. Earl McGrath, for example, who left the post of Commissioner of Education in 1953, appeared several times at congressional hearings later in the 1950's as an NEA witness, while one of McGrath's successors, Lawrence Derthick, moved directly from his federal post to a position as an officer of the NEA. The educators, however, have never been fully satisfied with the extent to which the Office has been removed from political influence and have continued to press for a nonpartisan national board of education to head the federal educational establishment.

The closeness of these contacts was somewhat diminished in 1961 when the Kennedy administration passed over the nominees suggested by the NEA, the CSSO Council, and others, and appointed a Commissioner of Education drawn from the field of higher education, Sterling M. McMurrin, a professor of philosophy and academic vice-president of the University of Utah. Although his public relations with the NEA remained cordial and correct, the difference in spirit was suggested by the new Commissioner's willingness to become the first occupant of his position in many years to give a major address at the national convention of the American Federation of Teachers. At the same time Commissioner McMurrin cultivated closer relations with the school superintendents of the major metropolitan areas, possibly as a means of diminishing the Office's previous dependence on the state school authorities as represented by the Council of Chief

[3] Quoted in Anne Gibson Buis, *An Historical Study of the Role of the Federal Government in the Support of Education, With Special Reference to Legislative Proposals and Action* (unpublished doctoral dissertation, Ohio State University, 1953), 365.

State School Officers. McMurrin resigned as Commissioner during the summer of 1962.

The professional staff of the Office of Education cannot be regarded as homogeneous. Some who are administering the impacted areas programs are primarily interested with federal responsibilities in that area. Others are concerned exclusively with the categorical grants provided under NDEA. Some, especially those in the elementary and secondary divisions, the CSSO Council regards as sympathetic with its own goal of federal support and federal advice, but state departmental control. Other staff members, however, were responsible for the preparation of a planning report proposing a greatly expanded future role for the Office of Education, a report released with hurtful effect by the Chamber of Commerce during the 1961 debate on federal aid. And one or more of the staff members were strongly enough opposed to the direction in which the Office has been moving to leak a copy of the confidential report to the Chamber of Commerce in an effort to head it off.

In general, however, the basic constituency of the Office of Education is the public school system of the United States, and its administrators share the values widely held by American public school educators. Even when Commissioner McMurrin set out to broaden his contacts with the AF of T and with the big-city school superintendents, he was revising only that particular part of the public school system with which he dealt. Despite the fact that NDEA funds of some kinds go to parochial schools and that a minuscule proportion of funds in the Office's cooperative research program go to Catholic colleges, Office of Education personnel and the National Catholic Education Association deal with one another at arms' length.

Only once in recent years has the Office become seriously estranged from its major clientele. Dr. Samuel Brownell, the Commissioner of Education who presented the Eisenhower administration's first federal aid program, was a member of the NEA but under pressure to conform to administration policy. By 1955 the Office of Education was largely removed from NEA influence. When the administration's school construction proposal of that year came before the Senate committee, Dr. Brownell was interrogated closely on this point by Senators Paul Douglas (D., Ill.), and Lister Hill (D., Ala.).

> Senator DOUGLAS. Have you called on the NEA?
> Dr. BROWNELL. Have we called on the NEA in asking for advice on this matter?
> Senator DOUGLAS. Yes.

Dr. BROWNELL. I would say this: that we have discussed the matter with them. We haven't followed all of the suggestions of the NEA any more than we would expect to follow the suggestions of any other particular group, but we have asked for their suggestions; yes, sir.

Senator DOUGLAS. The same question frequently comes up, what is a bipartisan foreign policy? Frequently the Department of State thinks it has a bipartisan foreign policy if it announces to the members of the opposition party what the policy is, after it has been decided, and acquaints them with the decision prior to the public hearings or public announcements. Do you think your consultation with the NEA is of this type?

Dr. BROWELL. I should say for the record I happen to be a life member of the NEA myself, of which I am very proud, and have been for a good many years, and have many friends in the NEA.

Senator DOUGLAS. That is not a reply to my question, Doctor. Did you consult with the NEA in the preparation of these plans, or did you tell them after the plans had been worked out?

Dr. BROWNELL. Well, the question of when the plans have all been worked out is a question—I would say that we asked the NEA people to go over our plans in the formative stage before they were completed and asked their advice.

\*    \*    \*    \*    \*

Senator DOUGLAS. How many meetings with the NEA did you have?

Dr. BROWNELL. How many meetings with the NEA?

Senator DOUGLAS. Yes, with official representatives.

Dr. BROWNELL. With official representatives of the NEA? In reference to this, I should say that I can think of only one real meeting but we made changes after that, and in part I would say as a result of some of these suggestions made, but I again want to say this: on the question of meeting with the NEA, we also had representatives from other groups who were NEA people.

Senator DOUGLAS. Did you consult with the American Federation of Teachers?

Dr. BROWNELL. No, we didn't bring in official groups from organized educational groups.

Senator DOUGLAS. Did you consult with the Association of School Administrators?

Dr. BROWNELL. I consulted informally on parts of this with a good number of administrators.

\*    \*    \*    \*    \*

Senator DOUGLAS. In the main, then, this plan has been developed by the Office of Education in consultation, not with the NEA, but—

Dr. BROWNELL. Oh yes; I wouldn't want to say that this has the NEA endorsement, or any other group. We didn't ask for their endorsement on it.

Chairman HILL. I don't think it is so much a question of endorsement, Doctor. The fact is you really didn't bring them right in and say, "Now, we are trying to work this thing out, sit down with us and see if you can help us work it out."

Dr. BROWNELL. No, sir.

Chairman HILL. You didn't do that?

Dr. BROWNELL. No, sir.

Chairman HILL. What you did after you had it pretty well worked out, was maybe to tell some of them about it, is that about right?

Dr. BROWNELL. And asked their criticism and judgment of it.[4]

In the end the result of this isolation from the established educational interest groups proved disastrous. Every educational organization that testified on the administration's 1955 school construction proposals opposed them. The partisan summary of the situation, made at the hearings by Senator Herbert Lehman (D., N.Y.), was not on the whole an unfair one:

It is a source of both regret and amazement to me that the administration has not been able to present, or hasn't presented, a single witness drawn from the educational field in support of the bill which is represented as an administration bill.

To me it would seem to be perfectly clear that the administration bill was drafted without adequate consultation with the educational authorities of this country who are responsible for the administration of the local units of education and represents not at all the public point of view of expert educators. It is merely a bill that was drafted by the administration without adequate consultation or study with those people who really know the field of education.[5]

Commissioner Brownell's experience illustrates the political difficulties the Office of Education may encounter when deserted by

[4] Senate Committee on Labor and Public Welfare, *Federal Assistance to Increase Public School Construction*, 84th Congress, 1st Session (1955), Vol. II, 105–7.

[5] *Ibid.*, 322–23.

its natural constituents, the public school educators. When, on the other hand, it has their support, no complaints are made to Congress, and since congressmen hear no evil, they are well-disposed toward the Office. This has been the usual situation in the past and congressmen have frequently expressed their favorable impressions of the Office of Education. Indeed, Senator Robert Taft (R., Ohio), in shifting to the support of federal aid, gave as one of his reasons his confidence that the Office could be trusted: "The record of the federal Office of Education has been very good. It has relied almost entirely on state boards of education. It has a history of not interfering in any way with their administration and of conducting a very simple operation."[6]

Other congressmen are enthusiastic champions of the Office. One of the most forceful probably was Congressman Carroll Kearns (R., Penna.). Kearns at times described the Office of Education as "three offices stuck in a corner,"[7] and the Commissioner as "a glorified clerk,"[8] but also informed the Commissioner, "your position in my opinion is one of the greatest positions in the federal government,"[9] and insisted: "Too many people are calling the signals. You ought to be the fellow in America that calls the signals and you ought to have the direct cooperation of every state officer in the Union right at your disposal. There ought not to be a question about it. New Jersey should not ask for one classroom if all those kids in Georgia are not in school."[10]

The relative lack of congressional criticism of the Office of Education is not, however, the same thing as political strength. One is negative, the other positive. When educators are satisfied with the Office, the Congress is reluctant to criticize, but when the Office of Education asks for something, Congress will not necessarily oblige. The Office is in one sense a victim of its own success in insulating its position against political pressure. Like public school educators generally in the country, it has ordinarily tried to be nonpartisan and has isolated itself from the centers of political power.

[6] 81:1 *Congressional Record* (1949), 5396.

[7] House Committee on Education and Labor, *Public School Assistance Act of 1949*, 81st Congress, 1st Session (1949), 55.

[8] House Committee on Education and Labor, *Federal Activity in the Field of Education*, 83rd Congress, 2nd Session (1954), 22.

[9] House Committee on Education and Labor, *Federal Aid for School Construction*, 83rd Congress, 2nd Session (1954), 396.

[10] House Committee on Education and Labor, *Federal Aid to School Construction*, 81st Congress, 2nd Session (1950), 159.

The relative weakness of education at the national level was dramatically illustrated in the early 1930's when the economic crisis pushed Congress into drastic action to reduce unnecessary government expenditures. On the recommendation of President Herbert Hoover, Congress set about the task of cutting expenditures by 10 per cent. But when it reached the Office of Education the Senate Committee on Appropriations cut deeper, slicing out 34 per cent of the funds. Despite protests by some senators the reduction was upheld on the floor. And even the senators who protested agreed that other matters were more important. Senator Royal S. Copeland (D., N.Y.), acknowledged: "We are at a time when the federal government must consider its costs, so I shall not press the matter, because I know what a difficult task it was for the committee." Senator George Norris (R., Neb.), after making his protest, admitted: "I would rather cut that appropriation than an item, for instance, of improvements such as Boulder Dam." The attitude of the senators was in striking contrast to the position of the Congress concerning vocational education, a matter of tangible economic importance, where all proposals for reduction were sharply rebuffed.[11]

The provocation is less severe and the congressional reaction less intense, but in recent years a political situation has arisen in many ways similar. As the federal aid issue has become a subject of increasingly sharp party controversy, the Office of Education has come under attack. Although the major administration bills on education have not originated in the Office itself—the initiative for major innovations in policy has ordinarily come from the HEW Secretary's level—the Office of Education has been called upon to supply the factual support to back up the departmental proposals. At first the opposition developed collateral lines of argument against federal aid; increasingly in the late 1950's the opponents began to challenge the factual premises behind the aid bills, denying, for example, the very existence of the "classroom shortage." In practice this has meant challenging the competence and trustworthiness of the research done in the Office. Premature publication of the task force report, *A Federal Education Agency for the Future*, added further to the Office's bad press, so far as many congressmen were concerned. Given the political weakness of the Office of Education, education bills have had to rely heavily upon the prestige and influence of the President and of the Department of Health, Education, and Welfare.

[11] 72:1 *Congressional Record* (1932), 7962, 8035.

## THE DEPARTMENT OF HEALTH, EDUCATION, AND WELFARE

Commissioner of Education Brownell's appearance before the Senate Committee in 1955 was a difficult experience, placing him as it did in opposition to the views of every major educational group. In some ways, however, it was no more embarrassing than his non-appearance before the same committee in 1954.

At that time the Eisenhower administration was officially opposed to any action on school construction legislation, pending the White House Conference on Education and the report of the Commission on Intergovernmental Relations. A bill was introduced nonetheless and hearings were held before a Senate subcommittee. Early in the hearings the subcommittee chairman, Senator John Sherman Cooper (R., Ky.), reported that he had talked to Commissioner Brownell, "and Mr. Brownell had said that he would be glad to come before the committee and give the committee any information that the committee wanted, and give his views upon this bill."[12]

Despite Senator Cooper's report that Brownell "still held himself available to the committee and to the chairman to appear and testify," Brownell's continued failure to appear produced sharply critical comment as the hearings proceeded. In the face of such criticism Senator Cooper was compelled to make another statement in defense of the administration. He explained Brownell's continued delay in coming before the Committee by a conversation between himself and the Commissioner: "In talking to me and saying that his testimony was upon the question of need which he had discussed at an earlier date, I think it was as much at my suggestion as anyone else that I suggested that perhaps his testimony would be more valuable later in the hearings." In answer to a question as to whether Brownell would appear later, Cooper replied: "My idea is that he will probably appear."

In the end result, he did not. On the last day of the hearings the Commissioner was "out of the city" and thus "unavailable to appear." The lameness of this explanation was underscored when the hearings were subsequently reopened to permit an appearance by Senator John McClellan (D., Ark.). The same could have been done for Brownell, but he preferred to rest content with a filed statement. Senator James Murray (D., Mont.) commented as the hearings closed:

[12] Senate Committee on Labor and Public Welfare, *Construction of School Facilities*, 83rd Congress, 2nd Session (1954), 41-42.

The United States Commissioner of Education, Dr. Samuel Brownell, was invited to testify at these hearings and, I understand was scheduled to testify on the very first day the hearings were opened. Commissioner Brownell did not appear at that time and has not appeared to give us the benefit of his thinking with respect to these bills since. I believe there is no parallel in the history of this committee—never before have we considered bills of major importance affecting the work of one of our departments or commissions without having testimony from the head of that department or commission, given in public and subject to committee interrogation.[13]

Senator Murray then proceeded to read into the record previous statements of Commissioner Brownell supporting a federal school construction program.

As Senator Murray's statement made clear, the reason for the Commissioner's embarrassment at testifying was the discrepancy between his own previous statements and the educational policies of the administration he was called upon to defend. This discrepancy made clear that executive policy regarding federal aid to education was being made at higher administrative levels and was in conflict with the recommendations of the educational specialists within the Office of Education.

In his filed written statement, and in subsequent testimony before a House committee, Brownell loyally defended the administration position "that the course of action promising the greatest immediate and long-range benefits to the most school children is to press for action programs in each of the 48 states, and to get the benefit of the studies and considerations of these 48 states as well as of the Commission on Intergovernmental Relations in determining the long-range place of the federal government in reference to the school-construction problem."[14] But as his answers to committee questions demonstrated, the Commissioner of Education was not close enough to the making of final decisions on educational policy to make commitments in the name of the executive. Thus when he was asked his reaction to specific proposals, he replied:

From the standpoint of the question of whether this committee

---

[13] *Ibid.*, 304.

[14] House Committee on Education and Labor, *Federal Aid for School Construction*, 83rd Congress, 2nd Session (1954), 368.

were to come out with a bill or not, and the question of what the Department's attitude would be, that is one of those things that would be very difficult for me to predict. . . . I would have to say that until we saw a specific bill and studied it. Until then I could not say what the position would be that the Office would take on any particular bill.[15]

The reply of Rep. Lee Metcalf (D., Mont.), was sympathetic: "I understand that. I frequently write the same sort of letters to my constituents when they ask me my position on a bill."[16] The exchange continued:

Dr. BROWNELL. I wish that I were in a position to speak for the administration to say whether it would oppose or not.

Mr. METCALF. I wish you were, too.

Dr. BROWNELL. I cannot. There are a lot of people involved in making that kind of decision. When you say "the administration" that involves the President and the Cabinet and the congressional leaders.

Mr. METCALF. I had hoped that someone would come up here and tell us about the attitude that we are going to meet if we brought out such legislation.

Dr. BROWNELL. I do not suppose that we can get that kind of reaction. I should like to have it on a number of things.

As you know, through the processes of finding out what the Bureau of the Budget position is and what the position of the Chief Executive is, and what the position of the congressional leaders is, that is trying to expect too much, I guess, to assume we can predict how they are going to balance all of their considerations.[17]

As Dr. Brownell indicated, the Office of Education was not close enough to the position of the Eisenhower administration to speak on its behalf. Under these circumstances the degree of enthusiasm of the departmental secretary determined in considerable part the vigor with which the education program was pursued by the administration. Mrs. Oveta Culp Hobby, as HEW Secretary in 1955, presented the first Eisenhower school construction program, but was not excited about the need for federal aid. Her successor, Marion Folsom, was. The contrast was so striking that it attracted partisan comment as Democrats sought to pit Secretary Folsom's testimony against that of Secretary

[15] *Ibid.*, 385.
[16] *Loc cit.*
[17] *Ibid.*, 385–86.

Hobby. At the 1957 House hearing, for example, Representative Stewart Udall (D. Ariz.), commented: "I am sure it serves no particularly constructive purpose, but we are still politicians to some extent—that it does seem to me that your predecessor did a disservice to this committee in attempting to present a rosy picture to us two years ago."[18]

Dr. Brownell's testimony in 1954 had, however, suggested another point as well: that administration policy with respect to federal aid to education could not be exclusively a departmental concern but involved also other departments, the Bureau of the Budget, and the Republican leaders in Congress. The enthusiasm of the Office of Education for federal aid was, under Mrs. Hobby, restrained by the Department. Subsequently, the support given to federal aid by HEW Secretary Folsom and his successor, Arthur Flemming, was checked by opposition elsewhere in the administration. Limitations were imposed in three principal ways.

First, the educational proposals of the Department were scaled down before presentation to Congress. Thus, for example, in 1959 Secretary Flemming presented the administration's education plan to Congress. Using Office of Education figures, he argued that a serious classroom shortage still existed. He defended the notion that the federal government had a responsibility in the situation. But the reasons given for his own support of an administration plan that provided no grants-in-aid to the states were extraneous to the field of education. The Secretary explained:

> Other plans, I appreciate, are being considered by this committee. These plans, however, would unbalance the federal government's budget for 1960. The executive branch, therefore, cannot support them. We cannot support them because we believe that deficit spending on the part of the federal government under existing conditions would set into motion forces that would lead to serious inflationary pressures.[19]

At the Senate hearing Senator Jacob Javits (R., N.Y.), unkindly described this method of preparing a school construction bill as "the shoehorn plan. You have to fit it into the shoe, which is the budget."[20]

---

[18] House Committee on Education and Labor, *Federal Aid to States for School Construction*, 85th Congress, 1st Session (1957), Vol. I, 60.

[19] House Committee on Education and Labor, *School Support Act of 1959*, 86th Congress, 1st Session (1959), 87.

[20] Senate Committee on Labor and Public Welfare, *Federal Grants to States for Elementary and Secondary Schools*, 86th Congress, 1st Session (1959), 200.

On the House side another proponent of federal aid, Representative Frank Thompson (D., N.J.), commented: "With all due respect to you I can almost see the drops of sweat on the bills and on the testimony in the department's attempt to do something toward alleviating the need which it recognizes."[21]

A second line of Democratic criticism at the 1959 hearings illustrates the second major restraint on the efforts of HEW. Representative Udall, for example, complained: "Let me say in all candor I was somewhat dismayed, myself, that the President to this point has not identified himself with, did not send up a special message on your program." Secretary Flemming's defense was to point to the conventional clearance of administrative proposals by the Bureau of the Budget: "I am sure you noted the last sentence on the letter which said that I had been advised that I could inform the Congress that what I was proposing was in accord with the program of the President."[22]

Far more serious to the cause of federal aid legislation than this "deficiency of leadership" in 1959, as Udall called it, were the events of 1957. Aware that the school bill was in trouble in Congress, its Democratic managers withdrew their own proposal in the course of the House debate and offered to accept the complete and exact Eisenhower measure of 1956. Nonetheless, a motion to terminate the debate was adopted 208 to 203. Bitter Republican supporters of federal aid charged that President Eisenhower could have saved the bill with a few phone calls. The President made his reply at his next press conference.

President Eisenhower explained that he "never heard" that the House Democrats were willing to accept the administration formula for federal aid. The President asserted he

> spoke up plenty of times for the principles in which I believe.... I have compromised twice in the proposals that I have placed before the Congress, and I was even ready to accept further proposals, but I am getting to the point where I can't be too enthusiastic about something that I think is likely to fasten a sort of albatross ... around the neck of the federal government.... I will have another bill ready for the next session of Congress.
>
> The work of a President with Congress in my opinion is done in a quiet conventional way by the telephone and informal meetings.

---

[21] House Committee on Education and Labor, *School Support Act of 1959*, 86th Congress, 1st Session (1959), 89.

[22] *Ibid.*, 13.

You don't influence Congress . . . by threats, by anything except trying to convince them of the soundness and the logic of your views. . . . I am trying to get through a program that . . . I believe to be for the good of the United States, and I will talk to any congressman . . . about these things if he has . . . honest differences of opinion with me. . . . I don't get up and make statements every 20 minutes. I don't think that is good business.[23]

If the second limitation upon the capacity of HEW to work for federal aid was the lack of enthusiastic presidential support, it was closely related to the third limitation, the existence of contrary pressures within the administration itself. To Secretary Folsom's pleas to the President to speak out for federal aid, House Leader Charles Halleck (R., Ind.) offered counter-pleas to let events take their course. And when Eisenhower remained silent, Halleck informed his House colleagues: "I am going to follow the dictates of my own conscience."

While Secretary Folsom was calling for a new federal program of aid to education in 1957, the Secretary of the Treasury, George Humphrey, was predicting that continued increases in federal spending would bring a "hair-curling" depression, and President Eisenhower was giving his endorsement to both. With such divided counsels it was impossible for HEW to mobilize the full force of administration support behind its proposals.

### The Opinion of the Public

The President is not, however, entirely the creature of his subordinates. The position of the President also reflects the opinion of the public, as well as his own personal beliefs. The President is indeed the only elective office-holder with anything like a national constituency (even if the weight of individual constituents is distorted by the electoral college). In this sense he is the only office-holder who can read a national opinion survey and take it as a reading on his own particular electorate.

The evidence strongly suggests that for the past quarter of a century, if not longer, a substantial majority of the President's constituents have favored federal aid to education. A number of public opinion surveys on the subject, drawn from various sources, are summarized in Table 3. These polls show that from 1938 to the present between two-thirds and three-quarters of those questioned have consistently expressed approval of federal aid.

[23] Quoted in 13 *Congressional Quarterly Almanac* (1957), 592.

It would be dangerous, however, to place too much faith in the results as a demonstration of widespread and enthusiastic support for federal aid. A more realistic appraisal of the situation is indicated by two other opinion surveys in which those interviewed were asked if they had heard of the debate over federal aid to education. In both surveys, one in 1950, the other in 1956, 58 per cent responded that they had. Or, to reverse the results, 42 per cent reported that they did not know federal aid was an issue. Clearly, favorable attitudes toward federal aid held by persons who do not realize it is a subject of controversy are unlikely to have much impact on the political process.

TABLE 3

PUBLIC OPINION POLLS CONCERNING GENERAL FEDERAL AID TO EDUCATION
1938 TO 1961

| Date | Per Cent Favoring Federal Aid |
| --- | --- |
| 1938 | 68 |
| 1943 | 69 |
| May, 1948 | 79 |
| Dec., 1948 | 61 |
| 1949 | 66 |
| 1950 | 66 |
| 1955 | 68 |
| Jan., 1957 | 76 |
| June, 1957 | 66 |
| 1959 | 77 |
| 1961 | 73 |

SOURCE: American Institute for Public Opinion, 1938; May, 1948; December, 1948; 1949; 1955; January, 1957; June, 1957; 1961; Elmo Roper and Associates, 1950; Survey Research Center, 1959; National Opinion Research Center, 1943.

There is other evidence also to suggest that the poll results recorded in Table 3 are not reliable indications of broad, strong support for federal aid. The shallowness of the affirmative opinions is demonstrated by the variations in the answers received when the question asked is rephrased. Thus in 1938 the Gallup poll asked a national sample: "Do you think the federal government should give money to states to help local schools?" Some 68 per cent answered yes, the figure recorded in Table 3. But when a second, similar cross-section of the population was simultaneously asked: "Do you think the federal government should give money to help local schools in the poor communities?" the emphasis on need raised the percentage answering yes to 81.

Similarly, Table 3 omits one atypical percentage produced by a differently phrased question. When in 1947 the Gallup poll asked: "Would you be willing to pay more taxes to the federal government to raise educational levels in the poorer states of this country—or should the poorer states take this responsibility themselves?" only 35 per cent volunteered to raise their own taxes while the rest preferred to let the states "bear their own responsibilities." The form of the question was clearly "loaded" and encouraged a negative response, but when a loaded question produces such a drastic change the reasonable conclusion is that most of those interviewed lack deep feelings and are expressing opinions on the spur of the moment. Public opinion is not, in other words, crystallized.

It may be suspected likewise that the relatively high degree of support recorded in 1959 was encouraged by the way the Survey Research Center put the question: "If cities and towns around the country need help to build schools, the government in Washington ought to give them the money they need. Do you agree or disagree?" In this slanted form, 77 per cent agreed, the second highest percentage recorded in Table 3. It is at least plausible that the variations from poll to poll are as much the result of such changes in the way the question is asked as reflections of a changing mood of the public.

Finally, a further indication of the instability of opinion concerning the federal role in education is provided by the substantial support shown for some very extreme proposals. Thus a *Fortune* poll in 1939 showed 20 per cent supporting the proposition that the government should take over and operate all private and parochial schools, while a National Opinion Research Center poll in 1943 reported 21 per cent as agreeing with the statement that public school systems should be controlled primarily by the federal government rather than by the states.

For all these reasons the generally favorable character of public opinion on federal aid can hardly be regarded as a dependable source of support for an aggressive presidential campaign to get legislation approved. But even this does not exhaust the limitations inherent in the situation; for the general public, like the interest groups, is divided by attitudes on the subject of race and religion.

Of the two issues, however, the latter is by far the more serious. There is little indication, at least in the fragmentary data available, of widespread public support for the NAACP position that a federal aid program is intolerable if aid goes to segregated schools. In each of three surveys on the subject by the Gallup organization, about one-fifth of the respondents took the view that federal aid should not be given to segregated school systems. The percentages were:

|                 |        |
|-----------------|--------|
| January, 1957   | 17%    |
| June, 1957      | 18%    |
| 1961            | 23%    |

Even this probably overstates the opposition. When, in 1956, the Gallup poll asked those who had heard of the debate over federal aid: "Would you like to see the bill passed if some money is given to communities in the South where white and Negro children are segregated?" 62 per cent said that they would. The close similarity of this percentage to the proportions supporting federal aid in general principle (Table 3) suggests strongly that few opposed aid to segregated schools who were otherwise disposed to favor federal action.

The religious question is, however, a different story. This appears to cut deeply within the public. By a fortunate coincidence three opinion surveys are available, conducted by the American Institute of Public Opinion at intervals of about a decade, all asking the same question in similar forms: Should federal aid, if granted, be used to help parochial schools? The results are summarized in Table 4. For every two who believe aid should be given to religious schools, about three think it should not.

TABLE 4

THREE PUBLIC OPINION POLLS CONCERNING FEDERAL AID FOR RELIGIOUS SCHOOLS, 1938-1961

|      | Federal Aid Should Be Granted to: | | |
|------|---------------------|----------------------|-------------|
|      | Public Schools Only | Public and Parochial | No Opinion  |
| 1938 | 53%                 | 35%                  | 12%         |
| 1949 | 51%                 | 41%                  | 8%          |
| 1961 | 57%                 | 36%                  | 7%          |

SOURCE: American Institute for Public Opinion.

Despite the passage of 23 years the results show a striking similarity. And on this topic variations in the phrasing of the question have little effect upon the answers received. The contrast with general sentiment concerning federal aid is striking. On the related but separate issue of governmental support for religious schools the citizens appear to have made up their minds. Public opinion appears to be both crystallized and stable.[24]

This suspicion is reinforced by examination of an additional opinion survey dealing with several facets of the same subject. Soon after the

---

[24] A similar conclusion is suggested by one study of congressional mail concerning federal aid. Of the first 1000 letters on the subject received by Rep. Howard Robison (R., N.Y.), in June and July, 1961, the content was divided:

Barden bill controversy, Elmo Roper conducted a poll in which one question took the form: "To get down to cases, here is a list of six kinds of federal aid some people have suggested ought to be given to parochial schools. Would you agree or disagree that federal money should be given to schools run by churches to help pay for . . ." The results are shown in Table 5.

TABLE 5

PUBLIC OPINION CONCERNING SPECIFIED TYPES OF AID TO RELIGIOUS SCHOOLS, 1950

| Federal Aid Should Be Given to Church Schools for: | | | |
|---|---|---|---|
| | Agree | Disagree | Don't Know |
| Physical Examinations | 55% | 36% | 9% |
| Free School Lunches | 36% | 53% | 11% |
| Transportation of Pupils | 35% | 53% | 12% |
| Textbooks | 35% | 54% | 11% |
| New School Buildings | 28% | 60% | 12% |
| Teachers' Salaries | 26% | 61% | 13% |

SOURCE: Elmo Roper and Associates.

Clearly, the public distinguishes among the six programs in terms of their appropriateness. The order of their acceptability probably contains few surprises, although some may be startled to discover that the ongoing federal program to provide school lunches for children attending parochial schools is just about as controversial as the disputed and unapproved transportation and textbooks programs. Most relevant to the present argument, however, is the fact that the proportion approving the programs then considered most likely to be included within a federal aid bill—transportation and textbooks—is closely equivalent to the figures in Table 4.

Subsequent arguments over the parochial school issue have raised an additional question: whether the federal government should grant

---

| | |
|---|---|
| Altogether opposed | 234 |
| Opposed to violation of separation of church and state | 657 |
| For federal aid, but without aid to private schools | 28 |
| For federal aid | 23 |
| Against federal aid *unless* private schools *are* included | 58 |

It is difficult to gauge opinion from mail, and the constituency is not necessarily typical, but the results strongly suggest the dominant interest concerned the subject of parochial school education. The figures are taken from: Betsey Evans, *Congressional Mail: Its Implications for a Democratic Society* (unpublished senior thesis, Syracuse University, 1962).

Catholic schools long-term loans at low interest to provide more school buildings. In a 1961 AIPO poll approval of this proposal was expressed by 42 per cent, disapproval by 46 per cent, and no opinion by 12 per cent. The results recorded in Table 5, if they could be presumed to reflect the situation a decade later, would suggest that the loan program stands between physical examinations and free lunches in acceptability.

One final factor can be noted that serves to divide the general public in its support of federal aid. Previous reference has been made to the disputes over the purposes for which federal grants should be made. Although the issue is a sophisticated one, it too finds its reflection in the opinions of the public. Some support aid for construction, others for teachers' salaries. A survey by Elmo Roper and Associates in 1957 found that 73 per cent of those questioned favored federal aid, but these divided in turn between 30 per cent who favored aid for construction only, and 43 per cent who sought federal aid for building programs and teachers' salaries.

In summary, the data strongly suggest the existence of a generally favorable public disposition toward federal aid to education, but little deep interest. Many are favorable, but many are uninformed. Some of those who are favorably inclined want segregated schools excluded. Still more want parochial schools included. Given these divisions and limitations, public opinion represents less a pressure forcing the President to act on the issue than an opportunity to take a position and develop support for it if he chooses to do so.

### THE POSITION OF THE PARTIES

Inevitably, the party managers have not overlooked the federal aid issue in their efforts to solicit support for their presidential candidates. Although federal aid was not mentioned in a major party platform until 1876, in other campaign materials as early as 1872 the Republican party boasted of its support for federal educational assistance.

The issue was not, however, joined directly between the parties in 1876. The Democratic platform unequivocally declared that the establishment and support of the public schools belonged exclusively to the states, but the Republican party was more concerned with the tangential problem of sectarian education. The Republican convention of 1876 pledged its support to a constitutional amendment forbidding the use of public funds for sectarian education. In 1880, in 1884, and again in 1888 Republican national platforms endorsed national support for education, but it was now the turn of the Democrats to keep silent;

from 1880 to 1920 Democratic party platforms made no mention of the subject.[25]

After the 1888 presidential campaign federal aid to education was abandoned as an issue by the Republicans and was not discussed again in a party platform until 1920. By that time the party positions had been reversed. To the Democratic call for "co-operative federal assistance to the states" for the removal of illiteracy, the increase of teachers' salaries, and instruction in citizenship, the Republican party replied equivocally. The platform endorsed "aid to the states for the purpose of vocational and agricultural training," but avoided direct reference to other kinds of educational assistance.

Neither party kept the issue alive for long. By 1924 the Democratic position was much more vague: "The federal government should offer to the states such counsel, advice, and aid as may be available through the federal agencies for the general improvement of our schools." The Republican platform urged the creation of a cabinet-level department for education and relief. Four years later the Democratic party reiterated the identical language of 1924, but the Republican convention made no reference to education. Indeed, it was not until 1948 that another Republican platform contained an education plank.

Through the 1930's Democrats claimed credit for aiding "youth to stay in school," for the National Youth Administration, the Civilian Conservation Corps, and the construction of school buildings with public works funds, but avoided endorsement of an expanded educational program. It was not until 1944 that the issue was again joined. The 1944 Democratic platform was unequivocal: "We favor federal aid to education administered by the states." In 1948 the endorsement was repeated, with specific reference to the $300-million-a-year aid bill defeated in the 80th Congress, and in 1952 the Democratic platform enumerated the specific purposes for which federal aid should be given: "new school construction, teachers' salaries, and school maintenance and repair."

In 1952 the two parties stood at maximum disagreement. In 1944 the Republicans had ignored the education issue and in 1948 they had dodged it with a generality: "We favor equality of educational opportunity for all and the promotion of education and educational facilities." But in 1952 the difference was clear-cut. To the Democratic endorsement of federal aid the Republican platform replied: "The

[25] Lee, *op. cit.* Quotations of party platforms in the following section are taken from Kirk H. Porter and Donald Bruce Johnson, *National Party Platforms, 1840–1960* (Urbana: University of Illinois Press, 1961).

responsibility for sustaining this system of popular education has always rested with local communities and the states. We subscribe fully to this principle."

By 1956 the parties were receding from their differences. A Republican administration had proposed a school construction program and the Republican convention now lauded it for its "five-year program of federal assistance in building schools to relieve a critical classroom shortage," promising to renew party efforts to secure approval. The Democratic stand was not far different. The Democrats endorsed legislation for federal aid "to assist states and local communities to build schools," for health and safety services, for the education of migratory workers, for programs for exceptional children, and for teacher training in technical and scientific fields.

Partisan controversy was renewed again in 1960. Both parties, at least in their platforms, supported federal aid in principle, but under quite different terms. The Republicans asserted: "Primary responsibility for education must remain with the local communities and the state. The federal government should assist selectively." The Democratic tone was quite different; after lauding the states and local communities on their educational efforts, the platform concluded: "Only the federal government is not doing its part." The Democrats called for "generous federal financial support" of the purposes the states "deem most pressing, including classroom construction and teachers' salaries." The Republicans, however, supported federal aid only for school construction, and declared: "We believe, moreover, that any large plan of federal aid to education, such as direct grants for teachers' salaries, can only lead ultimately to federal domination and control of our schools." The contrast between a Republican policy of aid for construction and a Democratic policy of aid for construction plus salaries became one of the major domestic issues of the presidential campaign.

### PRESIDENTIAL ACTION

Even this brief discussion of the use of federal aid as a presidential campaign issue is sufficient to show that presidential action has sometimes preceded party action, sometimes followed it, and sometimes ignored it. The explanation, of course, lies in the fact that a president in office is responsive to many forces in addition to his desire to conform to party platforms and campaign promises. Actually, the record of presidential action on federal aid is a puzzling one within which individual presidents have played sometimes surprising roles. As dynamic a presidential personality as Franklin D. Roosevelt, for example, studiously avoided committing himself on the issue, while the first president actively to support federal aid was the unlikely figure of Ulysses S. Grant.

Although President Andrew Johnson had given his approval to the act creating a Department of Education, Grant was the first president to urge federal grants to the states for primary education. In his message to Congress on March 30, 1870, Grant, after referring to the needs of the freed Negroes, declared: "I would therefore call upon Congress to take all the means within their constitutional powers, to promote and encourage popular education throughout the country."[26] This statement was the prelude to the struggle for federal aid that began with the Hoar bill, introduced the same year.

President Grant returned to the subject in subsequent messages, reiterating his concern both for the support of the public schools and for the exclusion of sectarian influences from them. President Rutherford Hayes continued Grant's policies in this respect, urging Congress in 1879 to devise "appropriate measures of financial aid to education, supplemental to local action in the states and territories."[27] Garfield, his successor, was likewise reported to have favored national support for education, and had run on such a platform in 1880. His death occurred before he could take any action, but both Chester Arthur and Benjamin Harrison as presidents in the 1880's supported federal aid in their messages to Congress. Only the Democratic President, Grover Cleveland, was silent on the subject.

With this display of nineteenth-century energy, however, presidential initiative lapsed. Although President Woodrow Wilson endorsed the original Americanization bill, the struggle for federal aid and a cabinet Department of Education in the 1920's was almost exclusively a congressional show. President Warren G. Harding opposed it and President Calvin Coolidge ignored it. The supporters of federal action were encouraged by the statement of President Hoover in his inaugural address: "Although education is primarily a responsibility of the states and local communities and rightly so, yet the nation as a whole is vitally concerned in its development everywhere to the highest standards and to complete universality."[28]

Supporters of federal aid were still more encouraged by Hoover's appointment of the President of Stanford University, Dr. Ray Lyman

---

[26] Quoted in Lee, *op. cit.*, 40.
[27] Quoted, *ibid.*, 74.
[28] Quoted in Buis, *op. cit.*, 92–97.

Wilbur, as Secretary of the Interior (the Office of Education was still at this time lodged within the Department of the Interior). But they were soon disillusioned when in a speech soon after taking office Secretary Wilbur firmly rejected both federal aid and a federal Department of Education. President Hoover's own response to the controversy over the proper educational role of the federal government was to appoint a study commission, the National Advisory Committee on Education.

Financed by a $100,000 grant from the Julius Rosenwald Fund, the 52-person Committee studied for two years before making its report in October of 1931. The first comprehensive survey of federal educational activities, the Committee report recommended: (1) immediate creation of a Department of Education to coordinate federal educational programs; (2) further studies by the Office of Education to determine whether federal financial support for education was needed; and (3) elimination of special educational grants, especially those for vocational education. If vocational education was to be subsidized, the Committee concluded, it should be supported by general federal grants used at the discretion of the state.

Of all the recommendations of the Advisory Committee on Education, President Hoover chose to follow only the suggestion that the vocational education program be terminated. As a part of his economy program to meet the economic crisis, he suggested in 1932 that all vocational funds be suspended for one year. This proposal was rejected by Congress. The struggle was renewed by his successor, President Franklin Roosevelt, who also sought to reduce appropriations for vocational education in the states. Instead of accepting Roosevelt's proposed reductions, Congress sought an increase, and in 1936 passed a measure enlarging the appropriation. President Roosevelt signed the bill, but appointed a Committee on Vocational Education to review the program. When the agitation for a general federal aid bill was renewed in Congress, the President sidestepped any immediate commitment by renaming the committee the Advisory Committee on Education, and referred the proposal to it, broadening its jurisdiction to all aspects of the relationship between the federal government and education.

The Advisory Committee made its report in February, 1938, recommending a program of federal aid to education that would have totaled $140 million in general aid by the sixth year, plus $62 million in various special grants. President Roosevelt accepted the report, but did not endorse it. As Congressman John J. Cochran (D., Mo.) pointed out in a congressional debate soon thereafter: "Bear in mind, however, that up to this moment the President of the United

States has in no way expressed himself as either for or against the recommendations of the committee he appointed."[29]

The President could not, however, postpone his decision much longer. When a bill, the Thomas-Harrison bill of 1939, was prepared on the basis of the Committee's recommendations and approved by the Senate Committee, Roosevelt could not avoid the issue. During the Senate hearing a letter was entered in the record from D. W. Bell, acting director of the Bureau of the Budget. It noted: "I have taken the matter up with the President and you are advised that the proposed legislation would not be in accord with his program."[30] The position taken by President Roosevelt in his speeches on the subject was that he would accept a federal aid program only if it confined assistance solely to those states unable to meet their own educational needs.

Despite Roosevelt's indifference to the issue, congressional supporters of federal aid continued to solicit his support. Senator Pat Harrison (D., Miss.) told the Senate of his difficulties: "I brought it to the attention of the highest authority in the country. I did not get anywhere." But when he asked the Senate Majority Leader, Senator Alben Barkley (D., Ky.), "Could the Senator conjure in his mind any reason why the Administration would be against the recommendations of a committee which was appointed by the Administration to study this matter?" Senator Barkley replied: "I have no idea that the Administration is opposed to it." Harrison agreed: "I cannot imagine it, and I do not think so. How welcome it would be if we could get a little lift on this proposal, if we could just hear a word of encouragement."[31]

It is difficult to determine precisely the source of President Roosevelt's opposition to federal aid. Certainly the subject was a controversial one within the executive department. As Federal Emergency Relief Administrator, Harry Hopkins chose to treat the educational problem of the 1930's as one of unemployment, hiring unpaid teachers to teach in rural schools, adult education programs, and other areas that seemed attractive. Commissioner of Education George F. Zook sought unsuccessfully to channel relief through the school authorities. Similarly, Aubrey Williams of the National Youth Administration preferred a federal program that would aid needy students directly to a decentralized program of grants to school districts.

Whatever the reasons, President Roosevelt continued to decline

---

[29] 75:3 *Congressional Record* (1938), 2479.
[30] Quoted in Mitchell, *op. cit.*, 181–82.
[31] 75:3 *Congressional Record* (1938) 8351–52.

to endorse federal aid through the 1943 Senate debate. Although a 1943 report of the National Resources Planning Board had supported the idea, the Bureau of the Budget again advised the Senate Committee that "enactment of this legislation would not be in accord with the program of the President." This did not settle the matter, however, and during the debate the following exchange occurred:

> Mr. ROBERTSON. The sole object of this bill—and I look for many more like it—is an attempt to purchase the votes of 1,000,000 people and to use the federal funds to do so. This is an administration bill and is in keeping, in perfect step, with many that have gone before it in the last ten years.
>
> Mr. BARKLEY. The Senator says it is an "administration bill." When did it become an administration bill and by what process?
>
> Mr. ROBERTSON. I understand it is sponsored by the administration.
>
> Mr. BARKLEY. The Senator is mistaken. The administration, as such, has taken no hand whatever in the sponsorship of this bill and is neutral, so far as I know, in regard to its passage.[32]

The first public commitment to federal aid made by President Roosevelt was a hesitant one in his last year in office. In his budget message to Congress in 1945 the President wrote: "The records of selective service reveal that we have fallen far short of a suitable standard of elementary and secondary education. If a suitable standard is to be maintained in all parts of the country, the federal government must render aid where needed—but only where it is needed."[33]

The federal aid cause was taken up more actively by Roosevelt's Vice President and successor, Harry Truman. Truman's first budget message called for: "Basic legislation under which the federal government will supplement the resources of the states to assist them to equalize educational opportunities and achieve satisfactory educational standards."[34] President Truman included funds for education in subsequent budgets and made federal aid one of his campaign issues in 1948. However, it would appear that Truman regarded it as one of the less important parts of his domestic program.[35]

---

[32] 78:1 *Congressional Record* (1943), 8558.

[33] Quoted in Buis, *op. cit.*, 487.

[34] Quoted, *ibid.*, 534.

[35] Although it is difficult to quantify the degree of presidential interest shown in a particular measure a suggestion of the relative importance of federal aid as viewed by President Truman is found in the space allotted it in his two

President Dwight Eisenhower, on the other hand, was actively hostile to federal aid at the beginning of his first term in office. His position was hardly surprising; he had been elected to office on a party platform that flatly opposed aid to education and had no compelling reason to repudiate that plank. The official position of the Eisenhower administration, however, favored postponement of any congressional action until after the White House Conference on Education, scheduled for 1954, and the report of the President's Commission on Intergovernmental Relations.

Not all congressmen were satisfied with this proposal for delay. Some were eager to hasten passage. Others objected to what they saw as an effort at executive domination of Congress. Thus Congressman Kearns, after first expressing "full sympathy" with the White House conference as "a step in the right direction," later showed suspicion of the idea as an attempt to limit Congress freedom of action. At the 1954 House hearings he asked the then subcommittee chairman, Ralph Gwinn (R., N.Y.),

> Mr. KEARNS. Mr. Chairman, would you as chairman, ask the Commissioner whether once this conference meets, everybody else is out of the picture, and must accept its recommendations?
>
> Mr. GWINN. I should not think they would go that far.
>
> Mr. KEARNS. That is what they want. Somebody wants to get off the hook some place on this deal. I do not know who it is.[36]

The outcome of the White House Conference came as a surprise to many. Suspicions had been expressed that the Conference would be stacked to produce a majority against federal aid. Instead a majority of the participants favored federal aid and a large majority favored

---

volumes of memoirs. Measured by lines and compared with other domestic issues of the time, this retrospective index of attention shows:

| | |
|---|---|
| Brannan Plan for Agriculture | 210 lines |
| Civil Rights Legislation Program | 226 |
| Displaced Persons-Immigration | 6 |
| Federal Aid for Education | 14 |
| Full Employment Bill of 1945–46 | 170 |
| Government Health Insurance | 290 |
| Post-War Price Controls | 373 |
| Public Housing Program | 147 |
| Taft-Hartley Labor Act | 131 |
| Tidelands Oil Issue | 302 |

*Memoirs by Harry S. Truman* (Garden City, N.Y.: Doubleday and Company, 1956), 2 volumes.

[36] House Committee on Education and Labor, *Federal Activity in the Field of Education,* 83rd Congress, 2nd Session (1954), 63–64.

aid for construction. The Conference results helped to shift the administration position and in 1955, 1956, and 1957 President Eisenhower gave his official endorsement to federal measures to aid in school construction. In 1958 the administration withdrew its backing in favor of support for the legislation that eventually became the National Defense Education Act. Subsequently, however, President Eisenhower returned to an official position favoring federal aid for construction.

There were three characteristics of presidential action at this time. Eisenhower favored federal aid only for construction, he favored only a very limited construction program, and he gave only limited support even to that. All three of these characteristics came under review during the 1960 presidential election. The Democratic candidate, Senator John Kennedy, sought to make federal aid to education a major issue in the election, criticizing the limited support given by President Eisenhower, criticizing Vice President Richard Nixon for proposing aid for construction only, and calling for federal aid to raise teachers' salaries as well as buildings. Although reluctant to intervene in a presidential campaign, NEA statements made note of the fact that the Democratic candidate's promises accorded with NEA policy.

It seems fair to say that in the long history of federal aid to education proposals, John Kennedy was the first president to make aid a major element in his domestic program and to give it vigorous personal support. By the time he took office, President Kennedy's position was clear-cut. His campaign statements plus his legislative record on federal aid as a senator had already filled in most details of his program. After receiving a task force report, he submitted to Congress legislative proposals calling for $866 million a year in federal aid for construction and teachers' salaries. This measure was coupled with renewal of the impacted areas aid program in an effort to broaden its base of support; the package bill was then identified as a key part of the administration's domestic legislative program. President Kennedy's principal addition to his earlier statements was to reiterate in increasingly strong language his opposition to federal aid for parochial schools.

Not every impact of President Kennedy's support was favorable to the cause of federal aid. The incentive to accept the bill because the President had asked for it was diluted in part by the narrow margin of Kennedy's election-day victory, and in part by the administration's greater interest in pushing other legislation. One great advantage of vigorous presidential leadership was its effect in spotlighting one particular proposal as the federal aid bill to be taken seriously. In this way at least a part of the tangle over multiple issues was cut away;

the President's bill, for better or worse, was the bill that Congress must approve or reject. Within a short period of time, however, this asset was partly dissipated by HEW Secretary Abraham Ribicoff's reiterated willingness to consider modifications. Even the position of opposition to aid for parochial schools was weakened as the administration promised to consider a compromise that would make available increased funds for private schools by appropriate amendment to the then pending extension of the National Defense Education Act. In practice these concessions meant reopening to every congressman the possibility of a federal aid bill just a little more to his own taste if only he could succeed in strangling the bill at hand.

In addition the involvement of federal aid as a major issue in the presidential campaign created for the first time a situation in which the President of the United States actively identified his entire administration with the struggle. By making federal aid a partisan issue in national presidential politics, the 1960 campaign hardened the position of the two parties in Congress. Passage of a bill with aid for teachers' salaries would be a Democratic victory; a bill with aid for construction would be a Republican bill. The consequences of this change are discussed in the next two chapters, focused upon decision-making in the congressional committees and in Congress as a whole.

# V. Action in the Committees of Congress

ONLY Congress possesses the authority to make the kind of policy decision—be it one of action or inaction—desired by the interests warring over federal aid. It is in Congress, therefore, that the most intense, the most critical, and the most climactic battles have been waged. It is here, in the votes of senators and representatives, that proponents must formally register any future victory. And it is here, in the record of congressional action, that they now find the authoritative evidence of past defeat.

The main functions of Congress are conflict resolution and consensus building. Important social conflicts are publicized and channelled through the legislative process; and they are resolved, with varying degrees of permanence, by legislative decisions. Once made, these decisions will serve either to reconfirm an existing policy consensus or to mark progress in the building of a new one. The condition of the federal aid controversy has long been, in spite of a series of negative legislative decisions, one of unresolved and continuing conflict. Disagreement has remained widespread and deep; the policy consensus in opposition to general federal aid, though reconfirmed year after year, has remained fragile. The unsettled character of the debate has kept Congress at the vortex of the struggle.

Congressional activity proceeds in accordance with the requirement of its decision-making machinery. There is, for example, the succession of formal stages through which legislative contests must proceed—from the introduction of a bill, through committee and to the floor in each chamber, through conference committee and to the president. There are well-established procedures and practices—some explicitly formulated (like those involving the Rules Committee in the House), others implicitly understood (like those circumscribing the informal processes of bargaining)—which must be observed by all participants. There are certain key legislators—committee chairmen, party leaders, or subject-matter experts—who can force the contest to flow through them and hence subject it to their special influence. Taken together, these institutional and personal factors shape the strategies of those interest groups, executives and congressmen who seek, in varying alliances, to produce congressional decisions favorable to their cause. The analysis which follows accommodates itself closely to these elements of legislative decision-making.

The most powerful institutions of the Congress are its committees. It is here that all demands for legislative decisions start their legislative journey; and it is here, in committee, that the overwhelming majority of these projected journeys come to an end. It is at the committee stage, concludes Bertram Gross, that "the real legislative infighting takes place" and that "the bulk of congressional decisions on legislative matters is unquestionably framed and digested."[1] For the advocates of positive legislative action, the basic problem is to generate sufficient power to move a bill from its introductory stage through the committee and to the chamber floor. This involves securing, first, committee hearings on the bill, second, committee meetings to discuss the bill, third, a favorable report by the committee, and fourth (in the House) a favorable rule from the Rules Committee. In addition to affirmative action at each stage, it is also necessary to produce the kind of a bill which stands a good chance of passing through each succeeding stage of the process.[2] The opponents of positive action face these problems in reverse. Their need is to stop the bill completely at any one stage or to cast the bill in such a mold at one stage that it will surely be defeated later in its legislative journey.

### The House and Senate Committees on Education

Primary jurisdiction over all general federal aid to education proposals has rested since 1946 with the Committee on Labor and Public Welfare in the Senate and with the Committee on Education and Labor in the House. Since legislation normally passes through the Rules Committee on its way to the House floor, this Committee, too, can have (and in this case has had) a crucial influence on legislative action. In the Senate, for reasons that are discussed in the next chapter, the Committee on Labor and Public Welfare has proved to be a uniformly congenial battleground for the proponents of federal aid to education. Since 1943 the proponents have been able to secure Committee hearings whenever they wished—on eight occasions. Nine times, they have reported a bill out of committee favorably and by

---

[1] Bertram Gross, *The Legislative Struggle* (New York: McGraw-Hill Book Company, Inc., 1953), 266, 309.

[2] For tactical purposes, proponents may occasionally support a bill they know will not be passed into law in the near future. This seems to have been the case with the Murray-Metcalf Bill in the House in 1959.

consistently wide margins.[3] And, following an early failure in 1943, the Senate has passed by substantial margins a general federal aid bill every time it has been debated on the floor—in 1948, 1949, 1960, and 1961. The Senate struggle in committee and on the floor has been remarkably one-sided. When the Senate has not acted it has normally been for external reasons and not because federal aid stood in any danger of defeat in committee or out.

The House Committee on Education and Labor has been, during much of this same period, a hostile arena for the proponents and a friendly one for the opponents of federal aid. Proponents have regularly mustered the minimum strength necessary to secure Committee hearings—eleven times in the last seventeen years. In four of these years, however, the proponents could not assert sufficient additional influence to secure even a Committee meeting to consider their bills. And on four more of these occasions, the Committee held hearings, met and formally voted not to report out a bill. With or without hearings, the House Education and Labor Committee has reported out a bill favorably in six of the past seven years. Three times, no further action was taken by the Rules Committee. Twice the bill was defeated on the floor. One bill passed the House but was stalled by the Rules Committee on its way to conference committee. Approximately half of the time, therefore, opponents of general federal aid have succeeded in blocking legislation in the House Committee. The rest of the time federal aid bills have been halted at later points in the process—particularly by the Rules Committee. For this result, too, the actions of the Committee on Education and Labor have been partially responsible.

Every congressional committee participates in the conflict-resolving and consensus-building functions of the Congress. From this viewpoint, the persistent problem of the federal aid proponents in the House Committee has been their inability to resolve the multiple conflicts at the committee level to help build a broader consensus in the House. To a large degree, their problem simply reflects the complexity of the issues previously described. But it is the very function of Congress to register this complexity and produce through its mechanisms some viable policy agreement. The various proponents have been relatively unable to use the Committee as a consensus-building mechanism. On the other hand, the problem for the opponents has been that of maintaining the status quo. To this end, they have manipulated the Committee machinery with great effectiveness. In a

[3] For the summary data, see Figure 1.

positive sense, the opponents of federal aid have been able to resolve the conflict in their favor. In a negative sense, they have succeeded in promoting and perpetuating division among the proponents. The Committee failures of the proponents and the Committee successes of the opponents have forestalled the formation of any new consensus in the area of federal aid.

The special characteristics of the Committee on Education and Labor as a decision-making institution have had a considerable effect on these patterns of success and failure. Nearly all of its members agree that it is probably the most difficult House committee in which to achieve a consensus and the easiest in which to promote and prolong conflict. In the words of a leading Democratic proponent of federal aid, "It's a very discouraging Committee. You can't get a resolution praising God through that Committee without having a three day battle over it. . . . It's about the most difficult Committee around. Our executive sessions are the most exciting things you ever saw."[4] A Republican opponent of federal aid uses a different perspective but arrives at a similar conclusion. "We work by trying to split the Democrats on the Committee. And, actually, we don't have to work very hard. They'll split off by themselves. . . . Not on the big issues on the final votes, but on amendments and in the Committee. They'll shout at each other, stand up and bang their fists on the table and stomp out."

Unlike its counterpart in the Senate, the House Committee on Education and Labor exhibits an almost classic incapacity as a consensus-building institution. Three basic reasons warrant extended treatment—the nature of the Committee's jurisdiction, the composition of the Committee, and its decision-making procedures.

## Jurisdiction

Most of the Committee's internal problems are consequences of the fact that within its jurisdiction fall a high proportion of the most controversial, the most partisan, and the most publicized issues of

---

[4] All unattributed quotations in this and the following chapter are taken from interviews held with 21 members of the House Committee on Education and Labor, one member of the Senate Committee on Labor and Public Welfare, and with staff members of both Committees. The interviews were held in Washington in June, 1961. They were semi-structured interviews, and the questions were open-ended. Notes were not taken during the interview, but they were transcribed immediately afterward. The quotations are as near verbatim as the author's power of immediate recall could make them. In all cases, the respondents were told that their comments would not be attributed to them.

American domestic politics. The Committee, activated in 1947, cut its legislative teeth on the Taft-Hartley Bill and has been a domestic political battleground ever since. In 1961, two out of President Kennedy's five major domestic programs came before it.[5] All members agreed with two of their colleagues—the first a Republican, the second a Democrat—whose explanations follow:

"This is where the basic philosophies of the two parties really come out strongly. It's a clash of philosophies. You don't get that on Merchant Marine and Fisheries. Oh, what battles! You should see the battles we have in executive session."

"This is probably the most partisan Committee in the House, because this is where the fundamental philosophical battles are fought. . . . The things that identify the administration's domestic program come out of our Committee. You take minimum wage. That's a black and white proposition there. And all of our issues are fundamental, philosophical questions. You don't get that on Space or Foreign Affairs."

If a committee is to function as a consensus-building institution there must be considerable opportunity for compromise and for mutual accommodation of views. Conditions must be maintained in which the legislative techniques of give and take, and of bargaining are possible. It is the chief consequence of nation-wide partisan and philosophical controversies that they seriously limit the development of such internal conditions. A former Republican member reflected on his experience in the 1950's. "Some of us were unalterably opposed to federal aid and some on the other side were just as unalterably in favor of it. . . . There weren't many minds changed by discussion. Everybody had a fixed position when he came there and nobody changed that opinion that I know of." A Democrat, speaking of the situation in 1961, agreed, "The lines are drawn pretty tight on this committee and there isn't much flexibility."

Issues involving the degree and direction of federal participation in such fields as labor-management relations, minimum wage, and education are among those which few legislators can avoid in their election campaigns. Several Republicans recalled debating their opponents on the federal aid issue in 1960; and they recalled, too, having taken a firm stand against all federal aid or a stand, following Vice President Nixon, in support of school construction aid only. Most

---

[5] The two were federal aid to education and minimum wage proposals. The other three of Kennedy's big five programs in 1961 were aid to depressed areas, housing, and medical care for the aged.

Committee Democrats, on the other hand, campaigned along with their standard-bearer Senator Kennedy in favor of both a construction and a teachers' salary program. Having assumed more or less unequivocal positions on federal aid before their constituents, members come to their Committee work in an advanced state of commitment and are denied that freedom of maneuver so basic to the production of legislative agreement. They come from their election campaigns trained, positioned, and girded for head-on, showdown Committee conflict.

In another way, too, the jurisdiction of the Committee has hampered consensus building in the field of federal aid. When the Committee was established in 1946, its main focus was considered to be the field of labor—not education. The great majority of Committee members were oriented toward labor problems and professed only minor interest in education. Though there has been a tendency for some members to specialize in educational matters, such members still remain in the minority on the Committee. Since the 1946 decision that the field of education did not warrant a separate committee, many large educational programs of the national government have been placed under the jurisdiction of other House committees.[6] The decision to combine education and labor has thus yielded a weaker and more fragmented effort on behalf of federal aid—by members of Congress and by supporting interest groups—than would surely have resulted from the concentration of educational matters in a committee on education.

Also, educational controversy has been infected with the by-products of labor controversy. Doubtless, internal conflict would be harsh enough in a single education committee, but the tradition of charge and counter-charge accompanying labor-management legislation has certainly not made it any easier for the building of consensus among the same people in another area. There is, of course, an affinity of philosophy between the supporters of organized labor and the supporters of federal aid to education. The record of the AFL-CIO on behalf of federal aid is proof enough. Nonetheless, the Democratic membership of the Committee has been chosen in such a way as to maximize unity on labor matters and with strictly secondary concern for unity on federal aid. The result is that while a Catholic Democrat and a non-Catholic Democrat or a Democrat with many Negro constituents and a Democrat with few Negro constituents can reach

---

[6] See Robert M. Rosenzweig, "The Congress—How It Deals With Educational Issues," 17 *Higher Education* (April 1961), 8-11.

agreement on labor matters, they may be pulled in many directions when confronted with the divisive racial and religious issues involved in federal aid.

The passage of time has increased the heat of the federal aid controversy and has done very little, therefore, to reduce Committee conflict. There was a period in the 1940's when information was scarce, when a variety of new approaches were being explored, when there was no legacy of controversy and when, therefore, some attitudes had not crystallized. Between 1943 and 1947, the conversion of Senator Taft to the cause of federal aid took place and helped to settle the issue once and for all in that chamber. But the issue that was settled in the Senate remained a standoff in the House. The opponents win but the proponents keep challenging. And each successive layer of legislative struggle compresses the participants into positions of increasing inflexibility.

The functions of committee hearings, for example, are to add current data to support old positions, and to add current reaffirmations of support or opposition to the store of old political intelligence. They may serve to promote communication between the interest group spokesmen and their own membership, but they have ceased to promote, if they ever did, the communication between proponents and opponents. One member described the federal aid hearings this way. "They don't do any good. And nobody listens to them anyway. The same people say the same things every year. Only the statistics change. But the lines are hard and fast on this issue and nobody changes his mind on or off the Committee. It's a formality. . . . The teachers groups and these other organizations can prove to their members that they are getting their money's worth for their dues. That's all. They don't change anything." For the newcomer, they may serve an informational function, but they do not convert. One freshman said, "I tried to keep an open mind. I went in there and listened with the attitude, 'let's see if you can convince me I'm wrong.' And the more I heard the more convinced I was that I was right." In the hearing rooms and out, Committee members say, they tend to maintain communications only with one set of interest groups and one set of lobbyists—those with whom they already agree. The only people who may have something new to present, who may represent a potential for change, and who are, therefore, listened to by both sides, are the spokesmen for the president and his administration.

### Membership

Conflict inside the Committee on Education and Labor is, ultimately, not a conflict among issues; it is a conflict among individual members. Issues do not battle one another; people do. The selection of Committee members is, therefore, critical in determining the degree, if not the main lines, of internal conflict. The Senate and House committees have dealt, after all, with the same controversial issues, but one has been far more successful at resolving them than the other. To a large degree, this difference is the result of a difference in the personnel of the two groups. The members of the Senate Committee have tended to come from among those of both parties who already are in substantial agreement on the issues of federal aid. The members of the House Committee, on the other hand, have tended to come from among those in their respective parties who already are in the widest disagreement on the issues of federal aid. What this means in the main is that a large minority of Senate Committee Republicans (such as Robert Taft, George Aiken, John S. Cooper, Clifford Case, and Jacob Javits) and Senate Committee southern Democrats (such as Lister Hill, Claude Pepper, Ralph Yarborough) have been far less conservative on the general problem of federal government-educational relations than their counterparts in the House. And it is worth noting that some of the sharpest and most crucial contrasts have been between the respective chairmen of the Senate and House committees—namely, Senator Robert Taft (R., Ohio) and Rep. Fred Hartley (R., N.J.), 1947-1949; Senator Lister Hill (D., Ala.) and Rep. Graham Barden (D., N.C.), 1951-1953, 1955-1961.

To concentrate, again, on the House Committee, those who control assignments to it exercise considerable care. On the Republican side, new House members are ordinarily discouraged from applying unless their convictions are firm, their talents for combat considerable, and their districts reasonably safe.[7] Those who cannot be dissuaded and those who must be solicited tend to lean toward the more conservative wing of their party. A rather senior Republican said that he advises anyone who desires a political career to stay off the Committee—unless he is deeply committed. Of himself, he said, "My people didn't vote for me. They voted for what I stood for, my principles. I was elected as a conservative and that's a wonderful thing. . . . It's an awfully unpopular Committee. I take a terrible pounding. But my future is behind me and I don't give a good God damn." "I'm the kind of person," echoed an equally conservative freshman member,

---

[7] See Nicholas A. Masters, "House Committee Assignments," 55 *American Political Science Review* (June 1961), 354-55. The four new members in 1961 all won election by less than 55 per cent of the vote; but all were young Republicans who won back normally Republican districts from Democrats who had benefited from the 1958 Democratic sweep.

"who jumps right into these hot spots. So I figured if this was the most controversial committee in the House I'd like to get on it." When the leadership has to fill a slot with some member who has not applied, they may try to ascertain his views beforehand. One member explained, "Halleck called a friend of mine in ——— and said, 'What kind of a guy is this ———? We're thinking of putting him on Education and Labor but we need someone who'll stand up—someone we can count on who won't waver in his views.' My friend replied, 'You don't have to worry about ———.'"

On the Democratic side, too, members are strongly issue-oriented, personally contentious and deeply committed. They tend to represent the more liberal elements of their party. Party leaders produce this result positively, by encouraging the appointment of labor-oriented congressmen, and negatively, by discouraging the appointment of southerners. To an individual representing a manufacturing or mining constituency a place on the committee dealing with labor matters will have positive electoral advantages. Many Democratic members (15 of the present 19 in either 1958 or 1960) receive financial assistance from the trade unions, and all of these, at least, are dependent upon labor support at the polls.[8] Union lobbyists may actively intercede with the Democratic committee selectors on behalf of congressmen known to be sympathetic to them. On the other hand, no more than four (and usually fewer) southern Democrats have ever been placed on the Committee at one time since its creation—despite the pleas of those southerners who were members of the group. No pretense is made at representativeness on this score; in 1961, 38 per cent of all Democratic congressmen (99 of 263) came from the 11 southern states, but only 11 per cent (2 of 19) of the Committee members did.

Despite the most careful attention to their appointment, the Democratic members of the Committee constitute an extraordinarily heterogeneous group. They are personally much more predisposed to intra-party conflicts than are the Republicans. Moreover, if there is a unifying bond among most of them, it is a bond on the issues involving labor and not education. Whatever other differences there may be among the Republicans on the Committee in 1961, they are all male, non-southern, non-border-state, and Protestant. They are all white, and not one of them represents a constituency with a non-white population of 10 per cent or over. Though 17 per cent of the Roman

---

[8] 17 *Congressional Quarterly*, April 10, 1959, 509-15; 18 *Congressional Quarterly*, November 11, 1960, 1857.

Catholic House members are Republicans, none is among the Committee Republicans. The 1961 Democratic members, by contrast, include two women, two southerners, two border-state members, seven Roman Catholics, and two Jews. The chairman is a Negro and four Democrats represent constituencies with non-white populations of over 10 per cent.[9] These demographic differences are, of course, overlaid with vast differences in personality and political style. Together they make consensus building on the Democratic side especially hazardous —particularly on the issues of school integration and private school assistance.

The combined result of Republican and Democratic appointment practices which is most significant for this study is not only that they guarantee sharp ideological and partisan division on the Committee, but that they intensify internal Committee division. The Congressional Quarterly selected 10 roll call votes in 1961 to distinguish those House members who supported a larger federal role in the nation's economic and social life (e.g., liberals) and those House members who opposed a larger federal role (e.g., conservatives).[10] A majority of Committee Democrats (12 of 19) voted on every occasion to expand government activity; and a majority of Committee Republicans (7 of 12) voted on every occasion in opposition to this expansion. Moreover, if the voting percentages are scaled, every Democratic Committee member voted more often for an expanded federal role than did any of the Republicans.

These ideological and partisan differences inside the Committee are significantly greater than differences on the same issues in the House as a whole. Whereas average percentages among House Democrats were 78 per cent in favor of a larger federal role and 21 per cent against, Committee Democrats averaged 91 per cent in favor and 8 per cent against. House Republicans averaged 12 per cent in favor and 87 per cent opposed, whereas Committee Republicans averaged 7 per cent in favor and 93 per cent opposed. (See Table 6.)

A similar set of 10 roll calls was selected in the Senate. In this case, voting by members of the Committee on Labor and Public Welfare indicates a convergence instead of a divergence of views on the role of the federal government. A majority of Committee Democrats (6 of 10) voted on every occasion to expand the federal role; but

[9] Data on the non-white population by congressional districts are taken from U.S. Bureau of the Census, *Congressional District Data Book* (Washington, 1961).

[10] The roll call votes used and the records of each Representative and Senator are listed in 19 *Congressional Quarterly*, October 20, 1961, 1751-63.

TABLE 6
IDEOLOGICAL REPRESENTATIVENESS OF LEGISLATIVE COMMITTEES, 1961

|  | Mean Percentage of Votes in Favor of Expanded Federal Role (10 Roll Calls) | Mean Percentage of Votes in Opposition to Expanded Federal Role (10 Roll Calls) | Index of Liberalism- Conservatism |
|---|---|---|---|
| All House Democrats | 78 | 21 | +57 |
| House Education and Labor Committee Democrats | 91 | 8 | +83 |
| All House Republicans | 12 | 87 | —75 |
| House Education and Labor Committee Republicans | 7 | 93 | —86 |
| All Senate Democrats | 67 | 33 | +34 |
| Senate Labor and Public Welfare Committee Democrats | 90 | 10 | +80 |
| All Senate Republicans | 32 | 64 | —32 |
| Senate Labor and Public Welfare Committee Republicans | 52 | 46 | + 6 |

SOURCE: 19 *Congressional Quarterly*, October 20, 1961, 1751-63.

only one of the five Republicans voted every time in opposition to such expansion. Three of the five Republicans voted more often for expansion than against it. When Committee voting is compared with Senate voting as a whole it becomes even more obvious that the Committee minimizes rather than magnifies the conflicts inherent in their subject matter. Committee Democrats averaged 90 per cent support for expansion and 10 per cent opposition to it, while the averages for all Senate Democrats were 67 per cent in favor and 33 per cent opposed. Committee Republicans voted 52 per cent in favor and 46 per cent opposed; whereas the averages for all Senate Republicans were 32 per cent in favor and 64 per cent opposed. Both groups on the Committee are substantially more inclined toward increased federal activity than their respective parties in the Senate. This fact is of the utmost significance in facilitating Committee action on federal aid in the Senate.

In the House, given the considerable degree of inflexibility between party groups, the ratio of Democrats to Republicans has assumed considerable importance. During the years of Republican control of the Committee, it was certain that no bill would emerge from the Committee. During the years of Democratic majorities on the Committee only a coalition of Republicans plus southern Democrats could prevent Committee action. Until the 86th Congress in January of 1959, the Republicans plus the southern Democrats constituted a majority of the Committee and, hence, a controlling influence whenever they could agree. In 1959, following the sweeping Democratic congressional victory of the previous November, the liberal Democrats and their interest-group allies succeeded in breaking the longstanding coalition majority. They persuaded Speaker Rayburn to recommend a new party ratio of 20 Democrats to 10 Republicans instead of the previous 17 Democrats to 13 Republicans. Under the previous arrangement 13 Republicans plus Chairman Barden and Georgian Phil Landrum could create a tie vote; and a third, more liberal southerner, Carl Elliott of Alabama, was placed in a strategic position at the ideological center of the Committee and in the eye of most internal storms. Six new Democrats, all supported by organized labor, were given Committee membership in 1959; those southerners who applied were turned down. This membership change constitutes one of the landmarks of the federal aid controversy in Congress.

*Procedures*

The resolution of internal strife and the formation of legislative consensus are affected greatly by the way in which a committee organizes itself for decision-making. The style of decision-making best suited to these ends would be one which emphasizes mutual accommodation within the group and develops procedures for cooperation and compromise. Frequently, informal and traditional techniques of accommodation will develop on committees—between majority and minority party leaders, between legislatively experienced members and the legislatively inexperienced, between the experts in a particular subject matter and the nonexperts. The Committee on Education and Labor has not devised this style of decision-making to any important degree. It tends to function in a fiercely competitive style in which the techniques are those of naked power and the decision goes to whoever can command a simple majority in a showdown vote. The rules of the game are the formal rules of the House, untempered by private Committee traditions or informal understandings. Committee members have no sense of the Committee as an entity worth worrying about. Sentiments of mutual regard and group solidarity are few. Group morale is not high. The Committee's decision-making procedures do nothing to lower tension or to increase cohesion inside the group.[11]

As described by two leading spokesmen, the atmospheric conditions in which the Committee's federal aid decisions of 1961 were made were typical:

Republican: "The Democrats haven't made a single concession to us on anything. . . . We've dug our heels in. We don't like their tactics and they don't like ours. But what we're doing against the bill isn't any worse than what they are doing to pass the bill. If they aren't going to do some of the things we think are reasonable, we're going to have to oppose the whole thing right down the line."

Democrat: "Boy were they mad. We were slick. But they were trying to be slick, too. They haven't got any interest in aiding parochial schools. They were trying to raise the issue, giggle, sit back and watch the bill die. They play the game right to the hilt."

Democrats and Republicans find it difficult to overcome their mutual suspicions sufficiently to establish even minimally harmonious working relationships. Throughout 1961, the Committee chairman and the ranking minority member, whose cooperation should provide the major lubricant of decision-making, conducted a ridiculous public feud over the amount of room space allotted to their respective staffs.[12] A marked lack of communication seems to exist at all other levels of the Committee as well.

Though it is doubtless true that, in the words of one Republican, "Some of our guys hate Democrats more than anything," it often appears that some Democrats hate some other Democrats with a similar passion. Democrats freely admit their natural propensity to fight one another, and a Republican remarked, "There's never that kind of fighting between Democrats and Republicans. They don't expect to convert us. It's like the old situation where they hate the heretic more than they do the infidel." In federal aid decisions, the injection of the segregation issue—splitting northerner from southerner and moderate from liberal—and the parochial school issue—splitting urban Catholic and rural non-Catholic—exacerbates the normal problems of consensus building on the Democratic side. Republicans, less beset by racial and

---

[11] For a study of a House Committee that contrasts sharply with the Committee on Education and Labor, see Richard F. Fenno, Jr., "The House Appropriations Committee as a Political System: The Problem of Integration," 56 *American Political Science Review* (June 1962), 310-24.

[12] Their battle was reported in the Capitol Hill newspaper *Roll Call* during March, April, September, and December, 1961. There is, predictably, almost no contact between majority and minority staff members on the Committee.

religious differences, and in the minority during all but four years since World War II, have tended to cohere much more frequently—though Eisenhower's support for federal aid split the group in the late 1950's.

One of the most common House traditions that functions as a check on intra-committee conflicts is the informal norm of apprentice-ship, which prescribes that committee newcomers should defer to those senior men more experienced in the work of the committee. The freshman should attend meetings, do his homework, say very little, and participate minimally in the making of the group's decisions. The Education and Labor Committee gives virtually no service to this tradition—a tradition which might help countervail against conditions of internecine conflict. The Committee's young men—who happen to be extraordinarily bright, able and disputatious—are expected to carry a major share of the decision-making burdens. A freshman Republican put this in the strongest language possible. "There isn't any bigger myth than the idea that new people can't do anything. After all this talk about seniority, I was surprised. You know you aren't going to be the Committee Chairman, and you know you aren't going to get to sponsor a major piece of legislation, but other than that you can participate as much as you want. You can even get to take leadership on a bill in Committee. . . . Every time a bill comes out the young members are asked to take five minutes or ten minutes to speak on the floor. They ask us, we don't have to ask. So it's just the opposite from what the myth and fiction of seniority would have you believe." A first-year Democrat spoke for his colleagues when he said: "I was amazed. I was hesitant to do all the things they asked me to do—being a newcomer. I'm the only lawyer on that subcommittee . . . and in drafting the law they relied on me a great deal. A new man has no restrictions at all." The weakness of seniority traditions is evident, also, in the fact that very senior members may be denied the sponsor-ship of a bill or the chairmanship of a subcommittee to which their rank would otherwise entitle them. Chairman Barden refused to give top Democrat Adam Clayton Powell the chairmanship he wanted, and Powell, when he became chairman, returned the treatment in kind to high-ranking Phil Landrum of Georgia.[13] Without the stabilizing in-fluence of these traditions, decision-making by free-for-all is en-

---

[13] Powell set up a battery of three subcommittees to deal with educational matters, but refrained from assigning them permanent areas of jurisdiction. He offered the chairmanship of the Special Subcommittee on Education to Landrum. Since, however, Powell had no intention of assigning any legislation to the subcommittee if Landrum became its chairman, Landrum declined to serve.

couraged. And one can understand the inability of the Committee to exercise any restraining influence whatsoever in regard to proposals such as the Powell Amendment.

Another force which often countervails against an every-man-for-himself technique of legislative decision-making is the presence of subject-matter experts. Committee members will acknowledge the expertise of one or two of their colleagues and will defer to them—not on matters of critical importance to themselves but on technical or factual matters. The expert may not be able to swing ultimate votes, but as the legislation works its way through subcommittee and committee his views will carry substantial weight. The success of federal aid to education bills in the Senate was in large part due to the fact that in committee and out a substantial body of senators were willing to follow an acknowledged expert—Senator Robert A. Taft. Taft's judgment in the Senate in 1947-48 sufficed to settle once and for all a series of questions which have been disputed regularly ever since in the House. It is important to realize, therefore, that there are no acknowledged experts on federal aid to education in the House of Representatives. If there were they would be found on the Committee. Yet every one of the factors thus far discussed militates against the unifying presence of expertise.

Inside the Committee there is no deference accorded even to the work of subcommittees. A subcommittee may have sat many days in hearings and worked long hours over their recommendations, but these are almost always changed by the full Committee. Long-time participants are hard put to remember occasions when substantial alterations have not been made. Regarding federal aid, one senior member remarked: "You can't take a bill before that group unless you know exactly what every section, every paragraph, every line, every word means. There are so many sharpies in there. . . . Someone will try to put another interpretation on it and if you can't refute it, it will stick. . . . Oh! it's a real circus." The Committee has, furthermore, never produced a staff of experts whose independent judgment has carried any weight at all with the members.

Since the Committee does not acknowledge within its own body of supposed specialists any experts on federal aid, it is hardly likely that the Committee will be viewed as conveying expert opinion to the floor. Committee views as such ordinarily carry little persuasion with House colleagues. The normal impression which Committee members manage to create on the floor is one of being wholly unable to agree among themselves—not only between but within parties. Individual Committee members may come to the floor prepared to introduce crippling amendments or, indeed, substitute bills. Members are not usually daunted should a pet amendment, e.g., the Powell Amendment, be defeated in Committee. Said one Democrat in reference to an education amendment, "I tried it in the Committee . . . and I'll try it again on the floor. I haven't told them [his Committee colleagues] I'm going to, but they know that I tried it in Committee and I suppose they know I'll try again. . . . I just believe in it—that's all." Other amendments may come to the floor because the Committee was incapable of dealing with them. "Lots of times . . . if a person has an amendment, he'll hold it back just so we can get the damn bill on the floor. Then he'll propose it on the floor."

To a House membership which already views the Committee as "stacked" via the appointment process, the picture of the Committee in wide disarray on the floor is not conducive to confidence. "Frankly," says one experienced Committee member, "It's not one of the authoritative committees of the Congress—not one of those whose word you take automatically. . . . It lacks stature. In fact most of the bills we report out get completely changed on the floor. . . . It's a power struggle that counts on the floor and not respect for the Committee or the influence of any one individual."

The Committee's modest rank in the prestige hierarchy of House committees operates as both cause and effect of its internal conflicts. Because it is not regarded as having great prestige, House members are only moderately attracted to it. Of the 21 members interviewed, eight had designated it as their first choice for a committee assignment six had listed it as their second or third choice, and seven members had been requested to go on, or were simply put on, the Committee. Moderate attractiveness means a relatively high rate of turnover among Committee personnel. Of the 30 members of the group in 1961, only three had been members since 1947, seven had been members since 1953, and less than half (14) had been on the Committee for as many as four years (since 1957). Instability of membership is, perhaps, a contributing factor to the Committee's lack of tradition, and lack of group-mindedness. These failures, in their turn, allow internal conflict to flourish, thus further decreasing the prestige of the group among House members.

To write a politically viable federal aid to education bill and to maneuver it successfully through the House Committee requires far more cohesion than the group normally displays. Only exceptional leadership within the Committee or extraordinary pressure without— or both—can produce the requisite internal unity. The many failures of federal aid proponents at the committee stage are due to their inability to combine sufficient Committee leadership, House leadership, administration pressure, and interest-group support to overcome the internal discord of the committee.

## Leadership

The Committee has had but one strong chairman since the war— Graham Barden (D., N.C.). Among the members of his Committee, Barden's legislative abilities are already legend. He is invariably described as "a shrewd, smart Chairman," "a very effective Chairman," "absolutely brilliant," "magnificent," and "one of the ablest congressmen in American history." For all of his eight years as chairman, Barden led the Committee in such a way as to create rather than resolve internal conflicts. Most of the time, he worked tirelessly to defeat federal aid legislation; and on the single occasion, in 1949, when he accepted a federal aid bill he did so on such restrictive and uncomprising grounds that he triggered the most acrimonious of all Committee conflicts.

His main tactics were those of delay, divide, and conquer. And his successes were in no small measure due to the fact that these tactics followed the natural grain of a conflict-ridden Committee. "Barden was trying to keep things from being done," said a Democratic member. "He just wanted to filibuster and sow confusion. If it lagged, he would introduce some more." Another Democrat recalled, "He never shut any one up. He'd let you talk yourself around the clock and in circles if you would. One year, he brought in 92 witnesses from the Chamber of Commerce on the school bill and was going to let them all talk. That was his way of doing things." In support of these tactics he relied heavily on the backstopping votes of the Republicans. A key Republican said, "He ran that committee 100 per cent. I must say that some of us on our side were in substantial sympathy with what he was doing. There was a good deal of support from the Republicans." From his perspective, a Democratic member concurred, "You never had any leadership under Barden—not majority leadership. Under Barden, you had a club. He was a Republican; there's no doubt about that. He was a Democrat in name only. Under him, you had a coalition. And it was very skillful. The coalition ran things until 1959 when Ways and Means decided to enlarge the Committee."

Barden's weapon was a skillful combination of formal prerogative, informal maneuver, and personal talent. During most of his tenure, for instance, he refused to institute formal Committee rules. Among other things, the Committee had no regular meeting day. "In my first year here," said one member, "we held our first Committee meeting in April and the next one in June." There was, in addition, no time limit placed on the questioning of witnesses during hearings. "I remember once," said a Republican member, "when the very suggestion of a five minute limitation [for each member in questioning each witness] was made, and he hit the roof. He wouldn't hear of any such thing. And he carried the day by sheer bravado or strength of character, call it what you will."

Another prerogative which Barden employed dexterously was his authority to terminate Committee meetings by declaring the absence of a quorum. "Even after 1959 Barden retained a lot of power," exclaimed one Democrat, "we tried holding rump sessions without him but with a quorum. Barden would come in, look around and say, 'I see there's no quorum present,' bang his gavel and it would be all over." A colleague recalled an occasion when the Committee had recessed during a crucial executive session to enable the members to go to the floor to answer a roll call. Barden, however, stayed in the Committee room and sent his clerk to the floor with instructions to call back as soon as the roll call was over and debate had resumed on the floor. "I was one of the first ones back, and Barden was sitting there. He got a phone call, put down the phone, looked around and said 'No quorum' and banged the gavel. I jumped up and protested. He said, 'No quorum' and left. . . . Technically, he was right. We were supposed to be sitting during debate and should have begun when the floor debate began again. . . . The time table was such that if we didn't complete our work that day we couldn't meet for some time."

In 1956 Barden, who was opposed to the federal aid bill, refused to relinquish his right to control and manage the floor debate on the bill. His allocation of disproportionate time to the opponents plus his dramatic resignation as floor manager near the end of the proceedings added important increments to the unbelievable confusion which accompanied the floor defeat of that year. In the absence of particular Committee rules and in the absence of compensating informal tradition, the rules of the group had to be the same as the rules of the parent House. And in his knowledge of these, Barden far outdistanced the young, aggressive, but legislatively naive liberals on his Committee. "He was a master of parliamentary strategy," said one inexperienced opponent. "He'd lull you to sleep and then hit you with an uppercut. You wouldn't know what the hell had hit you." Another agreed, "We're a young Committee . . . . And it takes a lot of time to learn how the legislative process works. . . . We learned a lot from Barden."

As chairman, Barden could manipulate the various units of the Committee—its subcommittees and its staff. For a considerable period of time, he refused to institute standing subcommittees with specific jurisdiction. The *ad hoc* nature of the Committee structure enabled him to exert close control over the tasks of each subcommittee and over its Democratic membership. In 1957, for example, Barden used his power over subcommittees to head off an incipient liberal revolt in the Committee. He won the support of one senior Democrat to his view on other procedural matters by agreeing to give him a permanent subcommittee of his own. As for the Committee staff, Barden kept it small and inactive as befitted his tactical goals. Democratic Committee members received little research help from the staff and confess to being ignorant of their names. An assistant to one, a veteran Democrat complained with great feeling, "This committee has the most incompetent, inept staff of any of the hill. Barden wanted it that way. He could manipulate a dumb staff easier than a smart one. . . . We haven't had a chief clerk or counsel on this Committee for years that knew enough to come in out of the rain." Whether true or not, this is the common perception which pro-federal aid members had of the Committee staff under Barden.

### FEDERAL AID IN THE HOUSE COMMITTEE, 1945–1954

Between 1945 and 1955 the Committee held federal aid hearings on seven separate occasions; and not until 1955 did a bill win the approval of a majority of the group. The peak years of controversy were those of 1949 and 1950. And for the decisions adverse to federal aid in those years, Barden was primarily responsible. In 1949 Chairman John Lesinski (D., Mich.), whose interest lay in labor matters, gave Barden the chairmanship of a 13-man Special Subcommittee on Federal Aid to Education. As Democratic members of the Subcommittee, Barden selected an unrepresentative group—all four of the Committee's southern Democrats, two of its four border-state members and only two of the Committee's seven northern Democrats. The year 1949 was a critical one because for the first time, in both 1948 and 1949, the Senate had passed a federal aid bill. This bill, the result of hard-headed political compromise, contained both equalization and flat-grant provisions. It could be used for teachers' salaries and other current operating expenditures (no construction). It provided money for transportation and textbook aid to non-public schools in states where such uses were permitted by state law. The 1949 bill, S.246, passed the Senate by a 58-15 margin on May 5. Twelve days later, when the House heard the first of its 58 witnesses and took the first of its 953 pages of testimony, the prospects for federal aid legislation seemed brighter than ever.

Expressing his devotion to federal aid at every opportunity, Barden staged a counter-offensive by proposing a substitute bill and by refusing to entertain serious testimony on S.246. At the outset, he set the ground rules. "There are some features in the Senate bill so objectionable to me that I could not find myself going over to it. I am not going to accept it; that's all."[14] The distasteful provisions included those requiring reports to the Commissioner of Education (e.g., federal control) and those providing for the possibility of aid to non-public schools. Barden dominated the hearings to a degree unequalled by any representative or senator in any federal aid hearing before or since. His colloquies with various witnesses consumed one-third of all the space devoted to questions and answers. Each witness was asked to testify and then subjected to questions on the Barden bill. Those groups, especially organized labor, who would not agree to support it were branded as uncooperative and given unsympathetic treatment. "I am frank to state to you that your idea will not pass" [to AF of L]. "I wanted some help, my friend, and you have had a tendency to add chaos to confusion. . . . I don't believe you yourself have the slightest idea in the world there would be a Chinaman's chance of getting that bill through Congress, do you?" [to AF of L]. "One ear is deaf and the other is partly closed when you talk to me" [to CIO].[15]

The issue which eventually rent the Committee—that of aid to non-public schools—was systematically avoided. On one of the few occasions when the question faced him point blank, Barden stated, "My reason [for a public school aid bill] was that it is just so much easier and more comfortable to go around a mud hole than it is to go through it. . . . So in this bill and in this legislation, I pray that we will be spared any controversy over that point because it should not be in here."[16] To the countervailing arguments of the NCWC representative he replied, "I am just as far in one direction as you can possibly be in the other. So we could not get together."[17] The fact that Barden's bill was a public school bill precipitated a national controversy as soon as it was reported (by a 10-3 vote) from the subcommittee to the full Committee. Chairman Lesinski attacked the

---

[14] House Committee on Education and Labor, *Public School Assistance Act of 1949*, 81st Congress, 1st Session (1949), 102.

[15] *Ibid.*, 628, 678, 768.

[16] *Ibid.*, 165.

[17] *Ibid.*, 744.

bill as "anti-Catholic" and filled with "bigotry." "It will never be reported out of the Labor Committee . . . ," he said. "It is my opinion that he [Barden] drew it up that way purposely because he didn't want any aid to education and wanted to kill it."[18] The parallel dispute between Cardinal Spellman and Eleanor Roosevelt flared and raged in the public press. The controversy over federal aid to non-public schools was not to dominate the educational policy struggle again until 1961. But in 1949 and 1950 it stirred a fatal division within the House Committee.

Two key votes were taken by the Committee in August of 1949. A motion to report out S.246 was defeated 11-14, a vote for which there is no record. Following the heavy defeat of two substitute Republican measures, Rep. John Kennedy moved to postpone action until the next session. The motion, which would have killed federal aid legislation for that year, was lost 13-12. (See Table 7.) Thus the possibility of favorable action remained—but nothing more was, in fact, done. The vote on the Kennedy motion revealed the toll which the private school controversy had taken of the proponents of federal aid. Four Catholic members of the Committee—Lesinski (Mich.), Kelley (Penna.), Kennedy (Mass.), and Burke (Ohio), all liberal Democrats, voted to kill federal aid legislation for that session. They were joined by the great bulk of the Committee's conservative members. The majority group, on the other hand, could agree only to keep the issue alive. They could not, especially against the opposition of Chairman Lesinski that late in the session, agree on a bill to support. For Barden it was all or nothing, and not all of the 13 were willing to pay his price.

Early in February of the next year the Committee met in executive session at the urging of President Truman to reconsider its negative action on S.246. A motion to report out S.246 was again lost—this time by 13-12. The voting alignment (Table 7) was similar to that of the previous August. Those who had voted to postpone the issue in 1949, voted against S.246; those who had voted to keep the issue alive in 1949 voted in favor of S.246. There were five exceptions. Rep. Augustine Kelley left his three colleagues and voted in favor of S.246. Rep. Barden voted against S.246, thus joining irrevocably with the Committee group opposed to federal aid. Rep. Thomas Steed, whose position had always been similar to Barden's, followed. On the Republican side, Reps. Carroll Kearns and Walter Brehm changed sides, Kearns voting against S.246 and Brehm in favor.

---

18 5 *Congressional Quarterly Almanac*, 1949, 266-69.

TABLE 7

FEDERAL AID VOTES—HOUSE COMMITTEE ON EDUCATION AND LABOR
1949 AND 1950

| | 1949 motion to kill federal aid for 1949 | | 1950 motion to report out S246 | |
|---|---|---|---|---|
| | Yes | No | Yes | No |
| *Democrats* | | | | |
| Lesinski (Mich.) | X | | | X |
| Barden (N.C.) | | X | | X |
| Kelley (Pa.) | X | | X | |
| Powell (N.Y.) | | X | X | |
| Wood (Ga.) | | X | X | |
| Kennedy (Mass.) | X | | | X |
| Lucas (Texas) | X | | | X |
| Bailey (W.Va.) | | X | X | |
| Irving (Mo.) | | X | X | |
| Perkins (Ky.) | | X | X | |
| Howell (N.J.) | | X | X | |
| Sims (S.C.) | | X | X | |
| Jacobs (Ind.) | | X | X | |
| Burke (Ohio) | X | | | X |
| Steed (Okla.) | | X | | X |
| Wier (Minn.) | | X | X | |
| *Republicans* | | | | |
| McConnell (Pa.) | X | | | X |
| Gwinn (N.Y.) | X | | | X |
| Brehm (Ohio) | X | | X | |
| Smith (Kans.) | X | | | X |
| Kearns (Pa.) | | X | | X |
| Nixon (Calif.) | X | | | X |
| Morton (Ky.) | | X | X | |
| Werdel (Calif.) | X | | | X |
| Velde (Ill.) | X | | | X |
| *Totals* | 12 | 13 | 12 | 13 |

SOURCE: *Congressional Quarterly Almanac*, Vols. 5, 6.

In view of the fact that S.246 permitted state option on the question of auxiliary services for non-public schools, the continued opposition of Lesinski, Kennedy and Thomas Burke requires further explanation. Since Kennedy proposed an amendment to S.246 specifically allowing aid for transportation to non-public schools (rather than leaving it permissive), it seems likely that the three were still dissatisfied with the treatment of the question in S.246. But it is also true that the three had spoken out against the equalization provisions of S.246 and in favor of the flat-grant principle. All came from states which were scheduled to give far more than they would receive, and all came from districts which needed assistance. The reluctance of representatives from needy districts in wealthy states to support equalization provisions has always caused more acute problems in the House than in the Senate. Republican Carroll Kearns, an NEA member and strong advocate of federal aid, reversed his decision and voted against S.246 on precisely these grounds. In the opinion of Senator Taft, it was Kearns' reversal that cost the proponents their victory in 1950. From that vote until 1962, Kearns was adamant and rigid in his opposition to any equalization provision whatsoever. Since Kearns was the ranking minority member of the Committee in the 86th and 87th congresses, his inflexibility provided a significant example of the absence of maneuvering room within the group. Kearns was, incidentally, defeated for renomination to Congress in the 1962 party primary in his home state of Pennsylvania.

Between 1950 and 1955 several extra-Committee factors combined to decrease the activity on behalf of federal aid—the disarray and exhaustion of the proponents, their search for an approach which would avoid "the religious question" (e.g., aid for school construction), the onset of the Korean War, the passage of the impacted areas bill, and the relative inaction of the Eisenhower administration. As chairman of the Committee in 1951 and 1952 Barden did not allow the full Committee to meet on federal aid questions. In 1953 and 1954, with the Republicans in control, a similar record was maintained by Chairman Samuel McConnell. In 1955, when the Republican administration finally sent a program to Congress, Chairman Barden was again successful in bottling up federal aid legislation in his Committee. In order to delay action, he designated the full Committee as the unit to hold hearings and refused to limit questioning. He prolonged the hearings from March 2 to May 24 during which time the Committee considered 11 separate bills, listened to 52 witnesses and took 1158 pages of oral and written testimony. Barden's foot-dragging ended only after he had been presented with an ultimatum by the 15 non-southern Democrats.[19] A bill was eventually reported out of the Committee (22-8) on July 28—but, as Barden had planned, too late to be acted upon that year. Having lost, temporarily, the support of the Eisenhower-oriented Republicans on his Committee, Barden was unable to avert floor action in 1956 and 1957. But when, in 1958, Eisenhower withdrew his support for federal aid legislation, Barden plus Landrum plus the Republicans once again succeeded—by a 15-15 vote—in keeping the legislation in the Committee.

[19] House Committee on Education and Labor, *Federal Aid to States for School Construction*, 84th Congress, 1st Session (1955), 1105-12.

## FEDERAL AID IN THE HOUSE COMMITTEE, 1955–1961

In recent years, with the exception of 1958, the proponents of federal aid have succeeded in moving their bills past the committee stage. The problem which they have not yet resolved, however, is how to shape and then maintain unified support for the kind of a bill that can clear all subsequent legislative hurdles. Since 1955 two types of Committee majorities have operated to promote federal aid. The first, which prevailed in 1955, 1956, and 1957, was a bipartisan coalition necessitated by divided party control of Congress and the Presidency. The second, which has prevailed since 1959, is an all-Democratic majority, resulting from the change in party ratios effected in 1959. Neither type of Committee majority has proved to be stable and cohesive enough to act as the spearhead of federal aid majorities in the House.

The bipartisan majority—usually 15 Democrats and 7 Republicans —of the Eisenhower years was a temporary and fragile alliance of factions which remained in suspicious disagreement throughout their three years of marriage. Eisenhower himself was never more than lukewarm about federal aid to education. One of his major Republican lieutenants in Congress, Rep. Charles Halleck, was in outright opposition to Eisenhower in the years when he did send down a modest program. The legislation which reached the floor in 1956 and 1957 was a compromise between the administration and the majority of Committee Democrats. In the words of one Republican, most of his party members "went along holding their noses because it was the President's program." Most of the Democrats, on the other hand, preferred a more ambitious program than any that President Eisenhower would support. Once given an opportunity to act on its basic desires, either faction might revert to a less flexible position. In the Committee their differences were papered over for the purpose of reporting out a bill, but disagreement broke through as soon as the coalition faced pressure on the floor. In 1956 Republican members of the Committee majority simply deserted amid cries of perfidy from their Democratic colleagues. In 1957 the Committee majority fragmented and was desperately seeking a new compromise when the bill was suddenly and skillfully put to death.

One issue which seriously ruptured the bipartisan majority was that concerning federal aid to segregated schools. This most deeply divisive of all domestic social questions had been placed squarely before the Committee by the Supreme Court's decision of 1954. It represented, perhaps, the sternest possible test for any consensus-building institution. The Senate Committee and the Senate as a whole, however, proved equal to the task on several occasions. Senatorial proponents of federal aid have refrained since 1943 from pressing the issue in the belief that a prohibition against aid to segregated schools would jeopardize the passage of federal aid legislation. The issue, as might be expected, nearly paralyzed the House Committee. It was agitated by Adam Clayton Powell (D., N.Y.) who, of all the members of that disharmonious group, was the least Committee-oriented, the least legislatively oriented, and the least amenable to appeals based on the necessity for compromise and cohesion.[20] Powell was supported out of conviction by some members of the bipartisan majority; he was opposed by most of them; and, to confound the problem further, he was supported by some Committee members who were strongly opposed to federal aid legislation under any circumstances. Consideration of the issue inside the Committee in 1955 was sufficiently heated to provoke at least one shoving incident between Powell and a Democratic opponent. The Powell Amendment was ultimately rejected 17-10 in the Committee. Six of the ten wrote additional views supporting Powell. Four of these were Democratic supporters of federal aid; two were Republicans opposed to it.[21] The lack of any Committee tradition of unity in support of its votes served the cause of federal aid ill in this instance. The Committee's inability to agree plus Powell's insistence on taking the issue to the floor forecast an even wider, more disastrous split within the bipartisan majority when the bill was debated and lost in 1956. As recently as 1960, a Powell-type amendment was instrumental in bringing about the demise of a federal aid bill.

Since 1959, when the Committee majority in support of federal aid became an all-Democratic majority, its problem of cohesion has

---

[20] Inside the Committee Powell was urged to adopt one of the following alternatives: attach his amendment to the appropriation bill for the Department of Health, Education, and Welfare; obtain a ruling from the executive branch that no funds would be distributed to segregated school districts; attach his amendment, as a first step, to the impacted areas program; and make a commitment in favor of federal aid regardless of the fate of his amendment. Powell declined to take any of these steps. Another Negro leader, Rep. William Dawson (D., Ill.), took a more compromising stand, as did Powell himself when he became Chairman of the Committee. Rep. Powell's behavior can be explained in part by his great disaffection from the Committee under Barden and by the political style he adopted in the light of his constituency. On the contrasting styles of Powell and Dawson, see James Wilson, "Two Negro Politicians: An Interpretation," 4 *Midwest Journal of Political Science* (November 1960), 346-69.

[21] House Committee on Education and Labor, *House Report 1504*, 84th Congress, 1st Session, 1955.

been two-fold. In the first place, as the clear necessity for bipartisan compromise in the Committee disappeared, the disposition to compromise was correspondingly weakened. The new Democratic majority found the key to its own cohesiveness in a type of permanent, flat-grant, construction and/or salaries bill quite unacceptable to President Eisenhower or to Committee Republicans. In 1959 the Democratic majority "picked up the Committee and ran away with it"; and the flimsy bipartisan majority of 1955, 1956, 1957 disintegrated. In 1958, 1959, and 1961, the Democratic bill was opposed unanimously by the Committee's Republicans. In 1960, two Republicans joined the Democrats, but didn't affect the outcome. The 86th and 87th congresses have, therefore, been marked by increasingly intransigent partisanship inside the Committee. These conditions do not prevent bills from getting out of committee. But they have cost the federal aid proponents increments of Republican (and southern Democratic) support at times and at legislative junctures when one or the other has been necessary.

The second problem faced by the new Democratic majority has been that of maintaining cohesion in its own ranks. With the advent of Rep. Powell to the chairmanship in 1961, the liberal majority gained complete control of the Committee. In his new role, moreover, Powell agreed to exert all of his influence in opposition to any provision concerning aid to segregated schools. These gains were partially offset, though, by the loss of three important federal aid leaders on the Committee—Rep. Lee Metcalf (D., Mont.), who went to the Committee on Ways and Means and later to the Senate; Rep. Carl Elliott (D., Ala.), who went to the Rules Committee after its enlargement, and Rep. Stewart Udall (D., Ariz.), who became Secretary of the Interior. Taken together, these three men had contributed a high proportion of the skill, the knowledge, the drive, and the disposition to compromise inside the Committee in the cause of federal aid. Chairman Powell organized his Committee for action rather than inaction. For the first time, he established a permanent subcommittee organization and a formal set of rules. By parceling out education legislation to three separate subcommittees, he speeded up the work of the Committee. At the same time, however, he created problems of priority within the Committee by giving to each subcommittee an institutional interest in its particular program—be it general federal aid, NDEA amendments, or college facilities and scholarships. Even under the new and more forceful leadership of Rep. Powell, Democrats continued to exhibit their natural tendency to fight other Democrats.

Specifically, the question of aid to non-public schools has again threatened Democratic cohesion. In 1960 the issue was raised but defeated in committee. The subsequent bill was carefully drafted so that a point of order could be (and was) made against any non-public school aid proposal raised on the floor. In 1961 one group of Democrats manipulated the Committee machinery adroitly to prevent another group of Democrats from adding a parochial school aid program to the public school bill. The issue, raised so strongly by the Catholic bishops and kept alive, perversely, by the very determination of a Catholic president to exclude it, then took a different form. A dispute broke out as to whether the public school bill or the amendments to the NDEA, which included a provision for loans to non-public schools, should be reported out of committee first. The faction supporting both the public and non-public aid programs and the faction supporting just a public school aid program eyed each other distrustfully, each fearful that the approach of the other would doom federal aid legislation entirely. Ironically, it was the standoff between these Democratic factions which killed the legislation. Behind each Committee faction stood a group of supporters within the House leadership group and within the Rules Committee. The standoff was broken within the House Education and Labor Committee, but not decisively enough to prevent a fatal recurrence in the Rules Committee.

### The House Rules Committee and Federal Aid

Once the opponents of federal aid lost their majority within the Committee on Education and Labor they repaired to a second line of defense in the Committee on Rules. Normally, any bill reported out of committee requires a majority vote in the Rules Committee before it can be brought to the floor of the House. When the first federal aid bill cleared the Committee on Education and Labor in July 1955, the Rules Committee refused to take action. It was not until June, 1956, when faced with a threat to bypass them and when urged by the administration, that the Rules Committee (by 8-3 vote; see Table 8) sent the bill to the floor. In the years 1956 and 1957 the bipartisan federal aid majority on the Education and Labor Committee was supported by a bipartisan majority on the Rules Committee. The membership of Rules during those years was composed of eight Democrats and four Republicans. And the proponents of federal aid were able to count on a majority of six or seven Democratic plus two Republican votes.

In 1959, however, the complexion of both the Education and Labor

TABLE 8

VOTES IN THE RULES COMMITTEE TO EXPEDITE FEDERAL AID LEGISLATION
1956-1961

| | 1956 Yes | 1956 No | 1960 1st Yes | 1960 1st No | 1960 2nd Yes | 1960 2nd No | 1961 1st Yes | 1961 1st No | 1961 2nd Yes | 1961 2nd No |
|---|---|---|---|---|---|---|---|---|---|---|
| **Democrats** | | | | | | | | | | |
| Smith (Va.) | | X | | X | | X | | X | | X |
| Colmer (Miss.) | | X | | X | | X | | X | | X |
| Madden (Ind.) | X | | X | | X | | X | | X | |
| Delaney (N.Y.) | X | | X | | X | | | X | | X |
| Trimble (Ark.) | X | | X | | | X | X | | X | |
| Thornberry (Tex.) | * | * | X | | X | | X | | X | |
| Bolling (Mo.) | X | | X | | X | | X | | X | |
| O'Neill (Mass.) | X | | X | | X | | | X | X | |
| Elliott (Ala.) | | | | | | | X | | X | |
| Sisk (Calif.) | | | | | | | X | | X | |
| **Republicans** | | | | | | | | | | |
| Allen (Ill.) | | X | | X | | X | | | | |
| Brown (Ohio) | X | | | X | | X | | X | | X |
| Ellsworth (Ore.) | X | | | | | | | | | |
| Latham (N.Y.) | X | | | | | | | | | |
| Reece (Tenn.) | | | X | | | X | | | | |
| Budge (Ida.) | | | | X | | X | | | | |
| St. George (N.Y.) | | | | | | | | X | | X |
| Smith (Calif.) | | | | | | | | X | | X |
| Hoffman (Ill.) | | | | | | | | X | | X |
| Avery (Kan.) | | | | | | | | X | | X |
| **Totals** | 8 — | 3 | 7 — | 5 | 5 — | 7 | 6 — | 9 | 7 — | 8 |

* Not present.
No record of 1957 and 1959 votes.
SOURCE: *Congressional Quarterly Almanac*, Vols. 12, 13, 16, 17.

and the Rules Committee changed. The changes were related to each other. In the first place, to the degree that the new Democratic majority refused to compromise with the Republicans inside the Education and Labor Committee, they increased Republican intransigence on the Rules Committee. In the second place, to the degree that the new Democratic majority failed to achieve cohesion inside the Education and Labor Committee, they encouraged disagreement among Democrats on the Rules Committee.

For the past three years, federal aid to education has been effectively killed by the Rules Committee. In 1959 an alliance between the four Republicans and two consistently anti-federal aid southern Democrats forestalled even a Committee vote on the subject. President

Eisenhower had declined to recommend any federal aid legislation and the flat-grant, teachers' salaries and/or construction bill of the Democrats faced a certain veto. One of the bill's architects recalled, "We got that bill out of Committee and we knew it didn't stand a chance of getting through the Rules Committee. But we just let it sit there. It put a few feet to the fire. We got enough pressure built up so that the next year when we came back with a construction bill we got one extra vote and got it through the Rules Committee." The extra vote came in 1960 from Republican B. Carroll Reece of Tennessee, who reportedly was under heavy pressure from his needy constituency to support federal aid. This bill became the first and only one to pass the House of Representatives. The Senate had already passed a similar bill. When a single objection to the projected Conference Committee was entered from the House floor, it became necessary for the Rules Committee to furnish a rule. At this point, the Committee voted 7-5 against sending the bill to conference. Rep. Reece of Tennessee and James Trimble, a moderate Democrat from Arkansas, changed their positions from the earlier vote. For Trimble, and probably for Reece, the primary reason was the inclusion by floor amendment of a provision denying aid to segregated schools.

One difficulty of the post-1959 liberal Democratic federal aid majority was that, although they had altered the membership and seized control of the Education and Labor Committee, they had not altered the membership and seized control of the Rules Committee. This latter step they proceeded to undertake in 1961 with the help of Speaker Rayburn and a Democratic president.[22] It was the adverse vote on federal aid in 1960 that furnished one of the main supporting arguments for the change to ten Democrats and five Republicans. In spite of this strategem, the Democrats again failed to achieve the requisite cohesion in their ranks. When the Education and Labor Committee reported out its public school aid bill, the Rules Committee voted 9-6 to take no action on it until the non-public school aid bill (the amendments to the NDEA) and a higher education bill had also reached their Committee. On this vote, the majority was comprised, as expected, by the five Republicans and the two anti-federal aid

[22] Accounts of the Rules Committee enlargement fight are to be found in Douglas Price, "Race, Religion, and the Rules Committee: The Kennedy Aid-to-Education Bills," in Alan Westin (ed.), *The Uses of Power* (New York: Harcourt, Brace, and World, Inc., 1962), 13-20; Milton C. Cummings and Robert L. Peabody, "The Decision to Enlarge the House Committee on Rules," unpublished manuscript, 1961.

southerners, who were joined, unexpectedly, by two liberal Democrats, both Catholics from heavily Catholic districts.

Thus the earlier dilemma in the Education and Labor Committee as to the order in which the public school bill and the parochial aid bill should come to the floor was being re-enacted in the Rules Committee. Three weeks later, when faced with all three education bills, the Rules Committee Democrats were still unable to agree on how to break the log jam. By an 8-7 majority, they voted to table all three education bills for the remainder of the year. On this vote, one of the two defecting Democrats, Rep. Thomas O'Neill of Massachusetts, changed his position; but the other, Rep. James Delaney of New York, still dissatisfied with the provisions for parochial school aid, again voted against sending the public school aid bill to the floor. A month later, an improvised federal aid bill was rushed to the floor on Calendar Wednesday—thus bypassing the Rules Committee—but it stood no chance of passage. The earlier defeat in the Rules Committee and in the course of regular legislative processes was decisive.

The Rules Committee is, by the very nature of its jurisdiction over the House's program and procedure, subject to the directive influence of the majority party leadership. And in 1961, the Democratic leadership group was itself badly split on the issue of priority and strategy. Speaker Rayburn, convinced that the only possibility for a public school program lay in its being considered first, insisted that the public school bill be taken up forthwith. Majority Leader John McCormack (D., Mass.) fearful that the bill containing aid to parochial schools would fail unless it reached the floor first, argued against Rayburn. Each was allied with a faction in the Rules Committee. Because the Rayburn faction took the initiative inside the Rules Committee, it was the two members allied with McCormack, *i.e.*, O'Neill and Delaney, who delivered the *coup de grâce* to federal aid. But, had McCormack's strategy been proposed in the Committee, federal aid would just as surely have perished at the hands of the Rayburn faction—men such as Trimble, Elliot, Homer Thornberry, and B. F. Sisk.

The Rules Committee Democrats had been presented with the issue in a form which made it virtually insoluble. The responsibility for their dilemma lay elsewhere—partly with the House leadership, and partly with the Education and Labor Committee. Even more, perhaps, responsibility lay with the Kennedy administration whose equivocations on the crucial questions of strategy—described earlier—had launched all these House decision-makers on an uncertain course. In any case, the necessity of commanding cohesive majorities in two separate House committees compounds the legislative dilemma of federal aid proponents.

The achievement of a substantial and stable consensus at the committee stage is a precondition for the passage of federal aid legislation. It is a precondition that has been repeatedly met by a Senate committee strongly in favor of federal aid; but it is a precondition that has been met only infrequently in the House of Representatives. In either instance, the record at the committee stage relates closely to actions taken or expectations held by the whole membership of the House and Senate. Logically as well as chronologically, therefore, the legislative struggle over federal aid must now be examined as it has occurred on the floor of Congress.

# VI. Action on the Floor of Congress

In CONGRESSIONAL POLITICS the important centers of decision-making are numerous and disparate. The committees of Congress are powerful units, but they are, after all, creatures of the House and Senate. A committee decision to report a bill necessitates still another decision on that bill by the total membership of the parent body. Four federal aid bills have reached the floor of the Senate and four have reached the floor of the House. The four Senate bills passed handily. In the House the formidable problems faced in pushing federal aid legislation beyond the committee stage also have been reflected in the decisions made on the floor. In three cases the legislation was defeated; and on the one occasion when it passed, the bill was not allowed to proceed to conference.

The disparity between Senate and House action has affected the sequence in which the eight bills have reached the floor stage. Senate supporters concentrated their efforts early and successfully in 1948 and 1949. But, having observed the total inability of their House colleagues to follow suit, the Senate gave priority to other matters until "the other body" could furnish some evidence of success. The next concerted effort, by the House, resulted in the unsuccessful floor attempts of 1956 and 1957. Somewhat encouraged, Senate backers again initiated and passed federal aid legislation in 1960 and 1961. They took action early enough in the session to put an additional impetus behind subsequent House action. In both years federal aid bills were voted upon in two chambers; but, again, House opponents succeeded, in one way or another, in blocking further action.

The three distinct waves of floor activity—1948–1949, 1956–1957, 1960–1961—provide a framework for the present analysis. In each of the eight instances of floor action particular emphasis is placed, as previously, on the conditions making for consensus building and those militating against it. Floor debate and roll call votes reveal a good deal about the relation between a policy position and the problem of building legislative support for it. The methods by which various legislative coalitions are formed remain hidden from view, but the results—in terms of who is aligned with whom on what issue—are recorded with a precision unequalled in any other public legislative record. Floor action also reveals the kind of payoffs which flow from

137

strategic decisions adopted in committee, thus linking activity at one stage of the legislative process with activity at another.

## SENATE FLOOR ACTION, 1948–1949

The debate which began in the Senate on March 23, 1948 was not the first federal aid debate in that chamber. It was the second. The first occurred in 1943, and had ended in a sudden defeat for the advocates of an enlarged federal role. The immediate cause was the passage of an amendment by Senator William Langer (R., N.D.) to prevent discrimination between white and Negro schools in the use of federal and related state funds. The amendment passed by a vote of 40-37. Republicans split 27-3 in favor of it; Democrats voted 34-13 against the amendment. This association of federal aid with the issue of segregated schools resulted in the immediate demise of the bill. A quick recommittal motion by Senator Robert Taft (R., Ohio) was carried 53-26 by a coalition of 19 Republicans and 34 Democrats. Every southern Democrat voted against the amendment and for recommittal. Eighteen Republicans voted for the Langer amendment and then (in what has become a classic maneuver) turned around and voted to kill the bill.[1]

For the supporters of federal aid the general lesson to be learned was the necessity of preparing in advance and holding firm against any amendment carrying divide and conquer potentialities. More particularly, the lesson of 1943 was the special vulnerability of the Democratic party—the party which had to provide the backbone for any federal aid majority.

The main provisions of the 1948 and 1949 Senate bills were virtually identical. They were the result of years of Committee experimentation in search of a politically viable bill, and they embodied a number of compromises deemed essential to secure its passage. Basically, the bill was an equalization measure designed to raise educational levels in needy areas and reduce state-to-state disparities in educational opportunity. The debate of 1943 and the Senate hearings of 1945 and 1947 had converted Senator Taft to the cause of equalization. It was Taft who played the most critical leadership role in behalf of federal aid in these years. Reminding his colleagues that "I was largely instrumental in defeating a federal aid to education bill in the fall of 1943," he stated that, "I will say that I changed my mind. Fundamentally, Mr. President, I think we have a tremendous obliga-

[1] 78:1 *Congressional Record* (1943), 8565-8570.

tion to provide equality of opportunity to the children of the United States. . . . No child can have equality of opportunity in my opinion unless to start with he has a minimum education. . . . Because of the way wealth is distributed in the United States . . . I do not believe we are able to do it without a federal-aid system."[2]

The bill which Taft originally helped write in subcommittee provided aid to only the 25 neediest states. In the Committee on Labor and Public Welfare, Senator Irving Ives (R., N.Y.) argued strongly on behalf of the large, wealthy taxpaying states for a flat-grant provision. Taft had compromised reluctantly by adding a $5 per child flat grant to those states that would not otherwise qualify. "I forget," he said later, "whether or not I voted for the amendment in the Committee. At any rate, I agreed to it finally."[3] Thus the basis was laid for widespread support from the wealthier (mostly northern) as well as the poorer (mostly southern) states.

A second important compromise involved the explosive problem of aid to private schools for current expenditures. Internal pressure in favor of such aid came from Senator George Aiken (R., Vt.), in whose state many private academies doubled as public high schools, and Senator Allen Ellender (D., La.), in whose state a large Catholic school-going population was receiving transportation and textbook aid under provisions of the state constitution. Opposition to any such aid was voiced persistently in committee by Senator Forrest Donnell (R., Mo.), whose questioning of witnesses on this matter dominated the hearings in 1945 and 1947. More importantly, the issue had been basic to the damaging split between the NEA and the AF of T at this time. The Committee resolved this conflict by permitting the use of federal funds for current expenditures, such as transportation and textbooks, where such was permitted by state law. It was argued that the bill thereby avoided federal control of education and endorsed the principle of state control.

Thus written, the 1948 and 1949 Senate bills commanded overwhelming majorities in committee and on the floor. The important feature of these majorities was their bipartisan character. The majorities which reported federal aid out of committee, the majorities which defended against crippling amendments on the floor, and the majorities which secured final passage were bipartisan majorities. On eleven of the twelve roll call votes taken in 1948 and 1949 a majority of Senate Republicans and a majority of Senate Democrats

[2] 80:2 *Congressional Record* (1948), 3291, 3350.
[3] *Ibid.*, 3350.

voted together. Every one of the nine amendments offered from the
floor was overwhelmingly defeated—all except one opposed by
majorities in both parties. Their margin of defeat ranged from a high
of 75 votes to a low of 19 votes. On final passage a majority of Republicans joined a majority of Democrats in running up margins of close
to 3 to 1. In 1948, 86.1 per cent of the Democrats voted with 61.4 per
cent of the Republicans to produce a vote of 58-22. In 1949, 92.3 per
cent of the Democrats were joined by 64.7 per cent of the Republicans,
resulting in a 58-15 vote for passage.[4]

On all twelve roll call votes the members of the Committee on
Labor and Public Welfare provided a stable, cohesive bipartisan spearhead of support. On seven of the twelve roll calls the Committee
members voted together unanimously. And in no case did more than
two members of the group vote against their Committee colleagues.
As measured by the index of cohesion reported in Table 9, Committee
unity was much greater than unity in the Senate as a whole. The unity
of Democratic members of the Committee was greater than the unity of
Democratic Senators generally; and the same relationship held true for
the Republicans.

TABLE 9

MEAN INDICES OF COHESION FOR PARTY MEMBERS AND MEMBERS OF LABOR AND
PUBLIC WELFARE COMMITTEE, U.S. SENATE, 1948-1949; 1960-1961

|  | Mean Index of Cohesion for 12 Roll Calls 1948-1949 | Mean Index of Cohesion for 24 Roll Calls 1960-1961 | Final Votes 1948-1949 1960-1961 |
|---|---|---|---|
| All members Senate | 61.4 | 32.6 | 35.5 |
| All members Committee Labor and Public Welfare | 92.1 | 54.5 | 79.2 |
| All Democratic Senators | 78.4 | 63.5 | 66.8 |
| All Democratic Committee Members | 93.3 | 91.0 | 100 |
| All Republican Senators | 46.3 | 45.5 | 35.0 |
| All Republican Committee Members | 90.4 | 48.2 | 58.7 |

NOTE: The index of cohesion is frequently used to measure the unity of legislative
groups. An index of 100 indicates unanimity within a group. An index of 0
indicates a 50-50 split among members. Arithmetically, the index of cohesion is
the difference between the percentage favoring and the percentage opposing a
given measure.

[4] Roll call votes examined hereafter are taken from the compilations of
*Congressional Quarterly.* Unless noted, the totals do not include paired votes.

The Committee and its party subgroups were more strongly united in favor of federal aid than their counterparts in the chamber as a whole. This is, again, a reflection both of the membership of the Committee and of its competence as a consensus-building institution for the chamber of which it is a working part.

In view of the experience of 1943, the organized vigilance against the recurrence of the racial issue is particularly noteworthy. A colloquy in 1948 between Senator Harry Byrd (D., Va.) and Senator Taft revealed the precautions taken prior to that debate.

> Mr. BYRD. I wish to say to the Southern Senators that there is no guaranty that a provision will not be adopted sooner or later to the effect that no part of this money will be available to states which practice segregation in the schools—a provision similar to the Langer Amendment to a previous bill. The Senator from Ohio [Mr. Taft] voted for it. I predict today that if a Senator were to offer the Langer Amendment to this bill, it would be accepted.
>
> Mr. TAFT: Mr. President, will the Senator yield?
>
> Mr. BYRD: I yield.
>
> Mr. TAFT: I assure the Senate that the Langer amendment would not be adopted today.
>
> Mr. BYRD: I do not understand how the Senator from Ohio can assure us as to that. He does not control the votes in the Senate.
>
> Mr. TAFT: I wish to say that I have made careful inquiry.[5]

The Senate's size and its unique traditions facilitate preliminary bargaining and informal understandings of this sort to a degree that seems impossible in the larger, more formal House of Representatives. In the area of federal aid, the smoothly managed and well modulated Senate floor action stands in vivid contrast to the chaos which typically engulfs the bill's leaders in the House.

In 1949 an amendment prohibiting aid to segregated schools was introduced by Senator Henry Cabot Lodge (R., Mass.). The response of the bill's proponents was as immediate as it was impassioned—and effective on both counts. The fight against the Lodge amendment was led by two long-time Senate supporters of federal aid—Elbert Thomas (D., Utah) and George Aiken (R., Vt.). Senator Thomas, co-sponsor of the 1943 bill, pleaded,

> As a supporter of the pending bill, as one who has worked with the bill through the years, as one who has known the devastating power of such an amendment as the one now proposed, and who

[5] 80:2 *Congressional Record* (1948), 3928.

has suffered defeat, I cannot but point out to my fellow Senators in all seriousness the great danger which lies before them. . . . All you have to do is go back and look at the votes on federal aid to education bills three or four years ago. A similar amendment was accepted and the supporters of the bill not by the tens, but by scores, walked out on it, the bill was lost and we were set back a quarter of a century thereby.[6]

Senator Aiken commented on the divide and conquer effects of the amendment.

In my opinion the most ardent supporters for the amendment offered by the Senator from Massachusetts would not be found among the colored race but would be found among the hard-shelled reactionary elements of some of our state chambers of commerce who are opposed to social progress of any kind at any price.[7]

The floor battle against the amendment was waged by a group of northern liberals favoring federal aid, including Senators Wayne Morse (R., Ore.), Paul Douglas (D., Ill.), and Hubert Humphrey (D., Minn.). On the subsequent vote not a single Democrat voted in favor of the amendment. Republicans, on the other hand, were less cohesive on this issue than on any other single one in the 1948-49 period, splitting almost equally.

The Senate, in 1948, had a Republican majority of 51-45; in 1949, the Democrats controlled by a margin of 54-42. The close party division necessitated bipartisan cooperation. It was Senator Taft's status as the intellectual leader of the chamber's Republicans that made his strong advocacy of federal aid critical. In 1948, in the Republican 80th Congress, he led the floor debate by dint of his position as Chairman of the Committee on Labor and Public Welfare. But his floor role was even more dominant in 1949, when his party was in the minority. At one point in the 1949 debate Taft held the floor for several hours engaging in colloquies, friendly and hostile, with seventeen different colleagues—an impressive performance continuing for seventeen pages in the *Congressional Record*. In 1948 twenty-two of his fellow Republicans did not vote against Taft on a single one of the five record votes. In 1949 a core of nine of his minority party colleagues voted or announced a position with Taft on all seven votes. These associations with Taft were not, of course,

---

[6] 81:1 *Congressional Record* (1949), 5473-74.
[7] *Ibid.*, 5471.

due simply to Taft's influence. They may have been a function of the ideology of many Republican Senators. And the greater support in 1948 may have been a function of majority party status. But a substantial number of senators whose conservatism on domestic issues was probably greater than Taft's own conservatism voted with him—several on every roll call and many more on final passage.[8] Taft was especially successful in uniting the Committee's Republicans. Since Taft's departure from the Committee its Republican members have voted less frequently with a majority of their Democratic colleagues, and they have been far less cohesive than was the case under Taft (See Table 8). The fact that Democratic Committee cohesion has not significantly changed, focuses attention on the Republicans and suggests the important consequences of Taft's leadership.[9]

During the Senate debates of 1948 and 1949, federal aid advocates faced prototypes of all subsequent amendments. No issue has been raised via amendment since then in either house that was not presented in those early years. Four categories of amendments have appeared—those altering the amount or distribution of funds, those dealing with aid to segregated schools, those treating aid to non-public schools, and those proposing that a proportion of some federal tax be remitted to the collecting state and earmarked for education aid. In 1948 and 1949, and in most cases since then, the two latter types of amendments have carried the greatest potential for disruption of federal aid supporters in the Senate. Each operated so as to lure a different segment away from the bipartisan coalition. An amendment allocating money for aid to private schools split the Democrats more seriously by far than any other vote. And the one roll call during the period on which a majority of Republicans voted in opposition to a majority of Democrats was a proposal to earmark a percentage of income tax receipts for educational use in the collecting state.

The remission of federal taxes, first introduced as a substitute proposal in 1949, has become a political staple of the congressional

---

[8] In 1948, for instance, Taft's followers on all votes included Republican Senators Jenner (Ind.), Brewster (Me.), Capehart (Ind.), Ferguson (Mich.), Watkins (Utah), Cordon (Oregon), Cain (Wash.), Revercomb (W. Va.), Knowland (Calif.), Dworshak (Ida.), and Vandenberg (Mich.).

[9] When the 1961 vote on federal aid was taken, nine Republicans who had voted with Taft in 1948 or 1949 or both (but never against him) remained in the Senate. Five of these nine, all fairly conservative, voted against the much milder 1961 bill. Their switch may furnish a crude measure of Taft's pulling power in the earlier years. The five were Senators Hickenlooper (Iowa), Dworshak (Ida.), Mundt (S. D.), Saltonstall (Mass.), and Capehart (Ind.).

opponents of federal aid. No fewer than seven separate roll calls (two in the House and five in the Senate) have been devoted to the idea. In six instances it has been put forward by devoted opponents of federal aid. And in every case it has been supported by the vast majority of those who eventually voted against passage. But its early success (in 1949) in attracting lukewarm backers of federal aid continues. Some see it as an alternative method of financing which, by remitting tax revenue to the state where it is collected, avoids the potential of federal control. For some representatives of wealthy states it meets their contention that the people of their states should not have to pay for the education of children in other states. Many, too, find it an eminently handy way of dealing with the political problem of how to appear to support federal aid without really supporting it.

Tax remission is, of course, in basic opposition to those advocates of federal aid who seek equalization through the redistribution of national income. It may have been Senator Taft's most durable legacy in the continuing federal aid debate that he fought resolutely against any earmarking proposal. He spoke as a conservative to the conservatives for whom the proposal has its greatest appeal, and his argument has been repeated in every debate, in House and Senate, where the amendment has been presented. As late as 1961, when four such amendments were offered in the Senate, federal aid proponents invoked the name and the argument of Taft. They attributed a large measure of their success to the lasting impact of Taft's objection in 1949 that "[This] amendment certainly violates every principle of federal finance. It is based on the supposition that in some way a state has some property right to the taxes collected from sources within its boundaries. If for one moment we admitted such a principle, the entire federal system will crash, because a state has no such interest."[10]

## House Floor Action, 1956-1957

As a result of their failure to report out the Senate bill in 1949 and 1950, federal aid supporters in the House sought an approach which would avoid the damaging entanglements of the parochial school conflict. They found it by shifting from a teachers' salaries plus current expenditures bill to one providing for the construction of school buildings. During a hearing late in 1950 a revealing colloquy

[10] 81:1 *Congressional Record* (1949), 5582.

took place between Chairman Lesinski and the Executive Director of the American Parents Committee:

Mrs. FAHY: While Mr. Lesinski is here, could I reiterate that I think you should pass a general federal aid to education bill as well as a school construction bill?

Mr. LESINSKI: Would you want the religious question to crop up again?

Mrs. FAHY: I think that this country has survived religious questions ever since the Puritans arrived on Plymouth Rock, and I think we are able to resolve it now, Mr. Lesinski.

Mr. LESINSKI: Of course, I have been on this committee 18 years and the same thing happened 20 years before I was here. And I am trying to avoid the religious question. That is why we are trying to do other things first, so that we do not revive the religious question.[11]

The bills which reached the House floor in 1956 and 1957 were school construction bills. They succeeded in avoiding the religious question. But they became involved in other equally divisive questions of American national politics.

Three dominant facts of political life shaped federal aid activity in the two-year period of 1956-1957. One was the fact of a Republican President and a Democratic majority in Congress. The second fact was the narrow margin by which the Democrats controlled Congress. In 1956 House membership was 232 Democrats and 203 Republicans; in 1957 it remained virtually the same, at 234-201. If the presidential and congressional elections of 1956 contained any mandate at all on federal aid to education, it called for legislative-executive compromise and bipartisan House majorities. The bills which reached the House floor were compromise bills. But bipartisan House majorities in their favor never materialized. A third political factor was the intensification and crystallization of domestic conflict over segregation in the public schools in the wake of the Supreme Court decision of 1954. Once this issue reached the floor of the House its potential for disrupting the Democratic members of the coalition was as great as the parochial school question.

In most congressional struggles there is a body of legislators who stand somewhere between the devoted advocates and the devoted opponents of change. They are lukewarm and tentative in their attitudes.

---

[11] House Committee on Education and Labor, *Federal Aid to School Construction*, 81st Congress, 2nd Session (1950), 258.

They are cross-pressured by a variety of influences. They do not care passionately one way or another about the outcome. In a close parliamentary situation this group is in a position to extract a price from the advocates of change without giving in return any very firm allegiance to that cause. They must be courted by legislative compromise. Yet there are dangers in the courting. Those who are successfully won over may remain essentially uncommitted to the main proposition. Hence their support may be too fragile to withstand the divisive impact of legislative combat. At the same time the support of the ardent proponents may be weakened by the series of concessions offered to the waverers. In either case a legislative majority may be artfully contrived on paper, but it is not a determined, cohesive majority on the legislative floor. Conditions such as this created the strategic dilemmas of 1956-57.

The federal aid bills which emerged from the House Committee in 1956 and 1957 did not command durable majorities. In their positive provisions they represented a shaky compromise between the desires of President Dwight Eisenhower and the desires of a majority of Education and Labor Committee Democrats. In a negative sense, they left wholly unresolved the explosive conflict over the issue of aid to segregated schools. Under the pressure of floor maneuver, these paper majorities crumpled. Republican supporters, reflecting Eisenhower's own lukewarm attitude toward federal aid, decided to exact a heavier price for their allegiance than they had settled for in the Committee bills. Southern Democrats, whose allegiance to federal aid was far weaker than their allegiance to segregated schools, left the majority as soon as the Powell Amendment had been added. The bipartisan majority was further whipsawed by those liberal Democrats who supported the Powell Amendment together with federal aid and by those conservative Republicans who supported the Powell Amendment but opposed federal aid. Legislative success depended upon a majority, like that in the Senate, which valued some federal aid legislation above all else. It depended upon a majority which would resolutely vote against the Powell Amendment and compromise on everything else. The possibility of such a floor majority occurred but once during the period—in 1957—and then only momentarily before debate was suddenly extinguished by a snap vote.

President Eisenhower's preference was for a debt service approach to school construction. If he had to compromise on some sort of grant program, he preferred equalization grants, to be matched by the states. The 1956-57 bills combined a grant program with a debt service program to assist local districts in financing construction. The

1956 bill called for flat grants on a matching basis; the 1957 bill provided for flat and equalization grants, also on a matching basis. Both compromise bills reached the floor with bipartisan Committee support.

In 1956 the Committee's Eisenhower Republicans accepted the compromise, but when the bill reached the floor they sought major changes in the grant distribution formula to conform to the President's preference. Their proposal, sponsored by ranking minority member Representative Samuel McConnell (R., Penna.), stirred confusion if not bitterness within the bipartisan coalition. Federal aid stalwart Cleveland Bailey (D., W. Va.) protested:

> I feel compelled to question the good faith of the gentleman from Pennsylvania in offering this substitute plan. He was a member of the subcommittee that drafted the legislation and it was agreed that the Kelley Bill would be a nonpartisan-bipartisan approach to the solution of the problem. That is why the proponents of Title I, the federal grants-in-aid, agreed to accept Titles II and III of the President's program as a compromise measure to insure the approval of this legislation. The gentleman is not satisfied with two Titles of the President's plan, he wants to substitute Title III of the President's plan for Title I of the Kelley Bill.
>
> I can assure you the distinguished gentleman from Pennsylvania [Mr. Kearns] was a party to this agreement that this would be fought out on a nonpartisan-bipartisan basis and that the Kelley Bill was to be defended against all crippling amendments right down the line.[12]

Other Democrats complained that McConnell's formula was too complicated to be dealt with on the floor and added that they themselves could not understand it. Chairman Graham Barden further revealed the Committee's disarray with his comment that "It is a little bit of an awkward position for the chairman to be caught in when the ranking minority member springs five pages of law on the committee of the whole without my ever having seen it."[13] The next day Barden formally withdrew as "floor manager" of the bill.

The public exhibition of Committee disunity did no service to the bill's supporters and gave encouragement plus a rationalization to its opponents. Representative Charles Halleck (R., Ind.), a Repub-

---

[12] 84:2 *Congressional Record* (1956), 11751.
[13] *Ibid.*, 11752.

lican leader and a key opponent of federal aid, seized upon the division to argue that:

> The Kelley Bill never was the administration program; it is not the administration program now. . . . I hope a motion to recommit is offered, with instructions to incorporate the Mc-Connell amendments thereby incorporating the President's recommendations.[14]

Representative McConnell did offer the recommittal motion. It was supported by 11 of the Committee's 13 Republicans (84.6 per cent) and by 76 per cent of the Republicans in the House as a whole. President Eisenhower was unwilling to state his own position positively enough to provide for Republican leadership one way or the other.

In 1957, on a bill which its architects said contained "85 per cent of the specifications laid down by the President," Eisenhower's silence was even more disastrous for aid proponents. For in this instance the bill was killed by a vote of 208-203. On the floor, Committee Republicans vied with each other in fathoming the presidential will. Representative Peter Frelinghuysen (R., N.J.), the strongest Republican aid-supporter on the Committee, admitted, "Perhaps he has not given it his unequivocal wholehearted support, . . . (but) this bill in my opinion incorporates all the principles which the President declared are vital to sound legislation in the field."[15] Representative McConnell, senior Committee Republican, attempted clarification. "The President is in favor of a bill for school construction. This is not the most preferred bill he wishes. He has made that very clear. He also realizes that legislation is a matter of compromise, and he understands an effort to compromise. He does say, however, that this is not his first preference; that he prefers a bill where financial need is more emphasized than in the compromise bill."[16] Representative William Ayres (R., Ohio), who had voted against reporting the bill out of committee, offered a substitute bill saying, "This is the bill that the President is really for. This is the bill he supported in the last session. This is the bill, in my judgment, after having talked with him at a breakfast at the White House, his heart is really in."[17]

Members announced at several points that a presidential statement

[14] *Ibid.*, 11869.
[15] 85:1 *Congressional Record* (1957), 12608.
[16] *Ibid.*, 12723.
[17] *Ibid.*, 12750.

was imminent, but the absence of such a statement allowed each legislator to interpret the Eisenhower position to suit his own preconceptions. As Representative Halleck declared:

> I am going to follow the dictates of my own conscience. I am going to be mindful of the views of the people I represent. . . . Certainly I shall not be unmindful of the loyalties that are mine to my party and the stand of the administration insofar as I am able to determine how those various things will come up as a matter of application.[18]

Unencumbered by presidential pressure, Halleck's conscience and that of 110 other Republicans dictated a vote to kill federal aid for 1957. A veteran federal aid supporter in the Senate summed up the sentiments of his cohorts when he exclaimed later:

> It was what the administration did—or didn't do—that killed the legislation. The truth of the matter was that Eisenhower never wanted federal aid. I think some of his friends on the golf course must have told him that it was creeping socialism. I really do. In 1957, the bill lost in the House by 5 votes. He could have had a bill. A few phone calls to members of Congress, "This is the President of the United States calling Congressman so and so"—and he'd have gotten the votes. If he had called up Charlie Halleck and Joe Martin and said "I want the votes," he could have gotten them. The struggle would never have been as close as it was. He just didn't want a bill. He did nothing. And in that situation, inaction meant, "No."

Amid great confusion on the floor, the Democratic supporters of federal aid struggled to repair the damaged bipartisan coalition. When Ayres offered his substitute bill (the Eisenhower preference of 1956 and the one embodied in McConnell's amendment of that year), the Committee's liberal Democrats agreed to support it. Representative Stewart Udall (D., Ariz.) said, typically, "If in order to get the bipartisanship we need, we must have precisely the bill the president said he wanted last year, I . . . will support the amendment of the gentleman from Ohio, as I want a school bill."[19] Republicans and Democrats rose to pledge allegiance to this new coalition and, briefly, it looked as if a timely if not hardy majority might coalesce. But before any new alignment could take shape Chairman Howard Smith

[18] *Ibid.*, 12721.
[19] *Ibid.*, 12751.

(D., Va.) of the Rules Committee offered a preferential motion to strike the enacting clause of the bill, *i.e.* to kill it, and "be through with this rather futile debate." Representative Udall made a last impassioned plea.

> Finally, after two years of thrashing around on this thing, we have finally reached an agreement. We on this side have decided to go all the way with the President, cross every "t" and dot every "i" and go right down the line with precisely what the President wants. We can join hands with you. We have obviously worked out a working agreement. It is feasible in this body. We can pass a school bill today. Therefore the purpose of this motion is to derail this new coalition that we have.[20]

The motion was carried 208-203. The time was ripe, as Judge Smith doubtless sensed, for disrupting a coalition, not creating one. That which Republican and Democratic supporters could not accomplish over a period of years in committee or at the White House they could hardly hope to improvise in a period of minutes on the House floor.

Ineffective bipartisan leadership contributed heavily to the federal aid failures of 1956-57. But even with the best of leadership the coalition might not have survived the divisive repercussions of the Supreme Court's 1954 segregation decision. Legislative attempts through the Powell Amendment to withhold aid from segregated schools raised an issue which splintered the prospective majority into a profusion of disparate minorities. Whereas a dearth of leadership cost the coalition vital Republican support, the superimposition of racial issues upon federal aid issues cost the coalition equally vital Democratic support.

In 1956 the Powell Amendment was attached to the bill by a coalition of 77 northern Democrats and 148 Republicans. The amendment was opposed by 115 southern and border-state Democrats, 31 northern Democrats and 46 Republicans. The voting alignment cut across and divided the ranks of proponents and opponents of federal aid. As such it bore little resemblance to the final alignment on passage of the bill. Ninety-six of the 148 Republicans who had voted for the Powell Amendment voted against the bill. Twenty-nine of the 31 northern Democrats who had voted against the Powell Amendment voted for the bill; but they could not offset the large Republican swing in the other direction. The 77 northern Democrats who voted for the Powell Amendment supported the bill, but they were un-

[20] *Ibid.*, 12753.

willing to vote against their civil rights convictions in order to improve the chances of federal aid. The very passage of the amendment, however, irrevocably detached from the coalition some southern and border-state congressmen who might otherwise have voted in favor of the legislation. Whatever their motivation may have been, the consequences of 76.3 per cent Republican support for the Powell Amendment and 61.3 per cent Republican opposition to final passage were first to divide and then to conquer the federal aid coalition.

It is difficult to know precisely how many Democratic supporters were lost to the bill through the passage of the Powell Amendment. Some measure of that loss, however, can be gleaned from comparing the vote on passage in 1956 with the vote to strike the enacting clause in 1957. At the time the 1957 bill was killed, the pending business was a vote on the substitute bill supported by the coalition leaders. The effect of this amendment would have been to strike out the Powell Amendment which had been proposed by Representative Stuyvesant Wainwright (R., N.Y.), an opponent of federal aid, and passed by a teller vote in the committee of the whole. A southerner who supported federal aid without the Powell Amendment could logically, therefore, have voted to keep the 1957 bill alive. Of the 94 southerners who voted against passage of the bill in 1956, only nine voted to keep the bill alive in 1957. Of the nine border-state members who voted against passage in 1956, four voted against killing the 1957 bill. Thirteen members, in other words, indicated by their 1957 votes that they might have been willing, in 1956, to support federal aid legislation free from desegregation provisions.[21]

The number of votes is not sufficient to have changed the result in 1956. How many other southern and border-state votes might have been forthcoming in 1956 if the racial issue had not been raised at all is problematical. Enough, perhaps, to have produced the 16 votes necessary to change the result. Certainly this was the contention of the northern liberals (including Negro Congressman William Dawson, D., Ill.) who voted against the Powell Amendment and pleaded with their fellow liberals to do likewise. By 1957 a greater number of northern liberals had been persuaded by this argument. They announced their change of mind and their intention to vote against

---

[21] The nine Southerners were Reps. Andrews, Elliott, Grant, Huddleston, Jones, Rains, Roberts, and Selden, all of Alabama, plus Reps. Trimble and Hays of Arkansas. The four border-state Reps. were Albert (Okla.), Steed (Okla.), Jones (Mo.), and Natcher (Ky.).

all antisegregation amendments in the hope of passing a federal aid bill.

But the issue of school segregation had been crystallized by the Court, and no southerner needed a Powell Amendment to be reminded of it. The political climate that had nourished southern support for federal aid in the Senate in 1948 and 1949 simply could not be re-created after 1954. On the racial issue, most southerners agreed with veteran Representative William Colmer (D., Miss.) when he said of the Powell Amendment in 1957:

> This is a case of tweedledee and tweedledum. It is immaterial whether this amendment is adopted or not. . . . This will be offered as an amendment on an appropriations bill. If that is not done, it will be done administratively. If that is not done, is there anybody so naive as to believe that the Supreme Court . . . is going to permit you to receive money and have segregated schools. So you lose any way it goes.[22]

The absence of a Powell Amendment would doubtless have increased the chances of federal aid passage in the House. But its absence would not have guaranteed passage. The likely effect of such an amendment on Rules Committee and Conference Committee delibera-tions is, of course, another matter.

Regardless of the segregation issue, the majority of southerners joined the majority of Republicans in conservative opposition to federal aid as a form of federal control. These hard-core opponents displayed skill in argument as well as in maneuver during the handling of the two bills. They filled the leadership vacuum left by President Eisenhower; and they held enough middle-of-the-road legislative support to prevent the passage of federal aid. In the debate of 1956 they keyed their opposition almost entirely to the generalized argument against federal control. In the words of Rules Committee Chairman Smith:

> This is an innovation. We are starting off on an entirely new road, a road that the American people, from the founding of the Republic, have said that we should never follow. That is to permit the control of our public education to go out of the hands of the local people. . . . They have to come with their hats in their hands, they have to comply with all the regulations, they have to grovel before a federal bureaucrat in order to get the money back for

their states which their states sent up here with the blood of taxation year after year in increasing amounts.[23]

In 1957, however, opposition arguments shifted to take advantage of President Eisenhower's publicly stated concern for the size of the budget. (This was the year of the "hair-curling depression" sentiment.) Typical was the explanation by Representative Leo Allen (R., Ill.):

> My chief reason for being opposed to the bill is that it will cost about $2,400,000,000. . . . There is not a state in the Union that is not in better financial condition than our own federal government.[24]

Aid opponents did propose, in 1956, an amendment to remit 1 per cent of federal income tax payments to the state where collected. This drew support from 26.7 per cent of the Democrats (61) and 54.9 per cent of the Republicans (107). Out of the total of 168 votes, 142 eventually voted against passage of the bill. Twenty-six supporters of federal aid (mostly Republicans) preferred this approach. By 1957 the opponents had developed, for the first time, the position that there was no need for federal aid, that the states and localities could do and were doing the necessary construction job. They laced this argument with an impressive array of statistics to demonstrate local fiscal capacity and to document the gradual decline of the classroom shortage. In so doing, they challenged for the first time an assumption that had been widely accepted by opponents as well as proponents of federal aid for ten years.

The Education and Labor Committee heard more witnesses (33) in 1957 than had appeared before or have appeared since in opposition to federal aid. And the tone of the House hearings in that year was more intemperate than ever before. The near success of the 1956 legislation had jolted opponents of federal aid into producing a more detailed rationalization of their position than they had heretofore thought necessary. Figures taken from the Chamber of Commerce, the Investment Bankers Association, the Kestnbaum Commission on Intergovernmental Relations, and state taxpayers' groups appeared in a strong minority report in the Committee and were then used to buttress argument on the House floor. It was the first statistical counterattack by the opponents—a counterattack which stressed lack of need and which has drawn increasing favor as a bulwark of opposition argument ever since.

[23] 84:2 *Congressional Record* (1956), 11299, 11300.
[24] 85:1 *Congressional Record* (1957), 12477.

The concerted effort in 1956 and 1957 to remove the parochial school aid question from the conglomeration of issues did meet with success. The 1956 Kelley Bill was sponsored by Representative Kelley (D., Pa.), a devout and unmistakably Irish Catholic Committee member. There was virtually no mention of private schools in the Committee hearings of 1950, 1955, or 1957. Within the Committee informal taboos operated against raising "the religious issue." A former Republican member recalled:

> I guess I was the first to breach a rule on that. I made a speech on the floor about it. When I came back, Sam McConnell said to me, "That's one thing I wouldn't have said if I were you." I said, "Well, I believe it." And he said, "I know, but that's one subject we shy away from."

On the floor, majority leader John McCormack called attention to the forbearance of parochial school supporters. Said McCormack:

> No complaints, no opposition, no obstructionist proposals have come from private or parochial school sources. . . . [they have] refrained from any action that might impede passage of this bill even though it will bring no direct benefit to their schools. These people have an unselfish, statesmanlike attitude. . . . I do not know whether we shall again need to consider federal aid for current expenditures. If we do, I hope we will be spared a repetition of the ordeal of a few years ago. I hope public school authorities will have a tolerant cooperative attitude if an effort is made to try in a small way to help private and parochial school children. . . .[25]

Neither McCormack nor those to whom he spoke demonstrated the requisite forbearance when the issue arose again in 1961.

The indisputable result of the 1956 and 1957 battles in the House was legislative stalemate. Comparing the final result of 1957 with that of 1956, proponents of federal aid increased their support by a very unimpressive nine votes. The striking contrast between Senate and House floor action requires some attempt at explanation. Most important would seem to be the differences in the constituencies represented by senators and representatives. Senatorial districts are larger and more heterogeneous than congressional districts. Large numbers of representatives find that they must respond to a single dominant constituency interest—whether it be that of federal control, private school aid, school integration, school construction, teachers' salaries,

[25] 84:2 *Congressional Record* (1956), 11844.

or economy. Most senators, on the other hand, face all of these interests in their constituencies. For instance, many representatives from rural constituencies can ignore the influences of urban areas, which tend to favor federal aid; few senators can remain unresponsive to urban interests. Except where the racial issue dictates their actions, senators must respond to a totality of social forces which touches far fewer House constituencies. The heterogeneity of their constituencies permits and encourages flexibility, moderation and compromise—three prerequisites for federal aid passage within the legislature.

The necessities of standing for re-election every two years instead of every six operate further to restrict the flexibility of House members on issues concerning large numbers of their constituents. "You're tied down a lot tighter to your constituency here than in the Senate," said one House Committee member. "Take Senator X. . . . He can afford to be a lot more independent than I can. Over there, at least one-third of the Senators can afford to be statesmen. Here, you've got to be a politician all the time because you have to run every two years." House members pride themselves on the fact that their short tenure keeps them "close to the people." But their constant accountability to their constituents may only reduce their autonomy in committee and on the floor. The frequency of House elections, together with the relative homogeneity of House constituencies, operates to exaggerate and perpetuate federal aid conflicts in that chamber.

## SENATE AND HOUSE FLOOR ACTION, 1960-1961

The Democratic sweep in the 1958 elections decisively altered the balance of congressional party power. Senate Democratic membership jumped from 49 to 66; House Democratic membership increased from 234 to 283. And in both cases the new members were of markedly liberal persuasion. As Democratic federal aid strength waxed in Congress, however, President Eisenhower's enthusiasm for any massive program correspondingly waned. His equivocal endorsements in 1957 proved to be the high-water mark of his enthusiasm. From then on federal aid programs faced the likelihood of a presidential veto. By 1961, however, the White House was in the hands of a sympathetic president—whose presence compensated for the 1960 losses (two in the Senate and 19 in the House) in Democratic strength in Congress. The net consequence of these party changes was a steady retreat from the strong bipartisanship of 1948-49 through the moderate bipartisanship of 1956-57 to the strong partisanship of 1960-61. (See Table 10).

*The Senate*

In both 1960 and 1961, the Senate passed bills providing aid for public school construction and/or teachers salaries. The formulas provided aid for all states on a per child basis and contained equalization provisions allocating more aid to the needy than to the wealthy states. The issues raised on the floor differed very little from those debated in the same chamber in 1948-49. Amendments were proposed involving aid to segregated schools (4), aid to private schools (3), changes in the amount and allocation of funds (9), remission of federal taxes to the states (4), and complete substitute bills (2). The great difference between the 1948-49 activity and that of 1960-61 was in the loss of strong bipartisan support for federal aid.

The major change has been a sharp drop in the degree of Republican leadership and support. Recent Republican leadership, in the White House and in the Senate, has not devoted itself, as did Senator Taft, to the cause of federal aid to education. President Eisenhower and minority leader Everett Dirksen (R., Ill.), for example, were as irrevocably opposed to aid for teachers' salaries as Senator Taft was determined to bring about such aid. Democrats still must rely upon Republican support, but it has come recently from a small minority. Democratic leadership and initiative in the enterprise are undisputed.

On the two votes of passage in 1948-49, Republican support averaged 63.1 per cent (equals 25 votes); in 1960-61, Republican support on the two final roll calls averaged 27.9 per cent (equals 8-9 votes). In 1948-49, a majority of Republicans voted with a majority of Democrats on 11 out of 12 (91.7 per cent) roll calls. In 1960-61, bipartisan majorities occurred on only five of 24 (20.8 per cent) roll calls. A similar erosion took place within the Committee on Labor and Public Welfare. Whereas, in the earlier period, the Committee furnished a unified bipartisan spearhead on the floor, it became, in the later period, an effective but unmistakably Democratic floor bloc. The mean index of Committee cohesion on roll call voting fell from 92.1 in 1948-49 to 54.5 in 1960-61. (See Table 9.) This precipitous drop was due to increasing splits among Republican Committee members—whose mean index of cohesion dropped from 90.4 in 1948-49 to 48.2 in 1960-61.

A second noteworthy shift in federal aid support has been the decline of enthusiasm among southern Democrats. In 1948-49 the 22 senators from the states of the Confederacy, states among the neediest and standing to benefit substantially from equalization formulas, voted overwhelmingly in favor of federal aid. On the two votes of passage, they voted 17-5 and 19-3 in favor. But the intervening years of racial controversy, writ large in the House struggles of 1956-57, have taken a significant toll among southern supporters. On both final roll call votes in 1960-61, they voted 13-9 against federal aid.[26] Thus in 1961 Senator John McClellan (D., Ark.), a passionate supporter of federal aid in the earlier period, said,

> Do not, I say to my Southern friends, vote for this measure with any thought that the segregation issue is not involved. We may just as well be frank about it and understand it. It is not openly present here at this moment, but let no one vote for this bill under any illusion or false conception that that issue is being bypassed. It is not. That issue cannot be evaded. We cannot escape it. In due time, it will be here to haunt us.[27]

TABLE 10
INCREASING PARTISANSHIP ON FEDERAL AID
FINAL VOTES
HOUSE AND SENATE 1948-1961

|  | 1948 | 1949 | 1956 | 1957 | 1960 | 1961 |
|---|---|---|---|---|---|---|
| Percentage of Democratic Senators Supporting Federal Aid | 86.1 | 92.3 |  |  | 77.8 | 77.4 |
| Percentage of Republican Senators Supporting Federal Aid | 61.4 | 64.7 |  |  | 29.0 | 26.7 |
| *Senate Index of Partisanship* | 24.7 | 27.6 |  |  | 48.8 | 50.7 |
| Percentage of Democratic Representatives Supporting Federal Aid |  |  | 53.1 | 56.5 | 62.5 | 66.7 |
| Percentage of Republican Representatives Supporting Federal Aid |  |  | 38.7 | 41.0 | 32.4 | 3.6 |
| *House Index of Partisanship* |  |  | 14.4 | 15.5 | 30.1 | 63.1 |

NOTE: The index of partisanship constitutes the difference between the percentages of Democrats and Republicans supporting federal aid. A value of 100 would indicate unanimous support by one party, unanimous opposition by the other; a zero value would demonstrate identical divisions within both parties.

[26] Including live pairs and announced positions as recorded in *Congressional Quarterly*.

[27] *Congressional Record*, Daily Digest, 87th Congress, 1st Session, May 25, 1961, 8339.

In view of Republican disenchantment, federal aid proponents have faced the strategic problem of retaining the crucial increment of southern support which still remains.

The shift in patterns of support became evident as soon as federal aid legislation reached the floor in 1960. In that year, the Committee on Labor and Public Welfare reported out a bill tailored, as usual, to attract bipartisan support. Accordingly, it provided for a two-year program of aid for school construction. Within the Committee only two of six Republicans opposed it. Written with an eye to winning President Eisenhower's support, it was, in the words of its sponsor, "not too different from the administration bill of 1957."[28] To a majority of Democrats and to their allies from the NEA, however, such a program was totally inadequate. They supported it as a vehicle for forcing floor debate, and immediately sought to transform it into a more expensive aid program, of indefinite duration, covering teachers' salaries as well as construction.

Their program, embodied in the so-called Clark Amendment of 1960, was the most far-reaching aid proposal ever to come to a vote in Congress. Its sponsors deliberately eschewed bipartisanship to place its legislative fate in the hands of the augmented Democratic majority. The amendment lost on a tie vote, 44-44. A motion was made to reconsider the vote, followed by a motion to table the motion to reconsider. On this latter motion a tie vote (44-44) again held and was broken by Vice President Nixon, who voted, in effect, against the amendment. It was symbolic of the decline in bipartisanship that the heir apparent of the Republican party should have cast the decisive negative vote. On that final roll call, Senate Republicans were more united than on any save one of the 24 roll calls in the 1960-61 period. On the vote 71.4 per cent of the Democrats voted in opposition to 87.5 per cent of the Republicans. Five of the six Republican members of the Committee voted against the Clark Amendment, including such federal aid supporters as Clifford Case (N.J.) and Jacob Javits (N.Y.). The partisanship of the vote was infused with the atmosphere of an election year in courting what was a certain presidential veto.

The defeat of the Clark Amendment pointed up the increased value of southern Democratic support and the impossibility of carrying even the Senate with a northern Democratic majority. Of the 22

[28] *Congressional Record*, Daily Digest, 86th Congress, 2nd Session, February 2, 1960, 1618.

senators from the states of the Confederacy, the amendment drew support from only five. Most noteworthy among the opponents was Senator Lister Hill (D., Ala.), chairman of the Committee on Labor and Public Welfare and a fighter for 22 years on behalf of federal aid for teachers' salaries. When, on a subsequent amendment, the size of the program and its duration were curtailed but the teachers' salaries option retained, Hill and three other southern senators closely associated with him changed their votes to yea.[29] Four Republicans also changed to vote in favor of this amendment, which put the bill in the form in which it was passed—a two-year program for salaries and/or construction. On the final vote, 77.8 per cent (42) of the Democrats joined 29.0 per cent (9) of the Republicans to pass the bill.

Federal aid proponents operated from the strength of presidential support in 1961.[30] With the support of three out of five Republicans, the Senate Committee reported out an administration bill calling for a three-year program of grants for salaries and/or construction. As an additional enticement to wavering senators (but considered more likely to entice House members), the bill had attached to it an extension of the impacted areas bill. Within the Committee, the administration's allocation formula was altered to the benefit of both the large northern taxpaying states (by broadening the population base) and the southern states (by increasing the equalization ratio). Floor leadership was placed in the hands of Senator Wayne Morse (D., Ore.), whose task was to bring the bill through floor action free from damaging amendments. For this, the classic problem of federal aid legislation, he was equipped positively by his long record of support. Negatively, his background left him freer from potential legislative embarrassments than those senior to him on the Committee—Senator Hill, a southerner, or Senator Pat McNamara of Michigan, a Roman Catholic. Morse's strategy and his performance were reminiscent of that of Senator Taft, whose name Morse invoked 20 times in the course of debate. What Taft accomplished with bipartisan majorities, Morse carried through by the cohesion of a hard core of liberal Democrats and shifting coalitions of other senators.

[29] Senators Sparkman (Ala.), Jordan (N.C.), and Ervin (N.C.).

[30] An excellent and more detailed analysis of the 1961 contest, in Senate and House, is to be found in Douglas Price, "Race, Religion and the Rules Committee: The Kennedy Aid-to-Education Bills" in Alan Westin (ed.). *The Uses of Power* (New York: Harcourt, Brace, and World, Inc., 1962), 1-72.

Morse employed the optimum legislative strategy for federal aid supporters. As he explained,

> At the very outset of our considerations on the bill—and I am not talking about the debate in the Senate but about the conferences on the bill even preceding the hearings on it—I made very clear to private school groups, to public school groups, to civil rights groups, and to anti-civil rights groups that I would do all within my power to pilot through the Senate a bill that did not have attached to it any private school amendment or any civil rights amendment. I have done my best to keep the faith. . . . I have been seeking to have the bill passed without having the feelings of the pro or anti-private school people aroused to the point where the bill will be damaged. I have also sought to prevent the development of a psychological situation in which people concerned with civil rights and segregation will become involved in a controversy which will damage the prospects for the passage of the bill. I cannot be more frank, can I? As the Senator in charge of the bill, I cannot state more frankly what my problems are.[31]

In the course of an eight-day floor debate, 15 amendments were offered. Morse accepted only one of those, an amendment which expanded the uses to which the funds might be put. It subsequently passed. But 14 others, which he opposed, were rejected. In successfully resisting crippling amendments, the Senator from Oregon relied on a hard core of 24 administration followers. Primarily from the Far West and Midwest, these 24 Democratic senators followed Morse's lead on every one of the 16 roll calls.[32] To this foundation, he added varying increments of support from eastern Democrats, southern Democrats, and Republicans sufficient to carry out his basic strategy. In the course of his maneuvering, every member of the Senate voted with Morse on at least one occasion.

Most treacherous, perhaps, was the thicket of civil rights amend-

[31] *Congressional Record,* Daily Digest, 87th Congress, 1st Session, May 24, 1961, 8180-81.

[32] This includes Senators paired or announced in favor of Morse's position. The bloc contained the following Senators: Carrroll (Colo.), Long (Hawaii), Church (Idaho), Hartke (Ind.), Muskie (Me.), McNamara (Mich.), Humphrey (Minn.), Symington (Mo.), Long (Mo.), Bible (Nev.), Cannon (Nev.), Williams (N.J.), Burdick (N.D.), Anderson (N.M.), Chavez (N.M.), Monroney (Okla.), Neuberger (Ore.), Gore (Tenn.), Moss (Utah), Jackson (Wash.), Magnuson (Wash.), Byrd (W.Va.), Randolph (W.Va.), and McGee (Wyo.).

ments (each one proposed by an opponent of the bill) through which Morse moved. A southern Democratic (Strom Thurmond, S.C.) amendment to prohibit the withholding of funds to segregated schools and a Republican (Prescott Bush, Conn.) proposal to prohibit the allocation of monies to segregated schools secured only 25 votes each. More moderate than these two were a southern Democratic proposal (Herman Talmadge, Ga.) to write into the law Secretary Ribicoff's written opinion that he had no authority to withhold funds from the states, and a Republican proposal (Kenneth Keating, N.Y.) to permit taxpayers' suits against the unconstitutional use of aid funds. The latter two proposals were less direct and hence potentially more dangerous to the federal aid proponents. The Talmadge amendment split the Democrats more sharply than any other of the 16 roll calls; but the Keating proposal resulted in the highest Democratic cohesion of any of the votes. The indices of cohesion for the Republicans, on the other hand, were higher on both amendments than on any other roll call.

In 1949, a civil rights amendment had caused the deepest rift among Senate Republicans. But as they have moved into increasingly greater opposition to federal aid, their unity on behalf of civil rights amendments has increased. Senate Democrats, on the other hand, will split only when such amendments are presented by other Democrats; against obvious Republican efforts to divide and conquer they remain highly cohesive.

For Senator Morse, who had authored an amendment in 1960 providing loans to private schools, the role of floor leader and administration spokesman necessitated a new posture. He faithfully implemented the ultimate administration strategy of passing the purely public school bill first and then bringing to the floor the NDEA extension with its private school loan amendments. A new version of Morse's 1960 amendment was offered by Senator Barry Goldwater (R., Ariz.), and was defeated 66-25. Democrats (except for nine with exceptionally large Catholic constituencies, *i.e.*, Rhode Island, Massachusetts, Connecticut, Ohio, Michigan, Illinois and Louisiana) held firm behind Morse. Most northern and western Democrats have constituencies heterogeneous enough to give them considerable maneuvering room on the parochial school issue. Republicans, on the other hand, demonstrated their second lowest degree of cohesion—just as they had on Morse's 1960 amendment. Constituency sentiment against aid to private schools seems strong enough to prevent Senate Republicans from utilizing this issue as a divide and conquer device.

Senate supporters had displayed once again the formula for success in that body. The really serious battleground of 1960-61 was in the House—most specifically, as we have seen, in its Committee on Rules.

## The House

The 1960 House bill was, like its predecessors, a school construction measure. For lack of teachers' salaries provisions, it was far less than the legislative proponents of the 1959 Murray-Metcalf bill and their allies from the NEA desired. It did, however, retain the flat-grant basis from the earlier bill; but in so doing, it eliminated the equalization provisions so basic to President Eisenhower's position. As a compromise with the Republicans, who were also devoted to the idea of matching grants, the bill provided direct grants for the first year and matching grants for the following two years. Representative Bailey, the chairman of the subcommittee which had drafted it, said, "It is particularly written and tailored to receive House approval. The job that faces me and other proponents of the legislation is to see that it is not muddied up from the introduction of a lot of side issues.[33]

The design of the bill did lead to the passage of the first twentieth-century federal aid legislation in the House. When the 206-189 vote for passage is compared with the 1956 vote 194-224 against passage, two facts emerge. In the first place, the number of Democrats in favor of the bill increased by 43, whereas the number opposed dropped by only eight. That is to say, the pro-aid Democratic vote, the heaviest ever cast by that party in the House, was made possible by the augmented Democratic majority arising out of the 1958 elections. Of the 49 Democrats who took seats away from Republicans in that election, 43 voted in favor of federal aid, 2 were paired in favor, 3 voted against it, and 1 had died.

In the second place, one-third of the House's Republicans voted for the bill. This represented a sizable drop in numbers (31), but only a slight drop in percentage (6.3 per cent). On the final vote, 162 Democrats (62.5 per cent) and 44 Republicans (32.4 per cent) combined to pass the bill. It was, however, the post-1958 Democrats who most directly altered the balance of power of 1956.

At the same time floor action constituted failure for the federal aid advocates. Representative Bailey, unlike his counterparts in the

---

[33] *Congressional Record*, Daily Digest, 86th Congress, 2nd Session, May 25, 1960, 10270.

Senate, was unable to prevent the side issues of which he warned from "muddying up the bill." Bailey's difficulty was underlined by the fact that during the floor action one of the key sponsors of the bill, Representative Frank Thompson (D., N.J.), offered a compromise amendment (affecting the grant provisions and the duration of the program) which was subsequently passed over Bailey's own vigorous opposition. When finally other items were tacked on to the Thompson amendment, Thompson and Bailey voted against it.

The key item which was added to Thompson's amendment was the Powell Amendment denying aid to segregated schools—first approved by a teller vote in the committee of the whole and later confirmed by roll call. The northern Democratic floor generals (Representatives Bailey, Thompson, and Udall) and some others voted against the Powell Amendment. But 100 northern and western Democrats, faced with a civil rights proposition and a fall election, voted for the amendment. Said Powell, "A vote against this amendment is a vote against the Supreme Court. A vote against this amendment is a vote against civil rights."[34] The strategic situation was the same as had existed in the Senate; and it was so recognized by the pro-aid floor leaders. A bill with a Powell Amendment might be endangered at several points—even if it could be passed. Yet House Democrats joined the anti-aid Republicans, just as they had done in 1956, in voting it into the bill. The Republicans achieved their greatest cohesion on this roll call out of the six taken in 1960. In line with their classic pattern, however, 77 Republicans who voted for the Powell Amendment subsequently voted against the bill. The presence of the Powell Amendment in the bill was a prime reason for the Rules Committee's ultimate refusal to send it to conference.

Throughout the debate, opponents of federal aid eschewed their philosophical objections to federal control to focus on the subject of need. Seven Republican Committee members had produced the most carefully documented minority report on record, stressing the rapidly improving construction picture. Their statistics and their conclusions furnished the floor ammunition for opponents. In the words of the report, "State and local school districts have mounted an effort in school construction over the past 10 years which, if maintained and encouraged by proper Federal action and restraint, will essentially eliminate the problem over the next 5 years."[35] The

[34] *Congressional Record,* Daily Digest, 86th Congress, 2nd Session, May 26, 1960, 10486.

[35] House Committee on Education and Labor, *House Report* 1426, 86th Congress, 2nd Session, 1960, 24.

flexibility of the opposition in floor debate has always been a source of strength. What was an emphasis on federal control in 1956 became an emphasis on budgetary considerations in 1957 and an emphasis on lack of proven need in 1960.

As in earlier years, federal aid opponents offered a tax remission amendment, the Bow Amendment, this time providing that 25 per cent of the cigarette tax be returned to the state in which it is collected. It was defeated 219-181—drawing support from two-thirds (95) of the Republicans but only one-third (86) of the Democrats, 82 of whom were southern Democrats. Of those favoring the amendment, 161 opposed federal aid on final passage. Of the 20 who favored the Bow Amendment but voted for federal aid, 16 were Republicans and only four Democrats.

With the passage of the bill, only the conference committee deliberations with the Senate remained. House rules provide, however, that unless there is unanimous consent to such a conference, the Rules Committee must grant a special rule sending the bill on its way. Following an objection by Representative August Johansen (R., Mich.), the Rules Committee procedure was invoked. There, at the hands of four Republicans and three southern Democrats, the bill perished. (See Table 8.) The ingredients of a conference committee compromise were clearly indicated. They involved the elimination of teachers' salaries coverage from the Senate bill, and the elimination of the Powell Amendment from the House bill. As one key prospective Senate conferee said,

> If we had had a conference, we'd have had a bill. It was killed by the Rules Committee. I've been on many, many conferences, but I've never known us to fail to get a bill. The Senate might have had to make some tremendous concessions with regard to teachers' salaries. But it's better to have a bill for school construction than nothing at all.

The Rules Committee took action on June 22; yet Congress did not adjourn until September 1. The opportunity remained, therefore, for aid proponents to urge reconsideration by the Committee. Working either through the administration or directly, pressure for the obvious compromise between Senate and House might have been generated. After all, two members of the Rules Committee— B. Carroll Reece (R., Tenn.) and James Trimble (D., Ark.)—had voted to send the bill to the House floor and would at least listen to arguments based on compromise. That is to say, a determined cohesive legislative majority might still have pushed the bill through to conference in the two months remaining to them. That they did not is evidence, once again, of the fragile and half-hearted character of the legislative majority and its allies.

Despite herculean efforts by subcommittee chairman Bailey and others, positions became ever more inflexible during the last weeks. Republicans feared that if a bill were passed, it might draw a presidential veto which could be a liability in the fall election campaign. Liberal Democrats were unenthusiastic because of the elimination of teachers' salaries and preferred a campaign issue to a watered down bill.

## The NEA

Among the decisive inflexibilities of the period, the most interesting was that of the National Education Association. At a point of legislative impasse, where a skillful lobbying group could be especially effective, they became deliberately inactive and uncompromising. Their enthusiasm was for a teachers' salary bill. Thus, they had worked hard for the Senate version of the bill. Said Senator Joseph Clark (D., Penna.), "We got a federal aid for public schools bill through the Senate this winter because the National Education Association knew what it wanted and lobbied its program across."[36] Failing to get their teachers' salary provision in the House bill, their zeal disappeared. Federal aid leaders were unable to state precisely what the NEA position was.[37] In the summer of 1960, they preferred to "wait till next year" rather than work to promote a compromise construction bill in conference. They did nothing, therefore, to move the House bill off dead center in the Rules Committee. *New York Times* education columnist Fred Hechinger went behind the Powell Amendment and the Rules Committee to place a large share of the blame for the 1960 failure on "the lack of enthusiasm for any realistically attainable compromise on the part of [the] . . . powerful association of public school educators representing more than 700,000 teachers."[38]

Since the NEA is the most important interest-group ally of the legislators favoring federal aid, their insistence on teachers' salary provisions as the price of their wholehearted support has severely

[36] *Congressional Record,* Daily Digest, 86th Congress, 2nd Session, May 10, 1960, A4014.

[37] *Congressional Record,* Daily Digest, 86th Congress, 2nd Session, May 26, 1960, 10476.

[38] *New York Times,* September 4, 1960, 17.

restricted the legislative maneuverability of their congressional cohorts. Perhaps the NEA attitude is simply a political naïveté not
uncommon to educators as a group. Perhaps, too, the NEA leadership
has grossly misread popular attitudes toward federal aid to education. As a teachers' organization engaged in building up its membership and justifying its existence, it may simply be unable to
compromise the crucial issue of salaries.

At the beginning of the 1960 session, the NEA memorialized
each member of Congress and stated its terms in flat, uncompromising language. "If no satisfactory school support bill embodying the
principles of the Murray-Metcalf bill is enacted in the next session
of Congress, the association will endeavor to make this matter a
major issue in the political campaigns of 1960 so that the American
people may again express their mandate for the enactment of such
legislation in 1961."[39] Their confidence is probably misplaced. In
spite of the fact that public opinion has been found to favor federal
aid as a general proposition, popular pressure cannot be generated
behind specific pieces of legislation—and surely not at the call
of the NEA. Nor does it seem possible to get any national "mandate" on the subject at the polls.

The political ineptitude of the NEA, both with regard to parliamentary flexibility and with regard to their reading of popular
opinion, is the cause of constant consternation and bitterness among
its legislative friends. Two sympathetic members of the Education
and Labor Committee commented in 1961:

> They are very disappointing. They want the moon. Their
> attitude is that they might as well try a big bite and go down
> fighting rather than to establish a new area of federal respon-
> sibility in a small scale reasonable way. I think they've done
> great damage to their own cause.

> They're the worst, most ineffective lobby around. . . . They
> don't get their people to do the one thing that gets bills passed
> around here—write letters. My desk should be piled that high
> with letters, but it isn't. They just don't do it.

A member of the Committee staff summed up:

> Their pavement pounders, the boys who are up here all the
> time, came to me when the construction bill was up and said
> they wanted a teachers salaries bill. They asked me what position

[39] Quoted in *Congressional Record*, Daily Digest, 86th Congress, 2nd Session,
May 26, 1960, 10476.

they should take before their convention. I said they should certainly take a position in favor of school construction and teachers' salaries both; but I said that didn't mean they couldn't support the school construction bill if that was up. There was that wondering whether they should hold out for all of their program. The AFL-CIO is much more realistic. They never backed down one inch on their position for construction and teachers salaries, but when the chips were down on the construction bill they were in there pounding away in favor of the construction bill long before the NEA. . . . The AFL-CIO was willing to take half a loaf. But the NEA has a tendency to want the whole loaf. They don't realize that if you get half a loaf you have taken the first step. That's the hardest step, and you may be able to get more. They're a little idealistic—and shortsighted. If you argue for a whole loaf and won't take half a loaf, you'll argue yourself right out of a job.

The foregoing comments were made before the 1961 bill became inextricably caught in the Rules Committee on its way to the floor. Having thus failed in their attempts to pass a facsimile of the Senate bill in the House, administration and legislative leaders hastily drew up a compromise measure. It called for a one year school construction program in particularly overloaded school districts plus an extension of the NDEA. The NEA withdrew its support completely from what it called a "woefully inadequate compromise," thus contributing again to failure.

House and Committee leaders combined to rush the bill through committee and bring it to the floor via the device known as Calendar Wednesday. Under Calendar Wednesday procedure, the standing committees are called in alphabetical order and given an opportunity to bring a bill before the House. Thus the Rules Committee can be circumvented. House rules, however, stipulate that debate on any such measure shall be limited to two hours. As soon as Chairman Powell called up his Committee's new bill, an undebatable motion was made on the question of considering the bill. On the roll call which followed, federal aid legislation was given its *coup de grâce* for 1961. The vote against consideration was 170-242. It was the most lopsided roll call defeat in the history of federal aid.

The revealing feature of this latest vote was the nearly unanimous opposition of House Republicans. Only six GOP members voted to consider the bill. The result had been forecast to some degree by the unanimous opposition of Committee Republicans to the original construction-plus-salaries bill. Neither Republicans nor Democrats were in a bipartisan mood in 1961. Party tensions were compounded even further by the manner in which the new proposal had been concocted and rushed to the floor. A normally sympathetic Republican, Representative Lindsay (R., N.Y.), explained his negative final vote as follows:

> It is insulting to those on the minority for the majority to slap a last-minute, strung-together, and totally inadequate compromise before us in this take-it-or-leave-it procedure. . . . My vote is a protest against the procedure used and the complete inability of the majority to put its legislative house in order.[40]

As always, the architects of federal aid had originally presented an artful contrivance for the capture of 51 per cent of the votes. A new component of the contrivance gave fresh illustrations (if any be needed) of the persistent dilemmas of aid proponents. As a device for luring votes to the 1961 general program, they had attached the renewal of the popular aid to impacted areas program to the legislation. In 1960, 319 members of the House had received a total of $314 million of impacted areas money for their constituencies. Even though these totals were reduced in the renewal legislation, it was felt that the threat of "no general aid, no impacted areas money" would be sufficiently persuasive to reluctant legislators to insure a vote for the whole package. So basic an element of strategy was this that even the midnight compromise proposal was keyed into the impacted areas program.

The heavy-handed manipulation could not have been less successful. It fooled nobody and succeeded only in highlighting the weakness of the federal aid cause. Members of the House knew all along that the impacted areas program was easily separable from the larger bill and would be renewed regardless of what happened to federal aid. This is precisely what happened. One week after the demise of the compromise bill, the House voted overwhelmingly (378-32) for a two-year renewal of the impacted areas program. Federal aid strategists, supported by the President and hoping to use the program as a lever in 1962, proposed a one-year extension. Republican insistence on a two-year renewal added injury to an already badly insulted pro-aid force.

The 1961 epitaph was spoken by Secretary Ribicoff when he

[40] *Congressional Record*, Daily Digest, 87th Congress, 1st Session, August 30, 1961, 16509.

stated, "They expected a miracle and I couldn't produce a miracle. It was impossible to bring together a majority for a bill when most members didn't want one."[41] Ribicoff's lament summarizes many years of struggle in the House. It is a commonplace of commentary on that chamber that when a determined and cohesive majority wants something, there is nothing it cannot accomplish. Persistence, perhaps, may be needed; but the federal aid proponents have not lost for lack of that commodity. It is doubtful, therefore, whether any firm federal aid majority has ever existed in the House of Representatives. Near the end of the 1961 session, Chairman Powell could only forecast in the language of guarded pessimism. "It is my personal opinion," he said, "and I may be totally wrong, that the temper of this House is of such nature that Federal aid to school construction, per se, is dead at least for the next year. I think it is deplorable, but we must face the stark, brutal, and disheartennig fact and not dissipate the energies of this Committee nor this House on that which will bring no results whatsoever.[42]" As prophecy Powell's assessment remained accurate through the 87th Congress and up to the Congressional elections of 1962.

[41] Quoted in *Wall Street Journal*, September 5, 1961, 14.
[42] *Congressional Record*, Daily Digest, 87th Congress, 1st Session, September 6, 1961, 17096.

# VII. Conclusions: Federal Aid and the Future

THIS STUDY has been concerned with the struggle to secure general federal support for education in the United States. In particular it has focused upon the effort to build consensus toward such a goal. In any study of this kind a constant danger exists—an unwarranted assumption of the ultimate inevitability of federal aid.

Sponsors of education bills have often explicitly made such an assumption. During the Senate debate on the Educational Finance Act of 1943 Senator Lister Hill (D., Ala.) assured his colleagues:

> Whether the bill shall pass or not, its enactment is as inevitable as that the day will follow the night.
>
> The longer we live, the more our country develops, the more complex becomes our civilization, the greater and more compelling becomes the need, the absolute necessity for the Federal government to meet its duty, accept its responsibility, carry out its obligation, and play its part in the training and the preparation of the citizenship of America.[1]

Such certainty may be consoling in defeat, but is not necessarily accurate as prophecy. The scenario for a Hollywood production must have a beginning, a middle, and an end; there is no guarantee, however, that such will be the case in a story of the making of public policy. For close to a century the federal aid story-line has run on without a break, rather in the manner of a daytime television serial. There is no particular reason to assume the end is now in sight, and some good reasons to suspect that federal aid will not be approved within the immediate future.

## THE PROBLEMS

On several occasions a federal aid bill has appeared to stand on the verge of passage. Each time some unanticipated difficulty has arisen to prevent final approval. So frequent has been this sequence

---

[1] 78:1 *Congressional Record* (1943), 8399.

of events that Douglas Price, in his study of the federal aid bills of 1961, has suggested that the measures should be regarded as "politically accident-prone" and, presumably, given prohibitive insurance ratings.[2]

Many of the reasons for the difficulties faced by federal aid bills have been discussed above; they may be summarized briefly here. One of the most important is directly related to the notion of passage of a federal aid bill of some kind as the final act in a story; congressmen believe—correctly—that passage of a bill will not be an ending, but a commencement. Subsequent sessions of Congress will not find the issue settled. Instead they will be confronted with educational groups seeking higher support levels to meet the continually rising costs of the educational establishment. This has been the experience of state legislatures with state aid programs, and would undoubtedly be repeated at the federal level.

To conservative congressmen this is a frightening prospect. And contemplation of this probable future helps explain what otherwise appears inexplicable, the vigor of the opposition shown by the U.S. Chamber of Commerce to what is, after all, a paltry sum by the standards of present-day federal finance. The Chamber and its allies assume that an appropriation of $300 million a year—or even a billion —will be only a small beginning toward the total cost of the most expensive domestic service provided by government within the United States. This is one of the principal themes in the writings of Roger Freeman on the subject, and helps explain his popularity among economy-minded congressmen.[3]

To justify such a risky commitment the Congress finds little in the way of public pressure to act. Opinion surveys show widespread popular support for federal aid, but only mild interest in it. The NEA to the contrary notwithstanding, few congressmen consider their chances for re-election endangered by the failure of Congress to approve federal aid. One answer to the lack of success of education bills was suggested at a 1955 House hearing by John Burkhart of the U.S. Chamber of Commerce, quoting in turn from an NEA official:

[2] Hugh Douglas Price, "Race, Religion, and the Rules Committee: The Kennedy Aid-to-Education Bills," 2-71 in Alan F. Westin (ed.). *The Uses of Power* (New York: Harcourt, Brace, and World, Inc., 1962).

[3] Roger A. Freeman, *School Needs in the Decade Ahead* (Washington, D. C.: Institute for Social Science Research, 1958); Roger A. Freeman, *Taxes for the Schools* (Washington, D. C.: Institute for Social Science Research, 1960).

Why, then, has this prodigious, long-sustained battle of NEA not yet attained the hoped-for goal? Perhaps the chief reason was discovered years ago by NEA Legislative Director Charl O. Williams who reported:

"It no longer makes any impression on Congress to have your secretary appear at a hearing and present a very fine statesman-like statement . . . which they say has been endorsed by a million or more men and women. Congressmen immediately want to know how many of these men and women believe in the legislation under consideration, how many of them made it their own, how many are willing to stand by it, how many are willing to fight for it in their respective congressional districts."[4]

Another of the significant obstacles to approval has been the skill in maneuver shown by its opponents, both within Congress and without. On the Senate side the federal aid cause profited for a number of years from the personal prestige of its sponsor, Senator Robert Taft (R., Ohio), but within the House of Representatives the bill's managers have never been able to match in agility such astute parliamentarians as Representatives Graham Barden (D., N.C.), and Howard Smith (D., Va.).

The comparison is not altogether a fair one, however, for the rules of the game are rigged to the advantage of the opponents of change. There are serious institutional obstacles to achieving legislative consensus for new departures in policy. The most serious consists of the large number of hurdles over which a bill must pass—action by two House committees, one Senate committee, two legislative chambers, and one president. Final approval of legislation, in practice, even requires a second decision by the House Rules Committee to permit a conference, a procedure so obscure it ordinarily is not mentioned in the textbooks, but which has nonetheless been used successfully to block action on federal aid. All this means that the legislature is favorable terrain for the opponents; without broad agreement on the need to act it is impossible to secure the separate majorities needed at each step of the road. If federal aid legislation has proved "accident-prone," it is, in part, because it travels a dangerous highway.

The "broad agreement on the need to act" so necessary in making the legislative system work is the consensus that has been the focus

---

[4] House Committee on Education and Labor, *Federal Aid to States for School Construction*, 84th Congress, 1st Session (1955), Vol. II, 437.

of this study. But if the analysis contained in the foregoing chapters is accepted, it would appear that the most important barrier to such consensus has been the multiplicity of conflicts concealed within the single label of "federal aid to education." Such a proliferation of issues is inevitable in a society in which education deals with all aspects of human values, but in a very real sense it doubles the task of the proponents of aid. First, they must break down resistance to the novel idea of federal financing for education. Second, they must eliminate these multiple controversies so that legislators may ultimately be led to line up for or against some single identifiable program. It may be suspected that the federal aid advocates have passed the first test; they remain baffled by the second.

Indeed it seems plausible that the difficulties faced by a federal aid bill have multiplied within the past few years and seem likely to increase in the immediate future. That conclusion emerges from a review of the principal issues dividing the proponents of federal aid.

## Race

In the early federal aid proposals of the twentieth century, race was a divisive issue due to the unwillingness of the southern sponsors to write in guarantees of an equal division of funds between white and Negro school systems. With the acceptance of such a provision in the late 1930's, however, the racial issue no longer divided the proponents despite its tactical use by the bill's opponents in 1943. Following the shift in NAACP policy at mid-century to uncompromising opposition to segregation, the racial issue has again become divisive. Confirmed by the Supreme Court decision of 1954, it effectively prevents the full mobilization of support by the advocates of aid.

Optimists might predict the waning of the racial education issue as the Supreme Court decision is implemented and segregation ended in the South. Such an outcome seems unlikely, however. Even if integration is formally accomplished in the southern states in the near future, it seems certain that the racial issue will express itself in new ways. Federal aid policy may then be proposed as a weapon to force the change from token integration to general integration, a proposal that would make it controversial in many *de facto* segregated school systems in both North and South. There is little reason to anticipate the banishment of the civil rights issue from the debate over federal aid.

## Religion

The 1949 federal aid debate was a breaking point as far as the racial issue is concerned; less change has occurred regarding involvement with the issue of parochial schools. Before 1945 Catholic groups opposed all aid. Since that time the official position of the Catholic hierarchy has been one of acceptance of federal aid if, and only if, some aid to religious schools is incorporated. Since a congressional majority for a general aid bill of this kind has never been visible, the sum and substance of the situation has not changed; Catholic influence has been exerted against the only type of bills public school educators are willing to accept.

Even a prophetic look into the future provides little reason for optimism. The most likely alteration in the situation would be a movement of the Catholic hierarchy toward direct support for a federal aid program that would include religious schools. Such a change in front is conceivable as financial pressures upon the parochial school system mount. Increasing support for legislation of this sort may also come from Jewish and other groups committed to religious day schools. The opportunity provided by this shift would pose a difficult choice to public school educators forced to weigh their relative preferences for no aid against aid to both public and private schools. It is difficult at the present time, however, to conceive of such a coalition producing a federal aid bill in the foreseeable future.

## Federal Control

The issue of federal control has likewise displayed a continuing ability to divide the advocates. Hopefully, it might be expected that the lengthy debate over federal aid would have clarified the subject, losing some support for aid among those unwilling to accept the minimum of necessary federal standards, while consolidating support for a defined program. This has not occurred; a substantial part of the blame probably belongs to the debaters who have consciously obscured rather than clarified the issues. Whatever the cause, the issue remains fundamentally unchanged.

## Equalization

Likewise the interminable disputes over the formula to be employed in the distribution of funds have been constant through the years, dividing the supporters of one aid bill from the supporters of another.

This, however, constitutes one area in which change is taking place. The sectional disparities in income within the United States have been declining. And as the differences in regional income become less, the differences in the impact of the various formulas grow less also. In specific terms, the changing economy will eventually make agreement on a flat-grant formula easier to secure. Unfortunately for the proponents, however, the impact of the change is double-edged; since the principal argument for federal aid has always been the need to equalize regional disparities in income, the Chamber of Commerce has been quick to point out that the alleged base of the need for aid is steadily disappearing.

## Construction and Salaries

The most important shift in the capacity of other issues to fractionalize the pro-aid coalition has concerned the purpose for which federal funds should be used. Although the efforts of the AF of T to secure guarantees for teachers' salaries divided it from the NEA in the late 1940's, there is little evidence of significant division among the legislative supporters of federal aid at that time. And when the shift to a strategy of construction grants occurred, it was a shift mutually agreeable to all parties concerned.

In the late 1950's, however, the friends of aid for construction and the friends of aid for salaries began to draw apart. This separation was confirmed by the partisan use of the issue in the 1960 presidential campaign. The line of cleavage hardened and was largely responsible for the lack of Republican support for federal aid in 1961.

These facts together suggest that the prospects for broad agreement on a single federal aid bill were probably at their height in the late 1940's. Such issues as federal control, religious schools, and the formula to be used were present, but the others were quiescent. After 1950, divisions over race were added to the controversies already plaguing the managers of the bill. In the decade of the 1960's a new issue has emerged with heavy partisan overtones, that of the purpose for which federal funds are to be employed. This issue further complicates the task of securing agreement on a single bill. The managers of federal aid legislation are not to be envied their jobs.

### The Possibilities

Faced with these problems, the bill's advocates have not, however, thrown up their hands and thrown in the towel. The principal strategic problem confronting them has been twofold: to maximize support for federal aid by minimizing the conflicts among its supporters, and to marshal their support at the critical points in the legislative process. Accordingly, their strategies have been of two interlocking kinds: strategies of substance concerned with the content of the legislation to be proposed, and strategies of approach defining the manner in which the aid bill should be advanced.

### Strategies of Substance

In their efforts to secure approval the supporters of federal aid have made use of every conceivable argument. After World War I the need for federal aid was portrayed as part of a war against illiteracy. Then it became a part of the struggle to Americanize the immigrant. Other proponents presented federal aid as an essential step to prevent the bolshevization of America, since ignorant citizens could not see through the appeals of communism. In the 1930's aid to the schools was a depression measure to solve the temporary fiscal emergency, to deal with unemployment, and to accelerate economic activity. During the war federal aid became a national defense measure that would help to mobilize more men for military service. As the immediacy of the issue of selective service rejections faded after the war, the bill's proponents turned to the gap between performance and need in school construction. Then in the late 1950's the national security argument was revived when it appeared that the Soviet Union was outdistancing America in some fields of scientific research. And so forth. There are substantial grounds, however, for suspecting that these changes in the style of the debate are fashions only, and that the new arguments convince only the same, already committed supporters. The principal variations in the content of the bills actually proposed have been of a different order.

*The Necessary Compromise.* The first problem facing the sponsors of any federal aid bill has been that of threading a way among the multiple conflicts earlier described. Most decisions concerning the provisions to be included in a specific bill are tactical in character, that is, they have been calculated in terms of what appears most likely to secure the most legislative support. As estimates of the political situation have changed, the measures to be proposed have been modified. When the principal educational groups have estimated the politics of the legislative situation differently, rival bills have emerged. But whether the educators are united or divided, they still face the same problem in each session: to secure a majority vote for what appears to be the most feasible compromise bill.

One effect of this strategy of compromise has been to multiply the inconsistencies in the record of the supporters of federal aid. Speaking for the American Federation of Teachers at the 1945 Senate hearings, Selma Borchardt derisively reviewed the past:

> Through the years, supporters . . . of federal aid have changed their reasons for wanting the legislation on practically every point involved. First, the supporters of this legislation made the request for a Department of Education; then they dropped it. Next they dropped their original request for State fund-matching programs; and then they condemned this formula. They dropped, picked up, and dropped again provisions for specific levels and kinds of education.
>
> They urged the allocation of funds on a basis of school population, on a basis of total population, on a basis of need, on a basis of a weighted formula combining the other methods; and then they dropped this formula. They first ignored the need of protecting the Negro's right to share in the benefits of a federal program; then, they opposed the right on a basis of state's rights; then they supported it halfway; then opposed it; then supported it.
>
> They have supported bills including the present set-up for vocational education, and they have deleted it. They have included, excluded, and included provisions for school-building programs. At first they ignored the question of aid to Catholic schools. Then they opposed the principle. Then they tacitly accepted it. Then they opposed it again. It is to be observed that this principle was most ardently opposed while many of these same opponents were endorsing WPA educational programs which aided private groups, and while they were urging support for NYA which made direct grants to Catholic schools. . . .
>
> The vast majority of the supporters of the principle of federal aid have adhered to a policy which has been vacillating in principle, opportunistic in tactics, and fatal in practice. As a result, the program has actually not advanced one bit while the teachers have been told that the legislation is on the way—for the last 25 years.[5]

[5] Senate Committee on Education and Labor, *Federal Aid for Education*, 79th Congress, 1st Session (1945), 749.

Miss Borchardt's criticism was expressed in 1945; it is still applicable seventeen years later. To a considerable extent it is an inevitable by-product of the necessary strategy of compromise; as noted in an earlier chapter, some of the testimony given on the religious issue by AF of T witnesses at the same 1945 hearing might be reduced to the summary: "I can argue that either way." It seems probable that the advocates of aid have injured their cause by making their strategy too obvious, and might have accomplished more by preparing one proposal and standing by it, but much of the inconsistency reflects a consistent willingness to compromise in order to get federal aid.

This is not, however, the only strategy that has been employed in the effort to prepare an acceptable aid bill.

*The Very Modest Proposal.* Another strategy recurrently employed has been to seek to disarm the opposition by the modesty of the sum sought. As HEW Secretary Arthur Flemming expressed it in 1959, urging Democrats to support the Eisenhower administration's bill:

> The only thing that I am impressed with as of this present time is that in order to get those 75,000 classrooms constructed we can get more support for this kind of approach as contrasted with the general grant because when we go to the general grant we are asking people not only to take one step in the direction of the federal government being of help on this classroom construction, but we are asking them to take a second step.
>
> I would like to see us take a step which would get us off dead center and get the federal government into the business of helping these school districts construct classrooms.[6]

In accordance with this strategy of what might be described as one-sixteenth of a loaf, the proponents of federal aid have scaled down their requests, asked only for small appropriations, etc. The only difficulty with this strategy of "a first step first" is that it is totally transparent. The opponents of federal aid recognize that the sums sought are only fractions of the total cost of education in the United States, assume that the first step will be followed by others, and fight vigorously against letting the camel's nose come under the tent.

*The Outrageous Proposal.* As a result some proponents of federal

---

[6] House Committee on Education and Labor, *School Support Act of 1959*, 86th Congress, 1st Session (1959), 105.

aid have at times abandoned the limited approach and instead asked for sums and programs far larger than they expect to get. The billion-dollar-a-year aid bill of the late 1940's was such a measure; so too was the Murray-Metcalf bill. The clearest example of this strategy, however, was the 1962 proposal by the American Association of School Administrators of eight billion dollars a year for federal aid. The reasons for suggesting such measures are various. The intention may be to emphasize the importance of the problem or the seriousness of purpose of its advocates. The proposal may be intended to establish a bargaining position from which further negotiation can be carried on. Or it may be hoped that it will frighten some of the bill's opponents. Or, again, such recommendations may be born of simple frustration.

*Trading Stamps.* A somewhat different strategy was employed during the 1961 effort for federal aid, a strategy which was a variant of the ancient legislative device known as logrolling. In an effort to broaden the base of support, the Kennedy administration tied renewal of the impacted areas educational program to its general grant bill. Wayne Morse (D., Ore.), the bill's manager in the Senate, accurately described the impacted area allocations as "the little green trading stamps" of the federal aid bill. The strategy proved unrealistic in the outcome, however, as the impacted areas program was too popular to be denied renewal. Confident that it would be approved in any case, its supporters could not be forced to accept general aid as the price of renewal.

*The Subtraction of Conflict.* The combination of the two bills in 1961 might be described as a strategy of addition, an effort to join together the advocates of two separate kinds of educational programs. At the same time, the bill's sponsors tried to pursue the strategy of subtraction, dropping off controversial features of the bill to minimize opposition. This they did by offering separate bills to provide grants for public schools and to renew and expand the National Defense Education Act, which included benefits for private schools. It was hoped that both could be passed, each supported by overlapping but distinct majorities. The strategy proved too clever as the mutually suspicious friends of the two bills deadlocked the House Rules Committee and blocked action on both.

The strategy is an old one and has been tried often in the past. Federal aid bills have been divided and subdivided in the effort to increase their palatability; the shift to construction grants was one such effort. In many ways the most ingenious attempt was Senator Hill's proposal of "oil for the lamps of education" in the early 1950's.

By substituting a measure to apply to educational purposes the revenues from federally owned tidal oil lands for a quitclaim bill to turn ownership over to the states, Hill sought simultaneously to secure the support of opponents of the quitclaim and to disarm the arguments of those who insisted aid for education must come from increased taxes. Unfortunately for Senator Hill, the substitution added more opponents than supporters and, like all the other trick proposals, failed.

### Strategies of Approach

All the strategies so far mentioned have one characteristic in common; they concern the content to be included within a specific federal aid bill. A second type of strategic question also faces the proponents: Whose sponsorship shall be sought for the bill and under what circumstances should it be presented? During the past two decades the advocates of federal aid have tried every conceivable strategy to manage their bill to legislative victory. Almost the only legislative strategy not employed was one that was unavailable: the attempt to slip "a quiet little bill" through Congress with a minimum of attention and controversy. The federal aid issue has been too widely publicized to permit such a procedure to work, and the opposition has been too alert to overlook any major educational proposal.

*Congressional Leadership.* The first choice of strategy was made for the advocates of federal aid by the presidents of the United States from Warren G. Harding through Franklin D. Roosevelt. Their indifference to federal aid made it necessary to build strength in Congress. And the internal structure of Congress made it almost inevitable that the leadership for any successful legislative drive must be bipartisan. From the decision of Senator Taft to support federal aid in the late 1940's down to the late 1950's primary reliance was placed upon bipartisan congressional leadership. In many ways this is one of the most interesting features of the federal aid controversy. In a political system in which presidential leadership in law-making has been constantly enhanced, aid to education has been treated almost exclusively as a decision to be made by Congress.

*The Appeal to the People.* The failure of Congress to act, however, compelled the educational groups to devise other strategy. Their first response was to seek to go beyond Congress, to take their case to the people, and to mobilize such popular support that congressional action must follow. To some opponents of federal aid, this was not playing the game. As early as 1948 Representative George Schwabe (R., Okla.), lamented:

> Pressure groups have been organized and propaganda has been inspired and broadcast among the members of Congress in an attempt to force us to vote for federal aid to education. Some have even written letters threatening to vote and work against the reelection of present members of Congress unless we support the pending measures. Of course, such letters are beneath the dignity of what we have a right to expect of the teaching profession.[7]

More serious than the suggestion that such strategy is undignified has been the fact that it has proven unsuccessful. Interest in education is widespread among the public. Support for federal aid is extensive. But the depth of involvement in the issue by the general public has been insufficient to coerce recalcitrant congressmen into supporting a bill for federal aid. And as long as the educational system appears to be reasonably satisfactory, this situation is likely to be perpetuated.

*The Sense of Crisis.* Concluding a study of federal aid legislation written in 1953, Anne Gibson Buis prophesied:

> The records reveal that the Congress has seriously considered federal aid to education bills only during periods of national stress when teacher shortages have forced school doors to close. Judging from the past, another teacher shortage threatening to close the doors of the schools will have to recur before the Congress seriously considers a federal aid to education bill again. The fact that teacher qualifications may continue to fall will probably have no influence as long as the doors of the schools do not close and excite the "constituents" to prod inert legislators to action.[8]

Since such total disaster in American education seems unlikely under present circumstances, the conclusion is a pessimistic one. Efforts have been made, however, to promote lesser crises into convincing evidence of the need for federal aid. Unfortunately for the

[7] 80:2 *Congressional Record* (1948), 1460.

[8] Anne Gibson Buis, *An Historical Study of the Role of the Federal Government in the Financial Support of Education, with Special Reference to Legislative Proposals and Action* (unpublished doctoral dissertation, Ohio State University, 1953), 659-60.

advocates of general grants, the fright that followed Sputnik was turned to use in the NDEA rather than in the type of bill they sought. And subsequent events have largely diluted its impact on popular attitudes. On a different level of political behavior this is what Richard F. Carter found in his study of voters and their schools. Reporting his findings, he wrote:

> Within a few weeks after planning for this research had begun, American education faced a seeming crisis—Russia's Sputnik. Critics fell on the schools, questioning whether an education valued for its ability to give citizens a knowledge of and an occupation in our society could continue to serve the country's needs without drastic change and re-emphasis. Those critics still hold forth, and their listeners were found among the voters interviewed in this study. Has anything changed? Could the needs of a nation be installed as the wants of its people? Are there new values for education? To these questions the answer is *no.* The concern expressed about the schools, and particularly about curriculum, appears to have been absorbed into previously determined value positions. The arguments have changed, but the values have not.[9]

In the absence of any continuing concern over the scientific threat, the only crisis left for the advocates of federal aid to cite is the shortage of classrooms. And this produces an unhappy, if mixed reaction. Some congressmen have come to disbelieve in the shortage, convinced or brought to neutrality by the contrary statistics of the U.S. Chamber of Commerce. Other congressmen, while accepting the figures of the NEA and the Office of Education, have simply heard the argument too often. It is difficult to believe in the importance of a crisis which has demanded remedial action for a decade and a half, but has got along without receiving it; the position may be an illogical one, but the passage of time has dulled the sense of immediacy surrounding the problem.

*Presidential Leadership.* With all the other strategies tried over and over without success, the educational groups in 1960 tried a gamble by seeking to mobilize through presidential action the support they were unable to secure by themselves. When Congress balked at an aid bill including teachers' salaries, the NEA clearly expressed its preference for making federal aid into a 1960 campaign

---

[9] Richard F. Carter, "Voters and Their Schools," 42 *Phi Delta Kappan* (March 1961), 244-49, at 244.

issue rather than seeking to salvage a compromise bill. Without expressing an open endorsement of either candidate, widely circulated NEA literature during the fall of 1960 made it clear that the Democratic presidential candidate's stand on federal aid was in agreement with NEA policy while the Republican candidate's was not.

In the short run this frankly political strategy appeared to pay off. In contrast to the mild support of Presidents Truman and Eisenhower, and the indifference of their predecessors, President Kennedy declared himself an enthusiastic champion of federal aid and placed it high on his priority list of domestic legislation. In the outcome, however, the presidential endorsement did not bring success and federal aid was defeated once again.

The reasons for President Kennedy's failure are significant since they are the principal evidence by which the effectiveness of future presidential action in support of federal aid may be estimated. To the extent that the factors leading to the President's defeat were peculiar to Kennedy's situation in 1961, they may be disregarded as guides to future events. For example, Kennedy's identification as the first Roman Catholic to occupy the Presidency made it singularly difficult to bargain flexibly on the crucial issue of private schools. His narrow election-day victory made it harder for him to claim a popular mandate for his campaign promises. Mistakes were made, as in the expressed willingness to consider reasonable compromises, which further weakened the administration by opening again the Pandora's Box of alternative proposals.

To the degree that these causes for defeat might be avoided in future presidential action, even future action by President Kennedy, they do not necessarily indicate the bankruptcy of this strategy for securing federal aid. More serious are the indications of two weaknesses in the presidential position intrinsic to any presidential action. The first of these is the problem of partisanship. All of the above evidence suggests the impossibility of creating a strictly partisan majority for a federal aid bill under the present conditions of American politics. Yet forceful, vigorous presidential leadership on a domestic issue of this kind is almost inevitably accompanied by a tightening of party lines. To the many other conflicts already surrounding the bill is added a new symbolic conflict—which party will secure the credit for passage.

The second limitation upon presidential action might be summarized as lack of time. As Douglas Price has emphasized in his study of the 1961 federal aid fight, President Kennedy consciously refrained from committing his full resources of time and effort to the struggle for federal aid. With only limited reserves of strength, the President chose to hold back a part of his influence for subsequent efforts to impose his will upon Congress. Some of the future efforts might concern such domestic legislation as tax reform and medical care for the aged; most especially, however, the President was conserving his limited resources of power to secure his program objectives in the fields of foreign policy and national security.[10]

It is exciting to speculate on what might happen if the cold war were to be brought to an end. One of the incidental results would be an unleashing of presidential capacity for leadership in the field of domestic policy-making. But barring such an unforeseeable eventuality, it seems likely that future presidents will face the same problems as John Kennedy and find it necessary to sacrifice domestic program objectives for the overriding concerns of foreign policy and military security.

### THE PROSPECTS

On several occasions the advocates of federal aid have considered their struggle to be won; each time they have been frustrated. It would be as reasonable to expect that when the future seems blackest, hope may be greatest. But apart from such perverse logic, the argument of the preceding pages leads to a pessimistic conclusion concerning the prospects for federal aid to education in the immediate future.

Such pessimism should be confined, however, to the specific type of aid which has been the focus of this study, general grants for elementary and secondary education. Specific grants for special purposes can be devised which avoid the problems that block the approval of federal aid. The past experience has been that pressures for federal aid have most frequently found expression in the passage of just such specialized programs. The agitation of the 1870's and 1880's was capped by the enactment of a vocational education law. The struggles of 1948 and 1949 brought educational legislation for impacted areas. And the 1956-57 House battles culminated not in a construction bill, but in the NDEA.

At the present time the same trend seems apparent, but in this case the deflection of purpose has been toward higher education. Indeed it might be argued that if federal aid legislation of a general character for elementary and secondary schools is not approved in the next few years, the pressure for action at the federal level may

10 Price, *op. cit.*

begin to slacken. Since the passage of NDEA particularly, the interest of the Office of Education in the field of higher education has been growing rapidly. At the same time one of the Office's most active programs at the elementary and secondary level has been a cooperative research program which, in practice, largely consists of the awarding of grants for research to personnel at institutions of higher education.

The reasons for this shift in emphasis are not far to seek. A general aid program at the elementary and secondary level steps on many toes and generates much opposition; federal programs at the graduate professional level step on virtually no toes and are readily approved. Undergraduate programs, especially when associated with the natural sciences, encounter little more in the way of opposition. Even general aid programs for college facilities and scholarships appear to find easier going in the political world. The racial issue is largely irrelevant and the problem of aid to religious schools becomes more negotiable when it includes large numbers of non-Catholic religious colleges. It is within the realm of possibility that the Office of Education, if balked for a few more years in expanding into the general aid field within elementary and secondary schools, while scoring breakthroughs in higher education, may drastically redefine its conception of its own role. Although many other reasons were involved in his choice, it is at least interesting to note that the Kennedy administration's first Commissioner of Education, in a break with past practice, was drawn from the field of higher education.[11]

Such dramatic shifts in the direction of federal involvement in education are only speculative. What does appear clearly from the record is the strength of the forces holding the federal government back from a deeper commitment in elementary and secondary education. In 1937 the Senate Majority Leader, Joseph T. Robinson, described education as "the one last field into which federal activity is to be extended."[12] In 1937, at the high tide of the New Deal, it must have appeared incredible that any major field of government action could be maintained aloof from federal intervention. Twenty-five years later, education remains the one last major governmental function assigned primarily to state and local government.

---

[11] A consideration of many of these questions from a quite different viewpoint will be found in Homer D. Babbidge, Jr., and Robert M. Rosenzweig, *The Federal Interest in Higher Education* (New York: McGraw-Hill Book Company, Inc., 1962).

[12] 75:1 *Congressional Record* (1937), 3368.

# Index

Abrams, Albertina Adelheit, 20n
Advisory Committee on Education (1938), 7, 40, 100-01
Aiken, George, 113, 139, 141, 142
Allen, Leo, 133, 153
Alpha Kappa Alpha Sorority, 25
Alpha Phi Alpha Fraternity, 25
American Association of School Administrators, 12, 21n, 42, 47, 52, 77, 82, 179
American Association of University Women, 25, 29, 30
American Christian Foundation, 63
American Farm Bureau Federation, 25, 28-29, 38
American Federation of Labor, 24, 25, 26n, 49, 57, 61-62, 125
AFL-CIO, 22, 25-26, 71, 111, 114, 117, 167
American Federation of Teachers: 22-23; allied organizations, 24-25; and Office of Education, 80, 81, 82; and religious issue, 61-62; conflicts with DAR, 30; conflicts with NEA, 10, 39, 40, 41, 139; efforts for federal aid, 13, 177-78; influence on AFL-CIO, 25-26; preference for equalization, 38
American Home Economics Association, 24
American Institute for Public Opinion, 92, 93, 94, 96
American Jewish Congress, 71
American Legion, 28, 50, 73
American Legion Auxiliary, 3
American Protestant Defense League, 63
American Teachers Association, 25, 70
Americanization Bill, 5, 176
Appropriations process, see Budget
Arthur, Chester, 99
Association of Colleges and Secondary Schools for Negroes, 25, 70
Ayres, William, 148, 149

Babbidge, Homer D., Jr., 185n
Bailey, Cleveland, 29, 32, 37, 45, 127, 147, 162-63, 164
Barden, Graham, 10, 15, 48, 50, 52, 73, 74, 113, 117, 119, 122-24, 125, 126, 127, 128, 147, 172
Barden Bill, 10-11, 23, 63, 69, 125-26
Barkley, Alben, 101, 102
Bartel, Carl R., 3n
Bartley, Ernest R., 12n
Biemiller, Andrew, 71
Blair Bill, 3
Bonds for schools, see Fiscal issues
Borchardt, Selma, 177-78
Boushall, Thomas C., 27
Bow Amendment, 164
Bozeman, Herman H., 66n, 67n, 69n, 70n
Brand-Nye Bill, 38
Brehm, Walter, 126
Bricker, John, 12, 39, 50n
Brickman, William W., 32n, 63n
Brownell, Samuel M., 51, 81-83, 86-88
Budget: limits on federal aid, 15, 41, 89, 153; impact of formulas on, 35; projected increases in federal aid, 42, 171; size of appropriations sought, 40-42, 43, 178-79
Building authorities, see State school building authorities
Buis, Anne Gibson, 5n, 8n, 11n, 27n, 32n, 46-47, 80n, 102n, 181
Bull, Mrs. Fred, 32
Bureau of the Budget, 52, 53
Burke, Thomas, 126, 127
Burkhart, John, 20, 26, 171
Bush, Prescott, 160
Byrd, Harry, 141

Calendar Wednesday, 167
Campbell, Roald F., 33n
Capper-Robinson Bill, 5
Carter, Leslie Guy, 33n
Carter, Richard F., 182
Case, Clifford, 113, 158
Catholic attitudes: on federal aid, 46-47, 54, 56-61, 174; on Barden bill,

217 7230